# Bloom's Modern Critical Views

African American
   Poets:
   Wheatley–Tolson
African American
   Poets:
   Hayden–Dove
Edward Albee
Dante Alighieri
Isabel Allende
American and
   Canadian Women
   Poets,
   1930–present
American Women
   Poets, 1650–1950
Hans Christian
   Andersen
Maya Angelou
Asian-American
   Writers
Margaret Atwood
Jane Austen
Paul Auster
James Baldwin
Honoré de Balzac
Samuel Beckett
The Bible
William Blake
Jorge Luis Borges
Ray Bradbury
The Brontës
Gwendolyn Brooks
Elizabeth Barrett
   Browning
Robert Browning
Italo Calvino
Albert Camus
Truman Capote
Lewis Carroll
Miguel de Cervantes
Geoffrey Chaucer
Anton Chekhov
G. K. Chesterton
Kate Chopin
Agatha Christie

Samuel Taylor
   Coleridge
Joseph Conrad
Contemporary Poets
Julio Cortázar
Stephen Crane
Daniel Defoe
Don DeLillo
Charles Dickens
Emily Dickinson
E. L. Doctorow
John Donne and the
   17th-Century Poets
Fyodor Dostoevsky
W. E. B. DuBois
George Eliot
T. S. Eliot
Ralph Ellison
Ralph Waldo Emerson
William Faulkner
F. Scott Fitzgerald
Sigmund Freud
Robert Frost
William Gaddis
Johann Wolfgang
   von Goethe
George Gordon,
   Lord Byron
Graham Greene
Thomas Hardy
Nathaniel Hawthorne
Robert Hayden
Ernest Hemingway
Hermann Hesse
Hispanic-American
   Writers
Homer
Langston Hughes
Zora Neale Hurston
Aldous Huxley
Henrik Ibsen
John Irving
Henry James
James Joyce
Franz Kafka

John Keats
Jamaica Kincaid
Stephen King
Rudyard Kipling
Milan Kundera
Tony Kushner
Ursula K. Le Guin
Doris Lessing
C. S. Lewis
Sinclair Lewis
Norman Mailer
Bernard Malamud
David Mamet
Christopher
   Marlowe
Gabriel García
   Márquez
Cormac McCarthy
Carson McCullers
Herman Melville
Arthur Miller
John Milton
Molière
Toni Morrison
Native-American
   Writers
Joyce Carol Oates
Flannery O'Connor
George Orwell
Octavio Paz
Sylvia Plath
Edgar Allan Poe
Katherine Anne
   Porter
Marcel Proust
Thomas Pynchon
Philip Roth
Salman Rushdie
J. D. Salinger
José Saramago
Jean-Paul Sartre
William Shakespeare
William Shakespeare's
   Romances
George Bernard Shaw

# Bloom's Modern Critical Views

Mary Wollstonecraft
 Shelley
Alexander Solzhenitsyn
John Steinbeck
Jonathan Swift
Amy Tan
Alfred, Lord Tennyson
Henry David Thoreau
J. R. R. Tolkien
Leo Tolstoy

Ivan Turgenev
Mark Twain
John Updike
Kurt Vonnegut
Derek Walcott
Alice Walker
Robert Penn Warren
H. G. Wells
Eudora Welty
Edith Wharton

Walt Whitman
Oscar Wilde
Tennessee Williams
Tom Wolfe
Virginia Woolf
William Wordsworth
Jay Wright
Richard Wright
William Butler Yeats
Émile Zola

*Bloom's Modern Critical Views*

# Alice Walker
*Updated Edition*

*Edited and with an introduction by*
## Harold Bloom
Sterling Professor of the Humanities
Yale University

BLOOM'S
LITERARY CRITICISM
*An imprint of Infobase Publishing*

**Bloom's Modern Critical Views: Alice Walker—Updated Edition**

Copyright ©2007 by Infobase Publishing

Introduction ©2007 by Harold Bloom

Chelsea House
An imprint of Infobase Publishing
132 West 31st Street
New York NY 10001

**Library of Congress Cataloging-in-Publication Data**

Alice Walker / edited with an introduction by Harold Bloom.
    p. cm. — (Bloom's modern criticial views)
 Includes bibliographical references and index.
 ISBN-13: 978-0-7910-9614-7 (hardcover : alk. paper)
 ISBN-10: 0-7910-9614-9 (hardcover : alk. paper)
 1. Walker, Alice, 1944-  —Criticism and interpretation. I. Bloom, Harold.
 PS3525.I5156Z5145 2007
 812'.52—dc22                          2006102701

Chelsea House books are available at special discounts when purchased in bulk quantitie for businesses, associations, institutions, or sales promotions. Please call our Special Sale Department in New York at (212) 967-8800 or (800) 322-8755.

You can find Chelsea House on the World Wide Web at
http://www.chelseahouse.com.

Editorial Consultant, Brian L. Johnson
Cover design by Takeshi Takahashi/Joo Young An

Printed in the United States of America

Bang BCL 10 9 8 7 6 5 4 3 2 1

This book is printed on acid-free paper.

All links and web addresses were checked and verified to be correct at the time of pub lication. Because of the dynamic nature of the web, some addresses and links may hav changed since publication and may no longer be valid.

# Contents

# Editor's Note

My Introduction amiably questions Walker's firm assumption that her books do not engage in any contest with Hurston's.

Linda Selzer reasonably examines the issues of race and domesticity in *The Color Purple*, after which Marcia Noe and Michael Jaynes zealously expound the everyday, ideological use of Walker's writing.

*Meridian*, Walker's most ambitious novel, is related by Deborah A. Baker to the prevalence of visual dominance in our mass media, while Bonnie Braendlin defends the experimental *The Temple of My Familiar*, a New Age pastiche.

Gail Keating exalts Walker as a high priestess of black maternalism, after which Robert James Butler more temperately considers *The Third Life of Grange Copeland*.

For Felipe Smith, Walker is a redeemer, while Lynn Pifer joins the chorus of hosannas for *Meridian*.

Walker's prowess as short story writer is recognized by Alice Hall Petry, after which Louis H. Pratt finds Walker's male characters to be generally a motley ensemble of sexism and racism.

Mystical messiahship is granted to *Meridian* by Joseph A. Brown, S. J. while Deborah Anne Hooker acclaims Walker as an ecocritic.

HAROLD BLOOM

## *Introduction*

## ALICE WALKER (1944– )

### I

A contemporary writer who calls herself "author and medium" is by no means idiosyncratic, and Alice Walker certainly seems to me a wholly representative writer of and for our current era. The success of *The Color Purple* is deserved; Walker's sensibility is very close to the Spirit of the Age. Rather than seek to analyze verse and fictional prose that is of a kind I am not yet competent to judge, or a speculative essay such as "In Search of Our Mothers' Gardens" which eludes me, I will center here upon Walker's meditations upon her acknowledged precursor, Zora Neale Hurston. There is no book more important to me than this one," Walker wrote of Hurston's masterwork, *Their Eyes Were Watching God.* Perhaps the only literary enthusiasm I share with Walker is my own deep esteem for that admirable narrative, about which I have written elsewhere.

Walker associated her feeling for Hurston with her similar veneration for famous black women singers, Billie Holiday and Bessie Smith. That association is a moving trope or defense, since Hurston, like Walker, was a writer and not a vocalist. Here is another tribute by Walker to Hurston:

> We live in a society, as blacks, women, and artists, whose contests we do not design and with whose insistence on ranking us we are permanently at war. To know that second place, in such a society, has often required more work and innate genius than first, a longer, grimmer struggle over greater odds that first—and to be able to fling your scarf about dramatically while you demonstrate that

1

you know—is to trust your own self-evaluation in the face of the Great White Western Commercial of white and male supremacy, which is virtually everything we see, outside and often inside our own homes. That Hurston held her own, literally, against the flood of whiteness and maleness that diluted so much other black art of the period in which she worked is a testimony to her genius and her faith.

As black women and as artists, we are prepared, I think, to keep that faith. There are other choices, but they are despicable.

Zora Neale Hurston, who went forth into the world with one dress to her name, and who was permitted, at other times in her life, only a single pair of shoes, rescued and recreated a world which she labored to hand us whole, never underestimating the value of her gift, if at times doubting the good sense of its recipients. She appreciated us, in any case, *as we fashioned ourselves.* That is something. And of all the people in the world to be, she chose to be herself, *and more and more herself.* That, too, is something.

The strength of this rhetoric is considerable, and has the literary force of a medium. Walker's tribute to Hurston bears an eloquent title: "On Refusing to Be Humbled by Second Place in a Contest You Did Not Design." To write a novel indeed is to enter a contest you did not design, and to *fashion yourself* certainly is the ambition of every novelist or poet aspiring to permanence. To write *The Third Life of Grange Copeland*, *Meridian*, and *The Color Purple* is to have entered a contest Walker did not design, an agon with *Their Eyes Were Watching God*. No feminist critic will agree with that statement, which for them reflects my purely male view of literature. Yet we do not live forever. Do we reread *Their Eyes Were Watching God* or do we reread *The Color Purple*? And if we choose to reread both, do we repress the comparisons that the two novels provoke in regard to one another?

Walker's most poignant paragraphs on Hurston come at the end of her superbly personal essay, "Looking for Zora":

There are times—and finding Zora Hurston's grave was one of them—when normal responses of grief, horror, and so on, do not make sense because they bear no real relation to the depth of the emotion one feels. It was impossible for me to cry when I saw the field full of weeds where Zora is. Partly this is because I have come to know Zora through her books and she was not a teary sort of person herself; but partly, too, it is because there is a point at which even grief feels absurd. And at this point, laughter gushes up to retrieve sanity.

It is only later, when the pain is not so direct a threat to one's own existence that what was learned in that moment of comical lunacy is understood. Such moments rob us of both youth and vanity. But perhaps they are also times when greater disciplines are born.

This may not be Browning at the grave of Shelley, but it is close enough. The pain is familial, since the literary mother, like the poetic father, evokes in the ephebe all the terrible poignance of Freud's "family romances." Michael G. Cooke, writing on Hurston, states the particular dilemma of the black writer's quest for a voice:

> What gives singularity to the black writer's burden in searching for a voice is the twofold factor of frequency and context. Either directly or in projection through a central character, black writer after black writer, generation upon generation, from Frederick Douglass to Alice Walker, evinces the problem of voice. And it is appropriate to regard the most outspoken black writers of the protest movement as bearers of the burden in another guise. Theirs is not so much a free voice as the forced voice of reaction and resentment.

The School of Resentment, which has many factions both critical and creative, does not regard voice as a problem, since the celebration of community necessarily decries individuated subjectivity while exalting collective roarings (or murmurings) as the more moral mode. I fear that influence and its anxieties do not vanish even in the presence of the most self-abnegating of ideologies or idealisms. Our most distinguished critics of Hurston evade this burden, but it is there nevertheless. Here is Elizabeth Meese on "Orality and Textuality in *Their Eyes Were Watching God*":

> By extricating herself from cultural control, Janie/Hurston creates culture. Through the retelling of Janie's story, orality becomes textuality. Textuality is produced by Janie's learned orality, her participation in the oral tradition of the culture. She learns to be one of the people; thus, this is a story of her acculturation into black womanhood and her artistic entitlement to language. By chronicling Janie's development, Hurston transforms the status of narrative from the temporality characteristic of oral tradition to the more enduring textuality required to outwit time's effect on memory. In doing so, she presents feminist readers with a map of a woman's personal resistance to patriarchy, and feminist

writers—in particular Alice Walker—with the intertext for later feminist works.

If one is presented with an intertext, does one pay nothing for the gift? Janie/Hurston creates culture but does Meridian/Walker? Again, here is that dynamic deconstructive duo, Barbara Johnson and H. L. Gates, Jr., rightly praising *Their Eyes Were Watching God* for giving us (and Walker) "A Black and Idiomatic Free Indirect Discourse":

> Janie, in effect, has *rewritten* Joe's text of himself, and liberated herself in the process. Janie "writes" herself into being by *naming*, by speaking herself free. In *The Color Purple*, Alice Walker takes this moment in Hurston's text as the moment of revision, and creates a character whom we witness literally writing herself into being, but writing herself into being in a language that imitates that idiom *spoken* by Janie and Hurston's black community generally. This scene and this transformation or reversal of status is truly the first feminist critique of the fiction of the authority of the male voice, and its sexism, in the Afro-American tradition.

That is admirably precise and accurate; *The Color Purple's* Celie indeed writes "herself into being in a language that imitates that idiom *spoken* by Janie and Hurston's black community generally." The authority of the male voice, and its sexism, may well be subverted by Hurston (she herself would have disowned any such intention or accomplishment). But what has Walker subverted by imitating and so repeating a revisionist moment that she has not originated? No feminist critic will admit the legitimacy of that question, but it abides and will require an answer

LOUIS H. PRATT

# Alice Walker's Men: Profiles in the Quest for Love and Personal Values

Many literary critics, perhaps understandably, have viewed Alice Walker's work with a skepticism typically accorded those whose "places" in the literary mainstream have not been secured. However, these reservations suddenly became muted in 1983 when Walker shed her mantle of relative obscurity at 39 and became, in her own words, "a name brand." This was the year that *The Color Purple* held a place on the *New York Times* Bestsellers' list for over twenty-five weeks and distinguished her as the first Black woman to win the prestigious Pulitzer Prize for fiction. Nevertheless, several questions concerning Walker's art have continued to haunt her. One of the most significant (and current) of these is why she has chosen to create a super-abundance of kind, loving women who triumph in spite of the odds, played off against weak, self-centered, violent men.

In a 1973 interview, Walker declared her interest in analyzing social relationships and challenging the double standards so firmly entrenched in the assumptions made by the *status quo*. Consequently, all of her later works, most notably the short stories and the novels, reflect this point of view:

> . . . I wanted to explore the relationship between men and women, and why women are always condemned for doing what men do as an expression of their masculinity. Why are women so easily

*Studies in Popular Culture*, 12 (1); 1989: pp. 42-57. © Estate of Louis H. Pratt.

"tramps" and "traitors" when men are heroes for engaging in the same activity? Why do women stand for this? (O'Brien 197).

Walker's sense of outrage at these injustices led her to formulate an artistic stance which is sharply critical of the men in her novels. One of her *Washington Post* interviews, published nearly ten years later, provides an interesting and insightful footnote to her artistic philosophy: "If I write books that men feel comfortable with, then I have sold out." (*Washington Post* E1)

Perhaps it is not surprising, therefore, that the question of Walker's negative male images continues to emerge. During the Fall of 1985, she continued to find herself on the defensive. In a *Publisher's Weekly* interview on the impending release of *The Color Purple,* the movie based on her Pulitzer-Prize winning novel, Walker side-stepped the issue by arguing that she intended to write a woman's story without trying to "balance" it. Although she admitted to feeling more compassion for her "miserable" men, she finally acknowledged, "it's hard to be sympathetic to someone who has a fist over your face" (Goldstein 48). Thus, one of the major short-comings in Walker's fiction is that her Black male characters emerge either as tranquil men whose existence must be validated and filtered through the consciousness of her women, or they are presented as weak, self-centered, turbulent men whose humanity is placed in jeopardy by their inability to develop loving relationships with their wives and children.

The eminent critic Addison Gayle has argued that Walker's women also come across negatively because of the interrelationship and the interdependency of Black men and women: ". . . you can't very well do a hatchet job on Black men without also doing a hatchet job on Black women" (Bell 213). Although he makes a sweeping indictment of modern Black women writers, Gale's pointed analysis, nevertheless, rings true as he argues that all of us, again, have been victimized by racism:

Nothing that happens to Black men in this country does not happen to Black women, only indirectly. There's another tremendous problem, too. Black men have grown up in this country being very afraid of Black women, and a hell of a lot of Black women have grown up in this country, in too many cases, looking at Black men the way white folks looked at Black men. At that point, there are tremendous kinds of conflicts because we have not realized that the enemy is not each other. The enemy is this country. The enemy is not Black men, not Black women, it's this country . . . white folks have managed to have us believe that the enemy is poor Black folks on welfare as opposed to middle-class Black folks who want to be decent; light-skinned Black folks as opposed to dark-skinned Black folks; and Black men as opposed to Black women (Bell 214).

Essentially, then, the problem is one of images: how Black men and women view themselves and each other in relation to their universe. In an earlier article, Carolyn F. Gerald addresses this issue by using the term "image" to mean "self-concept" and by focusing on "created," as opposed to "real" images. She further categorizes these created images as personal and adopted, and she cautions us against adopting another person's view of reality because this places us within the realm of that person's influence and control. Since Blacks bear witness constantly to white racial and cultural images which produce a "zero" image of themselves and negate their "peoplehood," she calls upon us to:

> . . . reject white attempts at portraying black reality. They are valid only in terms of the white man's projection of himself. They have no place in the definition of blackness, for they reveal this white writer's attempt to work through their own cultural guilt, fascination with blackness, or sense of spiritual emptiness. . . . No one can hand us a peoplehood, complete with prefabricated images (Gerald 354).

Perhaps one of the striking features of Walker's prose is that she displays a penchant for portraying her men indirectly. Many never speak; they are presented to the reader through the eyes of another person—usually a woman. One such attempt in developing these tranquil men can be found in the short story, "Roselily." Here Walker uses the omniscient narrator to describe a wedding scene in which the groom is characterized as a Black Muslim whose severity is underscored by his gray car, his black suit, and his handshake, which is "like the clasp of an iron gate" (*Love and Trouble* 8). He is proud, black, and understanding of Roselily's *economic* condition: she has to provide for three children from a former marriage by working in a garment factory. He has promised her freedom from the pressures of a job, a freedom which she yearns to enjoy. What comes home to the reader in this brief episode, however, is that her husband-to-be has no understanding of her *spiritual* condition. He will expect her to exchange her job of sewing straight seams in overalls, jeans, and dress pants for one of making and caring for strong Black babies. He will bring love into her loveless life, and he will expend great time in reshaping and molding her into an appropriate wife. Roselily thinks of the smoke and cinders in the Mississippi air and savors the prospect of relief, a chance in Chicago to pursue the dream of a new neighborhood where she and her children can find peace and happiness. Yet, Roselily feels "old" and "yoked." She senses that her expectations are like flawed visions exposed to the harsh sunlight of reality:

Something strains upward behind her eyes. She thinks of the something as a rat trapped, cornered, scurrying to and fro in her head, peering through the windows of her eyes. She wants to live for once. But doesn't quite know what that means. Wonders if she has ever done it. If she ever will (8).

"A Sudden Trip Home in the Spring" is a short story, narrated by Sarah Davis, which focuses on the death of her father and the new, brief insight which she gains into the significance of her nameless grandfather's life. Both men are filtered through Sarah's consciousness, which provides a simple but positive frame of reference for the two men. Sarah remembers her father's threats, spankings, and frequent relocations in his effort to provide for his family, and she decides that all of these grew out of love. However, it is her grandfather who receives most of Sarah's attention. She describes him as "simply and solemnly heroic; a man who kept with pride his family's trust and his own grief" (*Good Woman* 135). What impressed Sarah most, however, was his determination to allow his Blackness to be defined by his family, rather than by whites. This produced in the old man a unique kind of toughness, a hardness that defied Sarah's efforts to capture him on canvas. Instead, Walker allows the old man one solitary line which summarizes his durability: "if you want to make me, make me up in stone" (135).

Several other female-filtered male characters also preset similar images. "Elethia" is the name of the short story and the narrator in a brief character sketch of Albert Porter, affectionately known as "Uncle Albert." Through Elethia's eyes, Walker presents two contrasting images of Uncle Albert, who was imbued with a special pride in his Blackness. Albert Porter's stuffed likeness stood in the window of Old Uncle Albert's segregated restaurant for whites and blacks alike to view. His neatly-covered tray, white napkin, and smiling teeth satisfied the patrons of the eating establishment. In fact, some of the older Blacks had come to believe that the docile, faithful waiter image before them represented Old Albert. Fortunately, however, there were those old-timers who remembered the time he removed the genitals of a murdered young Black boy from public display and defiantly buried them. They recalled that he was a stubborn man who never forgot the horrible injustices heaped upon Blacks by the system. This was the image Elethia admired and loved, and this was what prompted her and her friends to steal Uncle Albert, burn his stuffed likeness, and cherish the ashes of a one-man champion of Black pride and dignity.

Mr. Sweet Little, another of Walker's tranquil men, is the charming subject of her frequently-anthologized short story, "To Hell With Dying." "Mr. Sweet," as the children lovingly call him, is the recreation of a twenty-four year old female narrator whose reminiscences about one of her favorite people span an acquaintance of nearly two decades. His story is one of stunted ambition and thwarted romance, both of which cause Mr. Sweet to retreat from the real world of accelerated stress, high tension, and crass materialism and turn to his homemade alcohol and elaborate playacting for relief and satisfaction. Although Mr. Sweet never speaks, the narrator captures his "magic" through detailed and exquisite descriptions which thoroughly convince us that Mr. Sweet Little is a genuine, caring human. She recalls that he never attended his crops, but he was always ready to frolic with the children and make them feel special with his own unique magic. Having inherited the powers of revival from her brother, the narrator delighted in the episodes when she believed herself able to rescue Mr. Sweet from imminent death and coax him back into their world of make-believe.

Finally, Walker presents the reader with Samuel, the peripheral male character in *The Color Purple,* who is described entirely through the eyes of Nettie in her letters to Celie. Although Samuel plays a central role in Nettie's life—first as her teacher and benefactor, and later as her husband—he is never fully developed as a character. Early on in Nettie's story, we learn of his compassion and kindness when he adopts Olivia and Adam and takes Nettie in on the mistaken assumption that she is the mother of the children. Nettie describes him as a tall, big, black man with white hair and "thoughtful and gentle brown eyes. When he says something it settles you, because he never says anything off the top of his head and he's never out to dampen your spirit or to hurt" (*Purple* 128). In his association with the Africans, he is reported to be sensitive, patient, and kind, through whose eyes, "the vulnerability and beauty of his soul can be plainly read" (211). We are told that, philosophically, his concept of God has evolved into a kind of pantheism which is strikingly similar to Celie's, the sister-in-law he has never met; God is personal, a spirit which cannot be confined to things and people, to be pursued directly by each person by observing and appreciating the wonders of nature. Clearly, Samuel was intended as a foil for the other men in the novel. Yet, we are never permitted to grasp the full significance of his character. While we can identify with him, we never fully understand the complexities of his thoughts and actions.

These tranquil men, generally, have traditional values, and they have been transformed by love into sensitive, compassionate individuals. They have a profound concern for the preservation of the family unit and an abiding love for their women and their children. They have a faith and pride in Blackness, as well as a commitment to the progress and the preservation of the race. These qualities contrast sharply with Walker's turbulent men, as we shall see.

Why are Walker's turbulent men so "miserable," as she herself calls them? Why are these men unable to come to terms with their lives? Consideration of the aspects of the lives of Albert Johnson, Grange and Brownfield Copeland, and Truman Held reveal that each man is actively involved in a frantic, unrelenting quest for love. Each character wrestles with the trials and the errors of life and reaches "experience," which Albert tells us, "everybody is bound to get . . . sooner or later. All they have to do is stay alive" (237). The final stage for these men except for Brownfield, is the distillation and the conversion of that experience into new lessons, new ways of responding to people and to the forces in their environment.

The men in Walker's fiction are so miserable because there is an absence of love in their lives which leads them to abuse their wives and children. Shug Avery remembers Albert Johnson as a handsome, loving, kind human being who has a zest for life. He kept her dancing and laughing in the course of their wild, youthful adventures. Thus, when she returns to live in his house, she is unable to understand the change that has come over him. She asks Celie, "How come he ain't funny no more? . . . How come he never hardly laugh? . . . How come he don't dance? . . . Good God, Celie . . . . What happen to the man I love?" (116) Albert and Shug had "the kind of love couldn't be improve," (116) but his father had denied him permission to marry her because he disapproved of her lifestyle and the three children she bore Albert, the paternity of whom the old man questioned. Albert fought for the right to marry Shug, but finally he yielded and married Annie Julia, his father's choice, a wife he did not want to have. It was then that he exchanged a world of love and laughter and hope for a mere existence of spiritual poverty. He and Shug paraded their affection openly for all the world to see while Annie Julia nursed her babies, endured Albert's beatings, and took her lover who, finally, shot her down.

Then the cycle repeats itself. Needing someone to raise his children, Albert offers to marry Nettie, to whom he has been attracted. However, her stepfather chooses Celie for him, throws her cow in the bargain, and Albert finds his romantic ambitions thwarted once again. Still resentful and frustrated because he has never been able to marry the woman he loves, Albert takes out his feelings on Celie and unleashes his crude invectives in order to undermine her confidence and self-respect as his has been destroyed:

> . . . What you got? . . . You skinny. You shape funny. You too scared to open your mouth to people . . . You black, you pore, you ugly, you a woman. Goddam, . . . . you nothing at all (186, 187 *passim*).

And he beat her unmercifully because he believes that all women are stubborn and that this is his conjugal privilege, necessary to keep his wife in line (See Harris). During these eruptions of extreme violence, Celie shields herself psychologically by entering a world of make believe: "I make myself wood. I say to myself, Celie, you a tree" (30).

Albert's abuse of his children might be described as benign neglect. Although he rarely harms them physically, he virtually ignores them, except for his son Harpo, who is forced to do the plowing and work alongside of Celie in the field while the lovelorn Albert pines for Shug and yearns for the life together that they never had.

In many ways, the life of Grange Copeland also parallels that of Albert Johnson. Grange's family disapproved of Josie and the notoriety she had acquired through her house of pleasure, and so he had married Margaret to please them. Before long, however, Grange had pondered his lot and future as a sharecropper, settled into a kind of silent resignation, and begun a routine of Sunday quarrels, weeks of depression, gloominess, and despair, and Saturday nights at Josie's, which always ended when he returned home in a drunken stupor which belied his youthful vigor:

> He was thirty-five but seemed much older. His face and eyes had a dispassionate vacancy and sadness, as if a great fire had been extinguished within him and was just recently missed. He seemed devoid of any emotion . . . except that of bewilderment (*Grange Copeland* 13).

On those nights he would threaten to kill Margaret and Brownfield, and mother and son would run for the woods under the protective cover of darkness. During the week, they quarreled and fought. For release from the pain, Margaret had taken many lovers, but when she took Shipley, the white overseer, the oppressor, Grange could endure no longer. So he abandoned his wife and baby to the merciful death which brought a peace they had never known before.

Grange Copeland was especially cruel to Brownfield, to whom he rarely spoke. He seldom looked at his son or acknowledged his presence in any way. On one occasion, Brownfield had watched his father as he drank whiskey on the porch, and Grange had been particularly cruel when he caught him staring:

> Brownfield was afraid to move away and afraid to stay. When he was drinking his father took every action as a personal affront. He looked at Brownfield and started to speak. His eyes had little yellow and red lines in them like the veins of a leaf. Brownfield leaned nearer. But all his father said was "I ought to throw you down the goddam well" (9, 10).

Because he had no money, Grange had rejected Margaret's idea of sending Brownfield to school. Brownfield also blamed him for his mother's gradual change from a sensitive, kind, warm human being to a woman whose attention was captured by good times and the transient pleasures of her lovers' embraces. He insisted in believing that Grange had been an attentive, loving father, but he could not remember when that time had been, so he began to detest him for the love that Grange was unable to give:

> ... he hated him for everything and always would. And he most hated him because even in private and in the dark and with Brownfield presumably asleep, Grange could not bear to touch his son with his hand (21).

Brownfield Copeland's young life was devoid of love, and even when he was grown, he felt "very often depressed by the thought that his father had never really loved him" (164). Consequently, he emerges as perhaps the most unredeemably degenerate of all of Walker's men.

On the day of Brownfield's birth, Grange and Margaret sit as unanticipating parents to name their new son. As Grange looks indifferently across the brown fields, they agree that no name can change the fate of the baby and that "Brownfield" is as good as any other. Yet, in spite of this ominous, inauspicious sign of foreboding, Brownfield's adult life does begin with a modicum of hope.

After Margaret dies, Brownfield realizes that he must avoid the "beneficent generosity" of the Shipleys lest he find himself hopelessly entangled in debt. So he vacates the property, hoping to make a new, independent life for himself, one which his father had never known. He survives simultaneous relationships with Josie and her daughter Lorene to marry the educated, innocent Mem, who has yet to be introduced to the real world. This was a significant step for Brownfield because "he could still look back on their wedding day as the pinnacle of his achievement in extricating himself from evil and the devil and aligning himself with love," (49) and as he loved Mem and " ... sucked and nursed at her bosom ... he ... grew big and grew firm with love, and grew strong" (49). Soon, however, this dream dies when Brownfield realized that whites are in control of his welfare and his family's welfare as well:

> He no longer had, as his father had maintained, even the desire to run away from them. He had no faith that any other place would be better. He fitted himself into the slot in which he found himself; for fun he poured oil into streams to kill the fish and tickled his vanity by drowning cats (59).

Realizing the hopelessness of his situation, he returns to Josie for comfort and solace. Like Albert and Grange, he feels that his marriage has been a mistake.

In order to force her to his level and to make her a scapegoat for his failures, Brownfield forces Mem to give up her "proper" speech, her teaching position, and her lofty aspirations. Simultaneously, he begins to abuse her, the most brutal instance of which occurs when she refuses to move back to Mr. J. L.'s place from their house in the city. In the course of the argument, Mem speaks up for herself, and Brownfield hits her squarely in the mouth:

> Don't you interrupt me when I'm doing the talking, Bitch! he said, shaking her until blood dribbled from her stinging lips . . . You Goddam wrankly faced blacknigger slut! . . . You say one more word, just one little goddam *peep* and I'll cut your goddam throat . . . Mem closed her eyes as he dropped her abruptly against the bedpost and gave her a resounding kick in the side of the head. She saw a number of blurred pale stars, then nothing else (90, 91).

Relentlessly, Brownfield pursued Mem to break her spirit, destroy her will, her self-concept, her ability to triumph against the odds. Rather than give up these things, Mem threatened to leave him, a move Brownfield had difficulty in countering. So he waited for her one night on the porch, pointed his shotgun at near point-black range into her face, and fired.

Brownfield's relationship with his children was equally as stormy. After Grange has returned to Georgia, Brownfield confides that "My trouble is, I always *could do without* childrens" (73). As a result, Ornette, Daphne, and Ruth were paid only the slightest attention, and only when he was nearly drunk. Brownfield could not view them in their naivete as human beings. He scolded Ornette, the middle child, as if she were a whore, but Daphne, the eldest, withstood most of the physical abuse. She alone remembered his kindness, and like Brownfield himself had done as a child, she fought hard to "remember when daddy was good." Her nervous condition made her jumpy, and Brownfield delighted in swearing at her, calling her "stupid," "crazy," and "Daffy," instead of Daphne:

> . . . One time, when she was holding her stomach and crying, with sweat popping out like grease bubbles on her face, Brownfield had kicked her right where her hands were. He was trying to sleep and couldn't because of the noise, he said (119).

Brownfield never touched the baby Ruth. Yet, at the age of four, she observed him in his various acts of domestic violence and perceptively summarized the opinion of the rest of the family. "You know what," she cried after he had sworn after her mother, "Hey, I say, do you know what, . . . You nothing but a sonnabit" (108).

This unfulfilled quest for love leads Walker's male characters to view their women in purely sexual terms. In one of their rare father-to-son conversations, Harpo asks Albert why he beats Celie, to which Albert replies, "Cause she my wife. Plus she stubborn. All women good for—he don't finish. He just tuck his chin over the paper like he do," Celie tells us. "Remind me of Pa" (*Purple* 30). The same attitude is reflected in Brownfield's relationship with Mem. When his friends teased him and inquired how he was able to marry a school-teacher, Brownfield rubs his pants and brags, "Give this old black-snake to her . . . and then I beats her ass. Only way to treat a *nigger* woman" (*Grange Copeland* 56). Later one morning, in front of the children, he tries unsuccessfully to entice Mem to delay her departure for work and come back to bed. Frustrated and dejected, Brownfield exclaims, "Shit . . . One of these days I'm going on over to Jay-pan, where the womens know what they real job is!" (118).

Indeed, the men in *Meridian* are kindred souls to those in *The Color Purple* and *The Third Life of Grange Copeland*. Here Walker presents us with an intermittent panorama of lustful men who assume that sexual conquest is their privilege and responsibility. Perhaps the earliest influence on Meridian was her grandfather who slept with nearly all the women in town while his wife, pregnant with their twelfth child, was compelled to work to pay for their daughter's education by hiring herself out as a domestic after her work at home was done. Then, as Meridian grows into her teenage years, she suffers the same fate as Sofia in *The Color Purple*: she finds herself constantly bombarded by the sexual advances of the men with whom she comes into contact. Meridian submits to the frequent sexual encounters demanded by her teenage lover Eddie, who later marries her, "shotgun" style, and then deserts her and their daughter. There is George Daxter, the undertaker, who enjoys fondling her, and there is his young assistant who allows her to witness his seduction of another teenage girl in a nearby shed. Later, Meridian encounters the doctor who performs her abortion at Saxon College and offers to tie her tubes in exchange for "some of all this extra-curricular activity" and the retired professor, Mr. Raymonds, with whom she barters her sexual favors for a job as well as the little extras: cokes, cookies, cans of deviled ham, and tennis rackets. Finally, of course, there is Truman Held.

Truman and Meridian have been drawn together by their shared experiences of beatings and jailings as a result of their civil rights demonstrations and voter registration drives. They had arrived "at a time and place in history that forced the trivial to fall away—and they were absolutely together" (*Meridian* 84). She treasures him because he punctuates his conversations with French phrases which she had difficulty understanding, and he values her as "a woman to rest in, as a ship must have a port. As a train must have a shed" (141). They become sexually involved, and soon Truman discovers that she has been both mother and wife. Thus, he turns to Lynn Rabinowitz, another civil rights worker, after he has made it clear to Meridian that dating white girls is "essentially, a matter of sex."

It becomes obvious at this point that in spite of his veneer of sophistication and charisma, Truman Held is a victim of racism and sexism, and he is driven by the same animalism which motivates the other characters of the novel. Scene by scene, Walker reveals him as an ambivalent, fragmented personality who is symbolic of the classic "double standard." On the one hand, he desires virginity; on the other, he is driven toward physical conquest. For him, the ideal woman must be knowledgeable and experienced (she must read the *New York Times*). It is not surprising, then, that he soon comes to view Meridian as sullied, damaged goods because she has been intimate with another man. However, this does not fully explain Truman's rejection of Meridian. Walker tells us that:

> . . . Truman, also did not want a general beside him. He did not want a woman who tried, however encumbered by guilts and fears and remorse, to claim her own life. She knew Truman would have liked her better as she had been as Eddie's wife, for all that he admired the flash of her face across a picket line—an attractive woman, but, asleep (110).

Truman's inhibitions and inadequacies prohibit him from accepting and appreciating the intelligent black woman whose assertiveness and independence he views as a direct threat to his masculinity.

Truman turns to Lynne because, on first inspection, she embodies the qualities of a perfect wife. However, it is not long before he feels intimidated by her intelligence, "her imagination, her wishes and dreams . . . she annoyed him with her irrepressible questions that kept bursting out and bubbling up into their lives, like spring water rising beside a reservoir and undermining the concrete of the dam" (140, 141). Because of Truman's insecurities, their relationship begins to founder, but it is not until Tommy Olds has been shot in Mississippi that he begins to examine their circumstances. When Truman visits him in the hospital, Tommy refers to Lynne as "that white bitch," and he tells Truman that "All white people are motherfuckers" (132). Truman accepts this generalization, and he concludes that since Tommy's assailant was white, Lynne, by virtue of *her* whiteness, shared the guilt for the loss of Tommy's arm. But the most devastating blow to their relationship comes when Tommy betrays their friendship and rapes Lynn. Truman cannot accept the idea that she has, however unwillingly, "belonged" to another man. Thus, the marriage deteriorates rapidly, and Lynne moves to New York City where their daughter Camara is beaten, raped, and killed. In the final scene of the novel, Truman replaces Meridian as he begins the quest for "wholeness," for stability and permanence.

In spite of their relentless pursuit of love and personal values, the men in Walker's fiction present near-zero images which range from the weak and ineffectual to the violent and the miserable. On the one hand, we have the tranquil men who have no legitimacy except that which is assigned to them through the consciousness of her women. They do not act, they do not react, they do not interact. They function simply as cardboard, underdeveloped, one-dimensional characters who lay no real claim to viability, especially when they are compared with the finely-drawn women in her fiction. And on the other, we have the turbulent men, neither of whom is ever able to establish and maintain a warm, kind, loving relationship. They are scheming, overbearing, and vindictive. They come to us as oppressive, insensitive, and degenerate individuals who are unable to celebrate their own humanity as well as recognize that humanity in others.

Even when we consider the positive elements in these characters, there is not a single man among them who exemplifies the most basic attitudes of humaneness. Albert struggles with his hatred for Nettie, and finally he reaches a near-human state when he abandons (though involuntarily) his vendetta against her and restores communication between the two sisters. He gains an appreciation f or them, but his "experiences" never translate into a loving relationship with his son Harpo. Similarly, Grange learns his lessons in the North. He comes home full of love and compassion which he showers on his granddaughter Ruth, but his relationship with Brownfield borders on hostility and disdain. Truman Held may have profited from his experiences, but the novel ends before he is able to demonstrate his new awarenesses. And if these things stir within the readers a sense of compassion, we are compelled to remember the deaths (and the lives) of Annie Julia, Margaret, Mem, their babies, and Camara, and we realize the enormous guilt for which their husbands and fathers must be held accountable.

It is unreasonable and patently unfair to examine a single work by Walker (or any other writer) and expect to find a perfect balance of characters. Similarly, it seems unusual when the gamut of her fiction is surveyed in a futile search for a viable Black male character with a positive identity. Still, we wonder if the Albert Porters, the Sweet Littles, the Samuels, the Grange Copelands, the Brownfield Copelands, the Truman Helds, the Albert Johnsons, are representative of Black men. Where are the Frederick Douglasses, the W. E. B. du Boises, the Gabriel Prossers, the Paul Robesons, the Martin Kings, the Malcolm X's? Where is the unheralded, unsung, decent, hard-working John Black who treasures his family and works his fingers to the bone to insure their economic and spiritual survival? Herb Boyd contends that these men have no place in Walker's "insular world where black male chauvinism is the principal contradiction, black men the main enemy . . . The characters in this universe are forced to feed on themselves, allowing the enemy to escape indictment" (Boyd 62).

For the most part, the Black men in Walker's world are in need of redemption from the racism, oppression, and sexism still rampant in our society. They are in need of liberation from the near-zero images of themselves which has been propagated through the literature and the culture. However, it is equally clear that Walker's men have not been victims of a society where injustices have been imposed *individually*. Rather, they have functioned in a racial climate where oppression has been administered systematically to Black people *collectively*. This recognition reemphasizes the interrelatedness of Black men and Black women and lends credence to the idea that there if no "Black woman's story," for there is no "Black man's story." All of us, Black females and Black males alike, are involved in the struggle, to achieve a state of wholeness and reassert our humanity. Like Addison Gayle, Boyd reminds us that, "at this juncture in our struggle, mired as we are in retrenchment, we can ill afford to be further confused about the roots of our present dilemma"(62). Therefore, we must identify and resist things which are divisive; we must create and create those things which are harmonious, those things which will lead us into the state of oneness which we seek.

## WORKS CITED

Bell, Roseanne P., "Judgement: Addison Gayle" in her *Sturdy Black Bridges: Visions of Black Women in Literature*. New York: Anchor Press/Doubleday, 1979.

Boyd, Herb. "The Arts." *The Crisis* 93. No. 2 (February 1986): 10ff.

Gerald, Carolyn F., "The Black Writer and His Role" in *The Black Aesthetic*. Ed. Addison Gayle, Jr. New York: Anchor Books/Doubleday, 1972.

Goldstein, William. "Alice Walker on the Set of *The Color Purple*." *Publisher's Weekly* (September 6, 1985): 46–48.

Harris, Trudier. "On *The Color Purple*, Stereotypes and Silence." *Black American Literature Forum* 18, No. 4 (Winter 1984): 155–161.

O'Brien, John, Ed. *Interviews With Black Writers*. New York: Liveright Publishers, 1973.

Walker, Alice. *The Color Purple*. New York: Washington Square Press, 1982. Cited as *Purple*.

———. *In Love and Trouble*. New York: Harcourt, Brace, Jovanovitch, 1973. Cited as *Love and Trouble*.

———. *Meridian*. New York: Washington Square Press 1976.

———. *The Third Life of Grange Copeland*. New York: Harcourt, Brace, Jovanovitch, 1970. Cited as *Grange Copeland*.

———. *You Can't Keep a Good Woman Down*. New York: Harcourt, Brace, Jovanovitch. Cited as *Good Woman*.

*Washington Post*, October 15, 1982, E-1.

JOSEPH A. BROWN

# "All Saints Should Walk Away": The Mystical Pilgrimage of Meridian

Towards the end of *From Behind the Veil,* Robert B. Stepto expresses a difficulty he has with the narrative strategy employed by Zora Neale Hurston in *Their Eyes Were Watching God.* Having described both the "narratives of ascent and immersion," and speculating that Hurston's novel is "quite likely the only truly coherent narrative" before *Invisible Man* that combines both ascent and immersion into a single text, Stepto cites as the "one great flaw" in *Their Eyes* the fact that the narrative is told in the voice of the omniscient third person. Stepto refuses to call *Their Eyes* a failed text; aware of its greatness, he suggests that the novel might benefit from a new category:

> one might say that the example of *Their Eyes* calls for a narrative in which the primary figure (like Janie) achieves a space beyond those defined by the tropes of ascent and immersion, but *(unlike* Janie) also achieves authorial control over both the frame and tale of his or her personal history.[1]

*Ascent* and *immersion* are terms with a rich religious significance. The ritual space defined by these terms (in Stepto's reading of Afro-American narratives) has been associated by other perceptive and prophetic readers of Afro-American culture, the composers and singers of the Spirituals.

*Callaloo: A Journal of African American and African Arts and Letters,* 12:2 (39); Spring 1989: pp. 310-20. © Charles H. Rowell.

*Immersion* demands attention to the *deep river*, to the *Jordan* (which, chilly and cold, chills the body but not the soul), to the *valley* (where countless old believers went to pray and where their souls got so happy that they stayed all day). *Ascent* likewise has its equivalents in the Spirituals: from the *rock* where Moses stood, to the *mountain* from which Elijah caught the chariot ride, to the carnival of wheels-within-wheels of Ezekiel's vision way up in the middle of the air. Stepto suggests that there is a "continuum of narrative strategies" that must be employed in the study of Afro-American literature. In order to calibrate that continuum more carefully—whether a name is ever found for each point on the scale—it might be helpful to spend some time right smack in the middle of the air, as the old folks suggested. By arriving at what will be called, in this essay, "the mystic plain," where Hurston seems to place Janie Crawford in *Their Eyes*, other characters of Afro-American fiction who would otherwise be place-less in the ascent/immersion scheme, might be found to be quite at home.[2]

The main thrust of this essay will be tracing the inner growth of the title character of *Meridian*, understanding that a mystical journey, in the Afro-American religious tradition, brings heaven down to earth; and by watching Meridian learn to hear the voice of God in the stillness amidst the storm of her life, we might recover a sight of the middle ground of the sacred spaces. After all, there was a *den* where Daniel faced the lions; and a *wilderness* from which many a saint emerged; *Jacob's ladder* upon which the messengers of God traveled—to say nothing of the familiar *battlefield*, where many a war was fought.

Zora Hurston has served as the tutelary ancestor for Alice Walker so consistently that her value as a primary guide in this endeavor needs no justification. While Alice Walker has written of her indebtedness and bond to Hurston for *Their Eyes Were Watching God*, it would be helpful to consider—in dealing with *Meridian*—some of the occasional pieces Hurston wrote concerning various aspects of Afro-American religious practices.[3] Hurston, it might be argued, serves as a model for Meridian Hill. The journey to seek the wisdom of the old is a quest common to both. The deliberate odd behavior and quirkiness in dress and utterance, the arresting presence and the delphic aura noticed in the real Hurston are echoed more than coincidentally in the fictional Meridian. In the portrait "Mother Catherine," Hurston first describes her meeting with the "spiritual dictator," then quotes several aphorisms from the prophetess:

> She laid her hand upon my head.
> 'Daughter why have you come here?'
> 'Mother, I come seeking knowledge.'
> 'Thank God. Do y'all hear her. She come here looking for

wisdom. Eat de salt, daughter, and get yo mind with God and me. You shall know what you come to find out. I feel you. I felt you while you was sitten in de chapel. Bring her a veil.' (24)

'There is no heaven beyond dat blue globe. There is a between-world between this brown earth and the blue above. So says the beautiful spirit.' (26)

As could be expected, Meridian Hill's beginning quest for knowledge had none of the aggression often associated with Zora Hurston. Meridian is introduced to the reader as a focused personality at the end of her quest. The flashbacks that give the novel its particular rhythm show Meridian beginning her journey on the periphery of the road, attracted to the distractions, unaware of any pattern to her life. There are no older women physically present to instruct her in the eating of salt and the gaining of wisdom, especially not her mother:

> Meridian was conscious of a feeling of guilt, even as a child. Yet she did not know of what she might be guilty. When she tried to express her feelings to her mother, her mother would only ask: 'Have you stolen anything?'

> With her own daughter she certainly said things she herself did not believe. She refused help and seemed, to Meridian, never to understand. But all along she understood perfectly.[4]

Hurston was able, as she demonstrates in book after book, to find wise elders to further her journey to wisdom. For Meridian Hill, there is only the wind buffeting her onto the road; it is her mind alone that will seek, discover and re-create the world. Hurston, in her own authorial voice, named her journey as "dust tracks on the road," and wrote of the journey in such a way as to keep herself veiled by her eloquence. Meridian Hill is never known, but not because it is an authorial voice other than her own that tells her story. Meridian remains a mystery because she fashions herself not into an authentic witness, but into the very presence of God, a presence that defies all telling. It is for others to give witness to the deeds of Meridian. She weaves her own veil, and Walker writes of Meridian's life in such a way as to force the reader (through Truman Held, Lynne, and the various townspeople who are touched by her power) to seek the truth of Meridian in her silence.

Scholars have never been comfortable with mystics. (Nor for that matter have the families, friends, and acquaintances of mystics had an easy time with them.) Those whose business is the critical sifting of words and other symbols are generally frustrated with any who use their lives to discount the

ability to communicate in words. Even though the world of literary criticism
is periodically enthralled with theories that maintain that texts are unreliable,
in more mundane worlds the actions of people are held in more suspicion if
there are no words to provide a context of possible interpretations. From the
time of Jeremiah, wandering through Jerusalem breaking pottery, to Teresa
of Avila floating several feet above the chapel floor, the very souls who most
seek quiet have most seriously disturbed the peace of mind of all who interact
with them. Meridian Hill, fictional though she may be, joins this company of
unsettling saints:

> Meridian did not look to the right or to the left. She passed the
> people watching her as if she didn't know it was on her account
> they were there. As she approached the tank the blast of its engine
> starting sent clouds of pigeons fluttering, with the sound of rapid,
> distant shelling, through the air, and the muzzle of the tank swung
> tantalizingly side to side—as if to tease her—before it settled directly
> toward her chest. . . . And then, when she reached the tank she
> stepped lightly, deliberately, right in front of it, rapped smartly on
> its carapace—as if knocking on a door— then raised her arm again.
> The children pressed onward, through the remains of the arrayed
> riflemen up to the circus car door. The silence as Meridian kicked
> open the door, exploded in a mass exhalation of breaths, and the men
> who were in the tank crawled sheepishly out again to stare.
>
> 'God!' said Truman without thinking. 'How can you not love
> somebody like that!'
>
> 'Because she thinks *she's* God,' said the old sweeper, 'or else she
> just ain't all there. *I* think she ain't all there, myself.' (21–22)

Without thinking (a state that is common to him), Truman Held sees the
reality that Meridian has become. This incident appears at the beginning
of the novel, in the episode entitled "The Last Return." At the end of the
book, when this incident is once again the focus of the narrative, Meridian
writes one last poem:

> there is water in the world for us
> brought by our friends
> though the rock of mother and god
> vanishes into sand
> and we, cast out alone
> to heal
> and re-create
> ourselves. (213)

The mosaic of episodes that Walker fashions into *Meridian* are fused in the central character as the reader finally realizes that Meridian has become *the rock of mother and god*. The poem is the final blessing for Truman Held, left to hang over his sleeping-place, a kiss of words left upon his brow. Meridian is no longer cast out, alone; she has healed and re-created herself. She has left the dark night of the soul, the purgative journey. Because the novel is an assembly of incidents, fashioned in a circle, the poem must be placed at the beginning of the story, no matter where it is placed in the book. The congregation of witnesses see Meridian *after* her journey through the wilderness and their/our souls "look back in wonder" at how she made it over. Her example is the teaching message she aspired to: go ye and do likewise.

In many a kitchen in Afro-America, Meridian Hill would be described as a "marked child." Her fascination with mystic plains was inherited through her father, because of her father's grandmother, Feather Mae. If Alice Walker intended *Meridian* to be anything else but her first extended meditation on mysticism, the episode in which the story of Feather Mae is recounted would be called something other than "Indians and Ecstasy." Meridian's great-grandmother was a "woman it was said of some slight and harmless madness." When she first enters the coils of the Sacred Serpent (the Indian burial mound handed on to Meridian's father), "she felt as if she had stepped into another world, into a different kind of air." Possessing only the story of Feather Mae, Meridian goes to the Sacred Serpent and induces a vision:

> It was as if the walls of the earth that enclosed her rushed outward, leveling themselves at a dizzying rate, and then spinning wildly, lifting her out of her body and giving her the feeling of flying. And in this movement she saw the faces of her family, the branches of trees, the wings of birds, the corners of houses, blades of grass and petals of flowers rush toward a central point high above her and she was drawn with them, as whirling as bright, as free, as they. Then the pit where she stood, and what had left her at its going was returned. When she came back to her body—and she felt sure she had left it—her eyes were stretched wide open, and they were dry, because she found herself staring directly at the sun. (58)

She induces this vision because she sought to understand "her great-grandmother's ecstasy and her father's compassion for people dead centuries before he was born." Meridian becomes her name (in all of its variations as listed at the beginning of the book, but notably, "of or at noon or, especially of the position of power of the sun at noon") and, unknowingly, is invested with the powers of the crossroads. The rest of her life is an attempt to re-create this moment during which she stands ecstatic, consonant with the Greek understanding: withdrawal of the soul from the body; a mystic or prophetic trance. A trance so powerful that she is "out of time," able to confront the sun without harm. Maybe "she ain't all there," but the part that seems missing to the old sweeper, and to Anne-Marion, Truman, Mrs. Held, and others *is* somewhere—flying between heaven and earth.

Traditional understandings of mysticism would assert that the individual mystics aim at direct union with their gods. In every tradition, the attempt at mystical union is marked by an urgent disregard for the body. Among the anchorites of the ancient African desert to the 14th-century mystics of Europe; among the varieties of Buddhist, Hindu, Taoist holy women and men; and among the initiates and devotees of traditional Native American and African religions, there is a universal struggle against the physical, a yearning to recapture the ecstatic for longer and longer "periods" of time, until time can no longer chain them to the earth and its hungers. What for these men and women is a blessed state is often the manifestation of obsessive, delusional, or pathological behavior to others.[5]

For those moments when mystics must return from the sacred space and walk the streets of the world, there are tasks to be performed by them, obligations to be met. In her essay, "Conversions and Visions," Zora Hurston succinctly outlines the dynamics of acceptance of a call to preach. Alice Walker does not follow this outline simply, but there is an appropriation of the insights Hurston offers. Keeping in mind the fact that Meridian is re-creating a tradition with no proximate mentor to guide her, it is possible to see the essentials of conversion and the call to preach as applicable to much of the purification process displayed in Meridian's life. Hurston begins:

> The vision is a very definite part of Negro religion. It almost always accompanies conversion. It almost always accompanies the call to preach.
>
> In the conversion the vision is sought. The individual goes forth into the waste places and by fasting and prayer induces the vision. The place of retirement chosen is one most likely to have some emotional effect upon the seeker. The cemetery, to a people who fear the dead, is a most suggestive place to gain visions. The dense swamps with the possibility of bodily mishaps is another favorite. (85)

It is obvious that Meridian has sought a vision—for understanding the dead of centuries before. Along with the more orthodox forms of Afro-American religion, Meridian's faith quest is an attempt to restore the broken circle. She has only the stories of her foremothers as sustenance; there is none of their handed-over wisdom; none of the practical methods of understanding special to wise old women are accessible to her. Taking the outline Hurston provides, a coherent pattern emerges from the pages of Meridian's "book of life."

While there is no cemetery, there is a preoccupation with the dead, not the dead of centuries before, but the present newly-dead. Beginning with the confrontation with the tank quoted above, *Meridian* can be divided into stages of understanding how the dead compel the living to pay reverence. Meridian confronts society so that the children may learn to distinguish the varieties and economics of death:

> 'You make yourself a catatonic behind a lot of meaningless action that will never get anybody anywhere. What good did it do those kids to see that freak's freaky wife?'
>
> 'She was a fake. They discovered that. . . . They said she was made of plastic and were glad they hadn't waited until Thursday when they would have to pay money to see her.' (26)

Throughout the novel, the primary question Meridian negotiates is "Can you kill for the revolution?" Her ambivalence, her habit of being "a woman in the process of changing her mind," causes feelings of alienation within Meridian. Her overwhelming sense of being alienated from those she respects and loves distracts her from the insight gained by the reader—Meridian is not an outcast from the circle; she is its very center. Anne-Marion rejects her and cannot break communications; Lynne is jealous and angry with Meridian's presence in her family's life and yet seeks out Meridian during every domestic crisis or tragedy. Truman felt:

> . . . it would have been joy to him to forget her, as it would have been joy never to have been his former self. But running away from Lynne, at every opportunity, and existing a few days in Meridian's presence, was the best that he could do. (143)

The brief recounting of the tale of the Wild Child (pages 35–37) is a distanced representation of Meridian's status as she begins her indenture at Saxon College. Rootless; instinctual; haphazardly pregnant; subsisting on the castoff generosity of near-strangers, the girl and the womanchild reflect each other. This establishes the motive for Meridian's response to the death of Wile Chile in the "Sojourner" episode. At this point in her life, Meridian is described as existing in a "fog of unconcern," but the description is less than complete. She is distracted from the external realities, focused on better shaping and understanding the significance of the moment within the coils of the Sacred Serpent. Meridian's flight from the body has stayed with her:

> Meridian lived in a small corner room high under the eaves of the honors house [of Saxon College] and had decorated the ceiling, walls and backs of doors and the adjoining toilet and large photographs of trees and rocks and tall hills and floating clouds, which she claimed she *knew*. (38)

Her identification with the Sojourner Tree begins the spiritual merging process that will develop, by the end of her story, into a presence who is rock *and* god *and* mother, and the action that signifies this beginning fusion is the funeral of Wile Chile beneath the branches of the Sojourner. Whatever Meridian knows, she *becomes*. Staring at the sun intensifies her name. Bringing the past and the unwashed present into the womb of Saxon College—disrupting time and the order that flows from time—Meridian functions in a manner similar to the slave, Lavinie. When the unthinking college students attack the nurturing Sojourner, a part of Meridian remains silent for most of the rest of the novel, and she must take on the name and the responsibility of the tree itself. After all, she *knew* it. And she knows the necessity of seeking out the children who would otherwise die ungrieved and unavenged.

Meridian's own child is the second death (in the structure of the novel) that reduces her distracted state and allows her the freedom to attain a higher level in the atmosphere. By renouncing the proof of her flesh, she gives the child his life. When she is sought out to be the refuge from grief by both Truman and Lynne at the death of their daughter, Camara, Meridian acts with a calm, a self-possession, that seems assumed and not demonstrated within the narrative. It would be a flaw if the death of children (imagined, unattended, deliberate, and perverted) were not major connectives throughout the novel.

Like rocks, rivers, hills, clouds and ancient trees, Meridian belongs, as she is, to give direction, comfort. She has become another function of her name: compass point.

> It was Meridian who had led them to the mayor's office, bearing in her arms the bloated figure of a five-year-old boy who had been stuck in the sewer for two days before he was raked out with a grappling hook. The child's body was so ravaged, so grotesque, so disgusting to behold, his own mother had taken one look and refused to touch him. To the people who followed Meridian it was as if she carried a large bouquet of long-stemmed roses. The body

might have smelled just that sweet, from the serene, set expression on her face. They had followed her into a town meeting over which the white-haired, bespectacled mayor presided, and she had placed the child, whose body had begun to decompose, beside his gavel. The people had turned with her and followed her out. They had been behind her when, at some distance from the center of the town, she had suddenly buckled and fallen to the ground. (191)

If Meridian has learned to see death in life, life in death, the ancestors in the fog, the great-grandmother in the serpent's coils, why would it not be possible at the end of her "recorded sayings and doings," for her to see not only the decomposing body of the child, but also the cruelly cut flower that is every dead child? To have the mystic sight is not to be blind to the world, but see it as it really is, bounded and encircled by the world of eternity. The mystic must make her return among the people and show them a larger universe, give them a sense of their being that is expanded in its horizon *because* of the sights the mystic has seen and knows to be true.

One final death allows Meridian to break through the most oppressive wall of her spiritual imprisonment. Throughout her life, attending church had been a punishing frustration, because she could respond only to the rhythms and melodies of the music, finding the words of the sermons and the lyrics of the songs unintelligible. Given the fact that she had learned from Miss Winter during the Black History pageant that love meant forgiveness, Meridian did not hate the churchgoers; she was (in her mind) simply not a part of the circle. Feeling herself, once again, outside of the people, she is actually, to the observing reader, thoroughly immersed in the essence of the religious experience. The music induces a rapture inside her; yet one more form of the ecstatic state for which she yearns. The clearest glimpse of the simple grandeur of the true religious experience comes to Meridian as she stands among the people during the funeral of Martin Luther King, Jr. The vision is terminated when the marching mourners put off their grief and renew their sociability:

> 'It's a black characteristic, man,' a skinny black boy tapping on an imaginary drum was saying. 'We don't go on over death the way whiteys do.' He was speaking to a white couple who hung guiltily to every word.
>
> Behind her a black woman was laughing, laughing, as if all her cares, at last, had flown away. (186)

While the entire passage is shaped by Meridian's shame and revulsion for the lack of piety among people, does she not transform every funeral into a celebration, from calling down (with her untrained power) the petals of the Sojourner upon Wile Chile, to the investing of flowers upon the drowned boy? Part of her revulsion, it would seem, is aimed against the uncluttered humanity of those who would renew themselves with laughter in the midst of the profoundest grief.

Meridian, having for some time visited the neighborhood churches, finally "for no reason she was sure of, found herself in front of a large white church, Baptist (with blue and red in its stained windows, perhaps that was what drew her). . . ." Within this church the last layer of her often-tortured journey around and around the wheel is met, managed, and connected. This episode is entitled "Camara," and the name of Truman's child is the binding force that allows Meridian to answer the question, "Can you kill?" When the death of Camara is narrated earlier in the book, Meridian's focus is centered upon Lynne and Truman. The novel and the person of Meridian are silent on the death of this child. It is up to the reader to put the name of Camara into each sentence that mentions a child who is murdered by the world. On the wheel of mystic time there is only *now*, so that Meridian's grief is not late, it simply *is*.

The service Meridian attends is a memorial in honor of a young man slain while working in the Civil Rights Movement. His father, terminally shattered, attends this memorial to speak a word to the congregation. In one of the most beautiful passages in the book, the awe-inspiring acceptance of the truth of his sorrow by a community "well-acquainted by grief," ends with the perennial words of the surviving father:

> The words came from a throat that seemed stoppered with anxiety, memory, grief and dope. And the words, the beginning of a speech he had laboriously learned years ago for just such occasions as this when so much was asked of him, were the same that he gave every year. The same, exact, three. 'My son died.'

Since Alice Walker is, by any account, "a strict constructionist" of fiction, the utter simplicity of the words, "my son died," must serve as the still point around which the meaning of *Meridian* must swirl. So small a sentence demands a halting and a reckoning, both for Meridian and for her attending audience. Walker brings it all together as an *ENDING*.

> There was a reason for the ceremony she witnessed in church. . . . The people in the church were saying to the red-eyed man that his son had not died for nothing, and that if his son should come again they would protect his life with her own. . . . 'Understand this,' they were saying, 'the church (and Meridian

knew they did not mean simply 'church,' as in Baptist, Methodist or whatnot, but rather communal spirit, togetherness, righteous convergence), the music, the form of worship that has always sustained us, the kind of ritual you share with us, these are the ways to transformation that we know. We want to take this as far as we can.' (199)

This passage brings us back to the beginning of the essay, and the difficulty Robert Stepto noted in the narrative voice of *Their Eyes Were Watching God*. The title of that book could—and ought—very well refer to Janie Crawford herself, since the people of her hometown were looking at her, returning from the grave of the Florida muck. Janie was transfigured by her journey; so, too, Meridian. When Meridian speaks *in her mind,* in this passage, she has become possessed by the voice of the holy assembly. She is the votary of the people. All of her actions throughout the novel have been the signs of doing what the people dreamed of doing, but were afraid to attempt. Now she has become so emptied of particularized self, that when she thinks, she can discern the nuances of unarticulated spiritual meaning. It is not a question of "narrative strategies," of determining who is speaking, and when. The least complex answer is: everyone, and no one; then, now and never.

Meridian leaves the church and makes her own vow to the man whose son died. "Yes, indeed she *would* kill, before she allowed anyone to murder his son again." Digging deeply into that promise, Meridian wavers with her authentic ambivalence; perhaps, perhaps not. Within the promise were several other harmonious determinations. One especially fulfills the dream-quest of the journey into the Serpent's Coils, fusing compassion and the dead of centuries before:

> —and when they stop to wash off the blood and find their throats too choked with the smell of murdered flesh to sing, I will come forward and sing from memory songs they will need once more to hear. For it is the song of the people, transformed by the experiences of each generation, that holds them together, and if any part of it is lost the people suffer and are without soul.

In *The Religion, Spirituality, and Thought of Traditional Africa*, Dominique Zahan offers this summary of his understanding of what essentially unifies all traditional African religions:

> . . . it is important to fully apprehend the unity of traditional African religion, not so much through some of its elements as

through man's attitude towards the Invisible, through the position which he feels he occupies in creation, and through his feeling of belonging to the universe. In my view, in short, the essence of African spirituality lies in the feeling man has of being at once image, model and integral part of the world in whose cyclical life he senses himself deeply and necessarily engaged.

Moral life and mystical life, these two aspects of African spirituality, give it its proper dimensions. They constitute, so to speak, the supreme goal of the African soul, the objective towards which the individual strives with all his energy because he feels his perfection can only be completed and consummated if he masters and surpasses himself through divinity, indeed through the mastery of divinity itself.[6]

Meridian's vow unites the moral and the mystical: yes, indeed she would kill, before she allowed anyone to murder his son again. His son, Wile Chile, Camara, the drowned boy, Martin Luther King, and the litany of names punctuating the book will be protected because in the time that *matters*, they cannot die; they are, even now, being born.

Within the traditional theologies of Africa, and within the traditions of mysticism throughout the world, there is one final element that must be addressed. It is final, in several senses, since Walker introduces this theme at the ends of *The Third Life of Grange Copeland*, and *The Color Purple* as well as *Meridian*. St. Paul says, in his Letter to the Galatians: "and there are no more distinctions between Jew and Greek, slave and free, male and female, but all of you are the one in Christ Jesus" (Gal. 3:27). Walker has not exactly covered all of those categories, but she has made a point of re-creating a world in which men become complete only when they become female; not feminine, but female. Grange Copeland becomes the daughter of Ruth. Mister Albert allows his full person to unfold only when Miss Celie begins to clothe him in her specially designed fashions, and teaches him to sew.

The constant illness besetting Meridian throughout the novel is clearly named as the side effects of pregnancy.

'Of course I'm sick,' snapped Meridian. 'Why else would I spend all this time trying to get well!'
'You have a strange way of trying to get well!' (25)

His first thought was of Lazarus, but then he tried to recall someone less passive, who had raised himself without help.

Meridian would return to the world cleansed of sickness. That was what he knew. (219)

Truman felt the room begin to turn and fell to the floor. A moment later, dizzy, he climbed shakily into Meridian's sleeping bag. Underneath his cheek he felt the hard edge of her cap's visor, he pulled it out and put in on his head. (220)

. . . though the handwriting was grotesquely small. . . he recognized it as Anne-Marion's. It contained one line: 'Who would be happier than you that The Sojourner did not die?' She had written, also in minute script, 'perhaps me,' but then had half-erased it. (217)

The photograph of a shoot emerging from the base of The Sojourner is the sign from Meridian's heaven (the between-world space where she is most herself) that announces her health. She has healed the Sojourner, by attending to the dead and bearing them compassionately, ultimately vowing to undo death when it next appears. It is the time of passing-over. Truman begins the physical transformation of self, in the hermitage of the healing woman. He will take Meridian's place and assume her role. She has been both mother and rock, channeling the power of God—who is the community in concerted song and prayer—back into itself. She will be less and less, diminishing and dissolving into the people. The others marked by her passing will undergo the same rites and initiation. Their hungers can be only half-erased. If the world is to be re-created, they must first recognize that they have been cast out, alone; then come close to the rock and cling. Meridian has been the rock, nurturing her children until they are strong enough to crawl into her womb and give birth to their own powerful spirits.

. . . The only new thing now,' she had said to herself, mumbling out aloud, so that people turned to stare at her, 'would be the refusal of Christ to accept crucifixion. King,' she had said, turning down a muddy lane, 'should have refused. All those characters in all those novels that require death to end the book should refuse. All saints should walk away. Do their bit, then—just walk away. See Europe, visit Hawaii, become agronomists, or raise Dalmatians.' She didn't care what they did, but they should do it. (151)

And what should the people do; what is required of them? To choose life. "Magnetic Meridian: a carefully located meridian from which secondary or guide meridians may be constructed."

## Notes

1. Robert B. Stepto, *From Behind the Veil* (Urbana: University of Illinois Press, 1979), 164–166.

2. Significant dwellers on this mystic plain would include John in Baldwin's *Go Tell it on the Mountain,* Milkman in Morrison's *Song of Solomon,* and the most elusive of all the mythic characters of modern Afro-American fiction, Bigger Thomas in Wright's *Native Son.* The concept of a "mystic plain" has been discussed earlier in *Callaloo,* in this author's review, "With Eyes Like Flames of Fire," *(Callaloo,* No. 24, Spring–Summer, 1985).

3. These occasional pieces have been collected in *The Sanctified Church* (Berkeley: Turtle Island Press, 1983). All the references to Hurston will be taken from this edition.

4. Alice Walker, *Meridian* (New York: Washington Square Press, 1977), 49–51. All subsequent references will be taken from this paperback edition.

5. Richard Kieckhefer, in *Unquiet Souls: Fourteenth Century Saints and their Religious Milieu* (Chicago: University of Chicago Press, 1987) presents a most balanced view of the hunger of the mystics for the freedom to fly to the Divine, and of the methods they employed to induce and sustain the ecstatic union. His discussion of the limits of a psychoanalytic critique of mystic behavior is remarkable.

6. Dominique Zahan, *The Religion, Spirituality and Thought of Traditional Africa* (Chicago: University of Chicago Press, 1979), pages 4–5. It is obvious, given the subject of this essay, that the broom of "womanist prose" would have a salutary effect upon the narrative style of Zahan or his translator.

ALICE HALL PETRY

# Alice Walker: The Achievement of the Short Fiction

There's nothing quite like a Pulitzer Prize to draw attention to a little known writer. And for Alice Walker, one of the few black writers of the mid-'60s to remain steadily productive for the two ensuing decades, the enormous success of 1982's *The Color Purple* has generated critical interest in a literary career that has been, even if not widely noted, at the very least worthy of note. As a poet (*Once*, 1968; *Revolutionary Petunias*, 1973) and a novelist (*The Third Life of Grange Copeland*, 1970; *Meridian*, 1976), Walker has always had a small but enthusiastic following, while her many essays, published in black- and feminist-oriented magazines (e.g., *Essence, Ms.*), have likewise kept her name current, albeit in rather limited circles. The Pulitzer Prize has changed this situation, qualitatively and perhaps permanently. Walker's name is now a household word, and a reconsideration of her literary canon, that all but inevitable Pulitzer perk, is well underway. An integral part of this phenomenon would be the reappraisal of her short fiction. Walker's two collections of short stories— 1973's *In Love & Trouble* and 1981's *You Can't Keep a Good Woman Down*—are now available as attractive paperbacks and selling briskly, we are told. But a serious critical examination of her short stories—whether of particular tales, the individual volumes, or the entire canon—has yet to occur. Hence this essay. As a general over-view, it seeks to evaluate Walker's achievement as a short story

*Modern Language Studies*, 19 (1); Winter 1989: pp. 12-27. © 1989 *Modern Language Studies*.

writer while probing a fundamental question raised by so many reviewers of the two volumes: why is *You Can't Keep a Good Woman Down* so consistently less satisfying than the earlier *In Love & Trouble?* How has Alice Walker managed to undermine so completely that latest-and-best formula so dear to book reviewers? The answer, as we shall see, is partly a matter of conception and partly one of technique; and it suggests further that Walker's unevenness thus far as a writer of short fiction—her capacity to produce stories that are sometimes extraordinarily good, at other times startlingly weak—places her at a career watershed. At this critical juncture, Alice Walker could so refine her art as to become one of the finest writers of American short fiction in this century.

She could just as easily not.

. . .

One key to understanding the disparate natures of *In Love & Trouble* and *You Can't Keep a Good Woman Down* is their epigraphs. *In Love & Trouble* offers two. The first epigraph, a page-long extract from *The Concubine* by Elechi Amadi, depicts a girl, Ahurole, who is prone to fits of sobbing and "alarmingly irrational fits of argument": "From all this her parents easily guessed that she was being unduly influenced by agwu, her personal spirit." It is not until the end of the extract that Amadi mentions casually that "Ahurole was engaged to Ekwueme when she was eight days old."[1] In light of what follows in the collection, it is a most suitable epigraph: the women in this early volume truly are "in love and trouble" due in large measure to the roles, relationships, and self-images imposed upon them by a society which knows little and cares less about them as individuals. A marriage arranged in infancy perfectly embodies this situation; and the shock engendered by Amadi's final sentence is only heightened as one reads *In Love & Trouble* and comes to realize that the concubinage depicted in his novel, far from being a bizarre, pagan, foreign phenomenon, is practiced in only slightly modified form in contemporary—especially black—America. In the opening story of *In Love & Trouble*, "Roselily," the overworked title character marries the unnamed Black Muslim from Chicago in part to give her three illegitimate children a better chance in life, and in part to obtain for herself some measure of social and economic security; but it is not really a relationship she chooses to enter freely, as is conveyed by her barely listening to her wedding ceremony—a service which triggers images not of romance but of bondage. Even ten-year-old Myop, the sole character of the vignette "The Flowers," has her childhood—and, ultimately, her attitudes towards her self and her world—shattered by the blunt social reality of lynching: as much as she would love to spend her life all alone collecting flowers, from the moment she accidentally gets her heel caught in the skull of a decapitated lynching victim it is clear that, for their own survival, black females like Myop must be part of a group that includes males. Hence the plethora of bad marriages (whether legal unions or informal liaisons) in Walker's fiction; hence also the mental anguish suffered by most of her women characters, who engage in such unladylike acts as attacking their husbands with chain saws ("Really, Doesn't Crime Pay?," *IL&T*) or setting fire to themselves ("Her Sweet Jerome," *IL&T*). Must be that pesky agwu again—a diagnosis which is symptomatic of society's refusal to face the fact that women become homocidal/suicidal, or hire rootworkers to avenge social snubs ("The Revenge of Hannah Kemhuff," *IL&T*), or lock themselves up in convents ("The Diary of an African Nun," *IL&T*) not because of agwus, or because they are mentally or emotionally deficient, but because they are responding to the stress of situations not of their own making.[2] Certainly marriage offers these women nothing, and neither does religion, be it Christianity, the Black Muslim faith, or voodoo. That these traditional twin sources of comfort and stability cause nothing but "trouble" for Walker's characters might lead one to expect a decidedly depressing volume of short stories; but in fact *In Love & Trouble* is very upbeat. Walker manages to counterbalance the oppressive subject matter of virtually all these 13 stories by maintaining the undercurrent of hope first introduced in the volume's second epigraph, a passage from Rainer Maria Rilke's *Letters to a Young Poet:* . . . we must hold to what is difficult; everything in Nature grows and defends itself in its own way and is characteristically and spontaneously itself, seeks at all costs to be so and against all opposition" (ii). For Walker as for Rilke, opposition is not necessarily insurmountable: struggles and crises can lead to growth, to the nurturing of the self; and indeed most of the women of *In Love & Trouble*, sensing this, do try desperately to face their situations and deal with them—even if to do so may make them seem insane, or ignorant, or anti-social.

The sole epigraph of *You Can't Keep* lacks the relevance and subtlety of those of *In Love & Trouble:* "It is harder to kill something that is spiritually alive than it is to bring the dead back to life."[3] Fine words from Herr Hesse, but unfortunately they don't have much to do with the fourteen stories in the collection. Few characters in *You Can't Keep* would qualify as "spiritually alive" according to most informed standards. We are shown a lot of self-absorbed artistes (the jazz-poet of "The Lover," the authoress of "Fame," the sculpture student of "A Sudden Trip Home in the Spring"), plus rather too many equally self-absorbed would-be radicals ("Advancing Luna—and Ida B. Wells," "Source," "Laurel"), plus a series of women—usually referred to generically as "she"—who engage in seemingly interminable monologues on pornography, abortion, sadomasochism, and rape ("Coming Apart," "Porn," "A Letter of the Times, or Should This Sado-Masochism Be Saved?"). These women are dull. And, unlike the situation in *In Love & Trouble*, the blame can't really be placed on males, those perennial targets of Alice Walker's acid wit. No, the problem with the women of *You Can't Keep* is that they are successful. Unlike the ladies of *In Love & Trouble*, who seem always to be struggling, to be growing, those of *You Can't Keep* have all advanced to a higher plane, personally and socially: as Barbara Christian observes, there truly is a clear progression between the two volumes, from an emphasis on "trouble" to an emphasis on self-assertiveness.[4] The women of *You Can't Keep* embody the product, not the process: where a mother in *In Love & Trouble* ("Everyday Use") can only fantasize about appearing on *The Tonight Show*, a woman of *You Can't Keep* ("Nineteen Fifty-Five") actually does it! Gracie Mae Still meets Johnny! Similarly, a dying old lady in *In Love & Trouble* ("The Welcome Table") is literally thrown out of a segregated white church, but in *You Can't Keep* ("Source") two black women get to sit in an integrated Anchorage bar! With real Eskimos! Trudier Harris is quite correct that, compared to those of *In Love & Trouble*, the women of *You Can't Keep* seem superficial, static: "Free to make choices, they find themselves free to do nothing or to drift"[5]—and they do, with Walker apparently not realizing that in fiction (as in life) the journey, not the arrival, is what interests. Men and marriage, those two bugaboos of *In Love & Trouble* responsible for thwarting women's careers ("Really, *Doesn't* Crime Pay?"), mutilating hapless schoolgirls ("The Child Who Favored Daughter"), and advocating anti-white violence ("Her Sweet Jerome"), at least brought out the strength and imagination of the women they victimized, and the women's struggles engross the reader. In contrast, the men of *You Can't Keep* have declined, both as people and as fictional characters, in an inverse relationship to the women's success. Most of the volume's male characters barely materialize; the few who do appear are milquetoast, from the pudgy, racist lawyer/rapist/lover Bubba of "How Did I Get Away with Killing One of the Biggest Lawyers in the State? It Was Easy"; to Ellis, the Jewish gigolo from Brooklyn who inexplicably dazzles the supposedly cool jazz-poet heroine of "The Lover"; to Laurel, he of the giant pink ears who (again inexplicably) dazzles the black radical journalist in "Laurel." And many of the male characters in *You Can't Keep* meet sorry ends—not unlike the women of *In Love & Trouble*: Bubba is shot to death by his schoolgirl victim; the shopworn Ellis gets dumped; poor Laurel winds up in a coma, only to emerge brain-damaged. Curiously, we don't miss them; instead, we miss the kinds of conflicts and personal/social revelations which fully-realized, reasonably healthy male characters can impart to fiction.

For men, either directly or through the children they father, are a vital part of love; and it is love, as the soap operatic title of *In Love & Trouble* suggests,[6] which is most operative in that early volume. It assumes various forms. It may be the love between a parent and child, surely the most consistently positive type of love in Walker's fiction. It is her love for her dying baby which impels Rannie Toomer to chase a urinating mare in a rainstorm so as to collect "Strong Horse Tea," a folk medicine. It is her love for her daughter Dee that enables Mama to call her "Wangero Leewanika Kemanjo" in acknowledgment of her new Afro identity, but her equally strong love for her other child, the passive Maggie, which enables her to resist Dee/Wangero's demand for old quilts (Maggie's wedding present) to decorate her apartment ("Everyday Use"). Then again, the love of *In Love & Trouble* may be between a woman and God ("The Welcome Table"); and it may even have an erotic dimension, as with the sexually-repressed black nun of "The Diary of an African Nun" who yearns for her "pale lover," Christ (115). And granted, the love of *In Love & Trouble* is often distorted, even perverse: a father lops off his daughter's breasts in part because he confuses her with his dead sister, whom he both loved and loathed ("The Child Who Favored Daughter"); a young black girl and her middle-aged French teacher, the guilt-ridden survivor of the holocaust, fantasize about each other but never interact ("We Drink the Wine in France"); a dumpy hairdresser stabs and burns her husband's Black Power pamphlets as if they were his mistress: "Trash!' she cried over and over ...'I kill you! I kill you!'" ("Her Sweet Jerome," 34). But in one form or another, love is the single most palpable force in *In Love & Trouble*. This is not the case in *You Can't Keep*, and the volume suffers accordingly.

What happened to love in the later collection? Consider the case of "Laurel." What does that supposedly "together" black radical narrator see in wimpy Laurel? Easy answer: his "frazzled but beautifully fitting jeans": "It occurred to me that I could not look at Laurel without wanting to make love with him" (107). As the black radical and her mousy lover engage in "acrobatics of a sexual sort" on Atlanta's public benches (108), it is clear that "love" is not an issue in this story: these characters have simply fallen in lust. And as a result, the reader finds it impossible to be concerned about the ostensible theme of the story: the ways in which segregation thwarts human relationships. Who cares that segregation "was keeping us from strolling off to a clean, cheap hotel" (109) when all they wanted was a roll in the sack? Likewise, the husband and wife of "Coming Apart," who speak almost ad nauseum on the subjects of pornography and sadomasochism, seem to feel nothing for each other: they are simply spokespersons for particular attitudes regarding contemporary sexual mores, and ample justification for Mootry-Ikerionwu's observation that characterization is definitely not Alice Walker's strong suit.[7] Without love, without warmth, this ostensible Everywife and Everyhusband connect literally only when they are copulating; and as a result Walker's statements regarding the sexual exploitation of women, far from being enriched by the personal touch of seeing how it affects one typical marriage, collapses into a dry lecture punctuated by clumsy plugs for consciousness-raising essays by Audre Lorde, Luisah Teish, and Tracy A. Gardner. Similarly, its title notwithstanding, "The Lover" has nothing to do with love. The story's liberated heroine, having left her husband and child for a summer at an artists' colony in New England, decides—just like that—to have an affair with the lupine Ellis: "when she had first seen him she had thought . . . 'my lover,' and had liked, deep down inside, the illicit sound of it. She had never had a lover; he would be her first. Afterwards, she would be truly a woman of her time" (34). Apparently this story was meant to be a study of how one woman—educated, intelligent, creative—uses her newly-liberated sensuality to explore her sense of womanhood, her marriage, her career as a jazz poet. But the one-night-stand quality of her relationship with Ellis, not to mention the inappropriateness of him as a "lover"—he likes to become sexually involved each summer "with talkative women who wrote for *Esquire* and the *New York Times*" because they "made it possible for him to be included in the proper tennis sets and swimming parties at the Colony" (36)—makes the story's heroine seem like a fool. And that points to a major problem with *You Can't Keep a Good Woman Down:* whereas the stories of *In Love & Trouble* move the reader to tears, to shock, to thought, those of the latter volume too often move him to guffaws. Too bad they weren't meant to be humorous.

One would think that a writer of Alice Walker's stature and experience would be aware that, since time began, the reduction of love to fornication has been the basis of jokes, from the ridiculous to the sublime. And whether they come across as comic caricatures *(vide* Laurel and Ellis), examples of bathroom humor, or zany parodies, the characters, subject matter, and writing style of most of the stories in *You Can't Keep a Good Woman Down* leave the reader with a she's-gotta-be-kidding attitude that effectively undercuts its very serious intentions. Consider the subject matter. In stories like "Porn," "A Letter of the Times," and "Coming Apart," Walker *attacks* pornography, sadomasochism, and violence against women by *discussing* them: it's a technique that many writers have used, but it can backfire by (1) appealing to the prurient interests of some readers, (2) imparting excitement to the forbidden topic, or (3) discussing the controversial subject matter so much that it becomes noncontroversial, unshocking; and without the "edge" of controversy, these serious topics often seem to be treated satirically—even when that is not the case. This is what happens in many stories in *You Can't Keep,* and the problem is compounded by the weak characters. The story "Coming Apart" is a good example: the husband dashes home from his bourgeois desk job to sit in the john and masturbate while drooling over the "Jivemates" in *Jiveboy* magazine. None of this shocks: we see so many references to genitalia and elimination in *You Can't Keep* that they seem as mundane as mailing a letter. Worse, the husband himself (called "he" to emphasize his role as Typical Male) comes across as a rather dense, naughty adolescent boy. He is so clearly suffering from a terminal case of the Peter Pan syndrome that it's impossible to believe that he'd respond with "That girl's onto something" when his equally-vapid wife (called "she") reads him yet another anti-pornography essay from her library of black feminist sociological tracts (51). Walker's-gotta-be-kidding, but she isn't. Likewise, the story "Fame" has a streak of crudity that leaves the reader wondering how to respond. For the most part, "Fame" consists of the ruminations of one Andrea Clement White (Walker always uses all three names), a wildly successful and universally admired writer who returns to her old college to receive her one-hundred-and-eleventh major award (63). She doesn't much like her former (Caucasian) colleagues or the banquet they are giving her, as her thoughts on the imminent award speech testifies:

> "This little lady has done . . ." Would he have said "This little man . . ."? But of course not. No man wanted to be called little. He thought it referred to his penis. But to say "little lady" made men think of virgins. Tight, tiny pussies, and moments of rape. (60, Walker's ellipses)

As Andrea Clement White degenerates from Famous Author to a character type from farce—the salty-tongued granny, the sweet old lady with the dirty mind—everything Walker was trying to say about identity, success, black pride has dissipated. We keep waiting for Walker to wink, to say that "Fame" is a satire; but it isn't.

The reader's uncertainty about how to respond to *You Can't Keep a Good Woman Down* is not dispelled by the writing style of many of the stories. Funny thing about lust: when you confuse it with love and try to write about it passionately, the result sounds curiously like parody. The following passage from "Porn" reads like a Harlequin romance:

> She was aflame with desire for him.
> On those evenings when all the children [from the respective previous marriages] were with their other parents, he would arrive at the apartment at seven. They would walk hand in hand to a Chinese restaurant a mile away. They would laugh and drink and eat and touch hands and knees over and under the table. They would come home. Smoke a joint. He would put music on. She would run water in the tub with lots of bubbles. In the bath they would lick and suck each other, in blissful delight. They would admire the rich

candle glow on their wet, delectably earth-toned skins. Sniff the incense—the odor of sandal and redwood. He would carry her in to bed.

*Music. Emotion. Sensation. Presence.*
*Satisfaction like rivers*
*flowing and silver.*

("Porn," *YCK*, 78)

Except for the use of controlled substances and the licking and sucking, this is pure Barbara Cartland. Likewise, the narrator's passion for Laurel (in the story of the same name) makes one blush—over the writing: "I thought of his musical speech and his scent of apples and May wine with varying degrees of regret and tenderness"; their "week of passion" had been "magical, memorable, but far too brief" ("Laurel," *YCK*, 111).

One might be inclined to excuse these examples on the grounds that love (or lust, or whatever) tends naturally towards purple prose. Unfortunately, however, similar excesses undermine *You Can't Keep* even when the characters' hormones are in check. Here is Andrea Clement White once again, musing on her professional achievements while awaiting the award at her banquet:

If she was famous, she wondered fretfully . . , why didn't she *feel* famous? She had made money . . . Lots of money. Thousands upon thousands of dollars. She had seen her work accepted around the world, welcomed even, which was more than she'd ever dreamed possible for it. And yet—there remained an emptiness, no, an ache, which told her she had not achieved what she had set out to achieve.

("Fame," *YCK*, 55)

The theme is stale; worse, the writing itself is trite, clichéd; and frankly one wonders how anyone with so unoriginal a mind could be receiving her one hundred and eleventh major award. The same triteness mars "A Sudden Trip Home in the Spring," in which Sarah Davis, a black scholarship student at northern Cresselton College, is "immersed in Camusian philosophy, versed in many languages" (131) and the close personal friend of the small-eyed, milky-legged, dirty-necked blonde daughter of "one of the richest men in the world" (127). Sarah is BWOC at Cresselton: "She was popular"; "Her friends beamed love and envy upon her"; her white tennis partners think that she walks "Like a gazelle" (124, 125). There is a momentary suggestion that Sarah takes her situation and her classmates with a grain of salt ("She was interesting, 'beautiful,' only because they had no idea what made her, charming only because they had no idea from where she came" [130]), but this theme and tone are quickly abandoned as the tale lapses into a curiously un-black reworking of the you-can't-go-home-again concept. If irony is what Walker has in mind, it certainly doesn't come through; and the over-all impression one gets from "A Sudden Trip" is that, like her 1973 biography of Langston Hughes, this is an earnest story intended for adolescent readers who appreciate simplistic themes, characters, and writing styles.

The mature reader's uncertainty over how to respond to "A Sudden Trip" takes on a new wrinkle when one considers that Sarah Davis's prototype was another black scholarship student from rural Georgia attending an exclusive northern college: Alice Walker.[8] The least effective, most seemingly comic heroines in Walker's short fiction were inspired by Walker herself. These predominate in *You Can't Keep a Good Woman Down.*

Walker has never denied that there are some autobiographical dimensions to her stories. When "Advancing Luna—and Ida B. Wells" was first published in *Ms.* magazine, Walker included a disclaimer that "Luna and Freddie Pye are composite characters, and their names are made up. This is a fictionalized account suggested by a number of real events"; and John O'Brien's 1973 interview with Walker offers further details.[9] Similarly, Walker in a 1981 interview with Kristin Brewer discusses the autobiographical basis of her earliest story, 1967's "To Hell with Dying" *(IL&T).*[10] Anyone familiar with Walker's personal life will see the significance of the references to Sarah Lawrence, the doorless first apartment in New York, and the job at the Welfare Department in "Advancing Luna" *(YCK);* or the stay at a New England artists' colony in "The Lover" *(YCK);* or the marriage to a New York Jew, the baby girl, the novel, and the house in the segregated South in "Laurel" *(YCK).* There is nothing inherently wrong with using oneself as the prototype for a story's character; the problem is that the writer tends, of course, to present his fictionalized self in the most flattering—even fantastic—light possible; and too readily that self assumes a larger role in the story than may be warranted by the exigencies of plot and characterization. Consider "Advancing Luna," in which the speaker—who is "difficult to distinguish from Walker herself"[11]— takes over the story like kudzu. We really don't need to hear all about her ex-boyfriends, her getting "high on wine and grass" with a Gene Autry lookalike who paints teeth on fruit, or her adventures in glamorous Africa ("I was taken on rides down the Nile as a matter of course") (94, 96, 90). Her palpable self-absorption and self-congratulation draw the story's focus away from its titular heroine, poor Luna—the selfless victim of interracial rape who ostensibly is an adoring friend and confidante of the narrator. The reader's immediate response (after confusion) is that the story is really quite funny—and with that response, all of Walker's serious commentary on rape, miscegenation, and segregation have dissipated. We see the same inadvertently comic, Walker-inspired heroine in "Laurel" and "The Lover." In the latter, the jazz poet "had reached the point of being generally pleased with herself," and no wonder. What with her "carefully selected tall sandals and her naturally tall hair, which stood in an elegant black afro with exactly seven strands of silver hair," and her "creamy brown" thighs and "curvaceous and strong legs," she is able to stop meals the way other women stop traffic: "If she came late to the dining room and stood in the doorway a moment longer than necessary—looking about for a place to sit after she had her tray—for that moment the noise from the cutlery already in use was still" (34–35). (Really, who could blame Ellis for wanting her so?) If only there were an element of self-mockery in "The Lover"; if only Walker were being ironic in "A Sudden Trip"; if only she were lampooning the shopworn notion of the successful but unsatisfied celebrity in "Fame"; if only she were parodying romantic writing styles (and thereby puncturing those "love affairs" undertaken purely to prove one's "sexual liberation") in stories like "Porn," "Laurel," and "The Lover." But there is absolutely nothing in Alice Walker's interviews, nothing in her many personal essays, nothing in her friends' and colleagues' reviews of her books, nothing anywhere to suggest that she is being anything but dead serious in *You Can't Keep a Good Woman Down*.

What is especially unfortunate about the unintentional humor of *You Can't Keep* is that Walker is quite capable of handling her material very effectively; in several stories, for example, she excels at narrative technique. Consider "How Did I Get Away with Killing One of the Biggest Lawyers in the State? It Was Easy" *(YCK)*. At first glance, the narrative voice seems untenable: how is it that a poor little black girl from Poultry Street writes such perfect English? (Placed entirely in quotation marks, the story is "written" by her.) We learn the answer at the end of the story: having murdered Bubba, the white lawyer who became her lover after raping her, the narrator/confessor stole all the money from his office safe and used it to finance her college education. Hence her flawless English, and the irony of her "confession": there is no repentance here, and no reader can blame her. The point of view also is consistent and effective. The same cannot be said of the long and rambling "Source," which unfortunately occupies the second most prominent position in *You Can't Keep*—the very end. It has no identifiable point of view, and suffers accordingly. "Source" would have been far more effective had Walker utilized what has been identified as her "ruminative style": "a meandering yet disciplined meditation."[12] It is seen in those stories (first-person or otherwise) which essentially record one character's impressions or thoughts, such as "Fame" *(YCK)*, "Roselily" *(IL&T)*, and "The Diary of an African Nun" *(IL&T)*. The sometimes staccato, sometimes discursive third-person narration of "Roselily"—"She feels old. Yoked." (6)—is reminiscent of E. A. Robinson's account of another dubious love affair, "Eros Turannos" ("She fears him, and will always ask / What fated her to choose him"). Likewise, the barely-restrained first-person narration of "The Diary of an African Nun" is very evocative of Li Po's "The River-Merchant's Wife: A Letter," and it comes as no surprise that Walker attributes her fondness for short literary forms to the Oriental poetry she has loved since college.[13] Also effective is the shifting point of view: the black father's and black daughter's disparate attitudes towards her affair with a married white man is conveyed by the alternating perspectives of "The Child Who Favored Daughter" *(IL&T)*. This rhythmic technique is usually identified as cinematic, but it also owes much to the blues, as Walker herself is well aware.[14]

This blues quality in the narrative points to the bases of several of her best stories: the oral tradition. Whereas stories based on Walker's own experiences tend, as noted, to be over-written and hence inadvertently comic, her most memorable tales are often inspired by incidents which were told to her—be they actual accounts (e.g., "The Revenge of Hannah Kemhuff" *[IL&T]* depicts her mother's rebuff by a white woman while trying to obtain government food during the Depression) or black folk tales (e.g., "Strong Horse Tea").[15] A particularly striking example is "The Welcome Table" *(IL&T):* having been ejected bodily from an all-white church, an old black lady meets Christ on a local road, walks and talks with him, and then is found frozen to death, with eyewitnesses left wondering why she had been walking down that cold road all alone, talking to herself. It could be right out of Stith Thompson. The importance of the oral tradition in Walker's stories is further evident in direct addresses to the reader ('you know how sick [my husband] makes me now when he grins' ["Really, *Doesn't* Crime Pay?," *IL&T,* 11]) and parenthetical asides ("I scrooched down as small as I could at the corner of Tante Rosie's table, smiling at her so she wouldn't feel embarrassed or afraid" ["The Revenge of Hannah Kemhuff," *IL&T,* 61]). The oral quality of Walker's stories is as old as folk tales, ballads, and slave narratives, and as new as Joan Didion, who shares with Walker a flair for using insane or criminal female narrators: compare Maria in *Play It as It Lays* with the would-be chain saw murderess in "Really, *Doesn't* Crime Pay?" *(IL&T)* or the coolly-detached killer of "How Did I Get Away with Killing. . ." *(YCK).*[16] Curiously, when the teller of the tale is an emotionally-stable omniscient narrator, the oral tale techniques tends to backfire. For example, the narrator's remark at the opening of "Elethia" *(YCK)*—*"A* certain perverse experience shaped Elethia's life, and made it possible for it to be true that she carried with her at all times a small apothecary jar of ashes" (27)—sounds regrettably like a voice-over by John-Boy Walton.

Clearly the oral tradition is a mixed blessing for Walker's fiction; but it is a particular liability when, as in so many folk tales and ballads, there is a paucity of exposition. Consider "Entertaining God" *(IL&T),* in which a little boy worships a gorilla he has stolen from the Bronx Zoo. The story would make no sense to a reader unfamiliar with Flannery O'Connor's *Wise Blood,*[17] and where a lack of preliminary information tends to draw the reader into O'Connor's novel, it alienates him in "Entertaining God": the story comes across as a disjointed, fragmentary, aborted novella. Another *Wise Blood*-inspired story, "Elethia" (in which a character with a habit of lurking about museums steals a mummy which proves to be a stuffed black man), does not fare much better. Similarly, as Chester J. Fontenot points out, "The Diary of an African Nun" *(IL&T)*, although "only six pages in length, . . . contains material for a novella."[18] Expanded to that length, "The Diary" could take an honorable place alongside another first-person account by a disenchanted nun, *The Nun's Story*—assuming, of course, that Walker did not turn it into a series of socioeconomic lectures disguised as chatty personal letters as she did with African missionary Nettie's letters in *The Color Purple*. Lack of exposition can be extreme in Walker's short stories. Consider this extract from "Porn" *(YCK):* "They met. Liked each other. Wrote five or six letters over the next seven years. Married other people. Had children. Lived in different cities. Divorced. Met again to discover they now shared a city and lived barely three miles apart" (77). How is the reader to respond to this? Is Walker making a statement about the predictability, the lamentable sameness of the lives lived in the ostensibly individuality-minded 1970s? Or is she just disinclined to write out the details? The more one reads *You Can't Keep*, the more one tends (albeit reluctantly) towards the latter.

Walker's disinclination for exposition, and the concomitant impression that many of her stories are outlines or fragments of longer works, is particularly evident in a technique which mars even her strongest efforts: a marked preference for "telling" over "showing." This often takes the form of summaries littered with adjectives. In "Advancing Luna" *(YCK)*, for example, the narrator waxes nostalgic over her life with Luna in New York: "our relationship, always marked by mutual respect, evolved into a warm and comfortable friendship which provided a stability and comfort we both needed at that time" (91). But since, as noted earlier, the narrator comes across as vapid and self-absorbed, and since the only impressions she provides of Luna are rife with contempt for this greasy-haired, Clearasil-daubed, poor-little-rich-white-girl from Cleveland, the narrator's paean to their mutual warmth and friendship sounds ridiculous. No wonder critic Katha Pollitt stated outright that she "never believed for a minute" that the narrator and Luna were close friends.[19] Even more unfortunate is Walker's habit of telling the reader what the story is about, of making sure that he doesn't overlook a single theme. For example, in "The Abortion" *(YCK)*, the heroine Imani, who is just getting over a traumatic abortion, attends the memorial service of a local girl, Holly Monroe, who had been shot to death while returning home from her high school graduation. Lest we miss the point, Walker spells it out for us: "every black girl of a certain vulnerable age *was* Holly Monroe. And an even deeper truth was that Holly Monroe was herself [i.e., Imani]. Herself shot down, aborted on the eve of becoming herself" (73). Similarly transparent, here is one of the last remarks in the story "Source" *(YCK)*. It is spoken by Irene, the former teacher in a federally-funded adult education program, to her ex-hippie friend, Anastasia/Tranquility: "I was looking toward 'government' for help; you were looking to Source [a California guru]. In both cases, it was the wrong direction—*any* direction that is away from ourselves is the wrong direction" (166). The irony of their parallel situations is quite clear without having Irene articulate her epiphany in an Anchorage bar. Even at the level of charactonyms, Walker "tells" things to her reader. We've already noted the over-used "he"/ "she" device for underscoring sex roles, but even personal names are pressed into service. For example, any reasonably perceptive reader of the vignette "The Flowers" *(IL&T)* will quickly understand the story's theme: that one first experiences reality in all its harshness while far from home, physically and/or experientially; one's immediate surroundings are comparatively "innocent." The reader would pick up on the innocence of nearsightedness even if the main character, ten-year-old Myop, hadn't been named after myopia. Likewise, "The Child Who Favored Daughter" is actually marred by having the father kill his daughter because he confuses her with his dead sister named "Daughter." The hints of incest,[20] the unclear cross-generational identities, and the murky Freudian undercurrents are sufficiently obvious without the daughter/Daughter element: it begins to smack of Abbott and Costello's "Who's on First?" routine after just a few pages. Alice Walker's preference for telling over showing suggests a mistrust of her readers, or her texts, or both.

One might reasonably ask how a professional writer with twenty years' experience could seem so unsure about her materials and/or her audience, could have such uneven judgment regarding fictional technique, could seem so strained or defensive in her short stories. Part of the answer may be that she is a cross-generic writer. Leslie Stephen felt that newspaper writing was lethal for a fiction writer, and perhaps the same may be said for journalistic writing—especially when the magazine's target readership is a special interest group. Whatever the case, as a short story writer Alice Walker seems to alternate between (1) presenting editorials as fiction, (2) experimenting with the short story as a recognized literary form, and (3) rather self-consciously writing "conventional" short stories. At best, the results are mixed.

The magazine editorials which masquerade as short stories are among Walker's least successful efforts. The classic example of this is "Coming Apart" *(YCK)*. It began as the introduction to a chapter on violence against third world women in *Take Back the Night;* then, with the title of "A Fable," it ended up in *Ms.* magazine, for which Walker happened to be a contributing editor; and now, unrevised, it is being marketed as a short story in *You Can't Keep a Good Woman Down.*[21] The volume contains several stories which occupy this

No Man's Land between journalism and fiction: "Advancing Luna," "Porn," "A Letter of the Times"—and, somewhat less transparently, "Elethia," "Petunias," and "Source"—all exist so that Walker (or a mouthpiece character) can make some statement about pornography, racism, politics, sado-masochism, the Search for Self, whatever. Perhaps these "stories" have some impact when read in isolation, months apart, in a magazine such as *Ms.;* but when packaged as a collection of short stories they are predictable and pedantic. The omniscient narrators and mouthpiece characters rarely get off their soap-boxes; too often they resort to lecturing other characters or the reader. Consider this appraisal of the husband in "Coming Apart": "What he has refused to see . . . is that where white women are depicted in pornography as 'objects,' black women are depicted as animals. Where white women are depicted at least as human beings, black women are depicted as shit" (52). The insistence upon the points Walker is trying to make would be appropriate for editorials or magazine essays, but it doesn't wash in a short story.

Those stories in which Walker attempts to experiment with what is commonly held to be "the short story" are a bit stronger, although they often have that fragmentary, unpolished quality alluded to earlier. Frequently the experimental pieces are very short: "Petunias" *(YCK)* is a one-page diary entry by a woman blown up by her Vietnam veteran son; it is entirely in italics, as are "The Flowers" *(IL&T)* and "Elethia" *(YCK)*. As Mel Watkins notes in the *New York Times Book Review,* Alice Walker's shorter pieces tend to be "thin as fiction," and he is probably correct to classify them as that short story offshoot, "prose poems."[22] Longer pieces also can be experimental. For example, "Roselily" *(IL&T)* utilizes a point/counterpoint format, alternating fragments of the wedding ceremony with the thoughts of the bride: the phrase "to join this man and this woman" triggers "She thinks of ropes, chains, handcuffs, his religion" (4). The irony is as heavy-handed as the imagery, but the device does work in this story. Experimentation with structure just as often fails, however. "Entertaining God" *(IL&T)* offers three discrete cinematic scenes—one of the boy and the gorilla, another (evidently a flashback) of his father, and a third of his mother, a librarian turned radical poet; but the scenes never really connect. Perhaps it was meant to be what Walker has termed (in reference to *Meridian)* a "crazy quilt story,"[23] but if so the quilting pieces never do form a pattern. The same quality of uncertainty and incompletion is evident in "Advancing Luna," which offers four—count 'em, four—separate endings with such pretentious titles as "Afterwords, Afterwards, Second Thoughts," "Discarded Notes," and "Imaginary Knowledge." Apparently meant to be thought-provoking, instead they suggest that Walker is indecisive about why she even wrote the story—or, what is worse, is resorting to experimentation as an end in itself.

In light of all this, one might expect Walker's more "conventional" stories to be uniformly stronger than the essay/story hybrids or the experimental efforts, but such is not always the case. All too often, conventionality brings out the banal, the sentimental, and the contrived in Alice Walker. Not surprisingly, two of her earliest stories—"To Hell with Dying" (*IL&T*) and "A Sudden Trip Home in the Spring" (*YCK*)—are very conventional in terms of structure, characterization, and action. In each, a young woman returns to her rural Southern home from college up North at the death of an elderly loved one. Old Mr. Sweet in "To Hell with Dying" is a sort of dipsomaniac Uncle Remus, wrinkled and white-haired, with the obligatory whiskers, a nightshirt redolent of liniment, and a fondness for singing "Sweet Georgia Brown" to the narrator, who helps to "revive" him during his periodic fake deathbed scenes. In short, he is very much the sentimentalized "old darky" character that Walker challenged so vigorously in "Elethia," that O'Connoresque tale of the grinning, stuffed Uncle Albert in the white man's restaurant window. Sarah Davis, the heroine of the equally sentimental "A Sudden Trip," summarizes what she learned by attending her estranged father's funeral: "sometimes you can want something a whole lot, only to find out later that it wasn't what you *needed* at all" (136). Is it any wonder that black writer Ishmael Reed has called Walker "'the colored Norman Rockwell'"?[24]

Her sentimental streak has been noted by many of her commentators (Jerry H. Bryant admits to a lump in his throat), and Walker herself acknowledges she is "nostalgic for the solidarity and sharing a modest existence can sometimes bring."[25] Perhaps it does have a place in some of the stories from early in her career. But it seems frankly incongruous in the work of a woman who prides herself on being a hard-hitting realist, and it poses particular problems in her handling of the stories' endings. The potentially incisive "Fame" is all but ruined when the tough-as-nails Andrea Clement White melts at hearing a little black girl sing a slave song. Likewise, "The Lover" (*YCK*) ends with the jazz poet heroine in a reverie: she "lay in bed next day dreaming of all the faraway countries, daring adventures, passionate lovers still to be found" (39). Perhaps in part to avoid these final lapses into sentimentality, Walker sometimes doesn't "end" her stories: she leaves them "open." It can be a very effective technique in stories such as "Strong Horse Tea" (*IL&T*) or "The Child Who Favored Daughter" (*IL&T*), where the pain is underscored by the lack—indeed, the impossibility—of resolution in the character's situations. Probably Walker's strongest non-sentimental endings belong to three of the most conventional stories: "The Revenge of Hannah Kemhuff" (*IL&T*), "Nineteen Fifty-Five" (*YCK*), and "Source" (*YCK*). In "The Revenge," Mrs. Sarah Marie Sadler Holley, fearing that a black rootworker will be able to use them in spells against her, stores her feces "in barrels and plastic bags in the upstairs closets" rather than trust "the earthen secrecy of the water mains" (80, 79). Her psychotic behavior turns her husband against her, and she lets herself die in a chilling dénouement that would do Miss Emily Grangerford proud.

Walker has used the psychology of guilt and fear in lieu of the Jesus-fixed-her-but-good attitude held by Hannah's prototype, Walker's mother, and the refusal to sentimentalize enhances the story. Likewise, "Nineteen Fifty-Five," a strong story with which to open *You Can't Keep* but atypical of the volume, is a sort of docudrama tracing the career of Elvis Presley (Traynor) through the eyes of blues great Big Mama Thornton (Gracie Mae Still). Still never does understand this sleepy-eyed white man or his alien world, and her reaction to seeing his funeral on television—"One day this is going to be a pitiful country, I thought" (20)—is the perfect conclusion to the story. No sentiment, no commentary. Finally, "Source" offers a surprisingly non-sentimental ending to an insistently nostalgia-soaked story. Whether they are grooving in a Mann County commune with Peace, Calm, and Bliss (didn't nostalgia for the '60s end with *Easy Rider*?) or getting it together in the '70s in an Anchorage bar (sort of *"The Big Chill* Goes Alaskan"), the story of Irene and Anastasia/Tranquility has little for anyone. But the ending of the story—that is, after the now-reconciled heroines have hugged "knee against knee, thigh against thigh, breast against breast, neck nestled against neck" (167)—is quite provocative: a group of tourists, peering through the mists, believe they are seeing Mt. McKinley: "They were not. It was yet another, nearer, mountain's very large feet, its massive ankles wreathed in clouds, that they took such pleasure in" (167). Suggestive without being saccharine, and ironic without that "tinge of cynicism"[26] which undercuts so many of Walker's endings, it is an ideal fade-out conclusion to a collection that, with varying degrees of success, seeks to pose questions, to raise issues, to offer no pat answers.

• • •

The strengths and weaknesses of *In Love & Trouble* and *You Can't Keep a Good Woman Down* offer little clue as to the direction Alice Walker will take as a writer of short fiction in years to come. Surely she will continue to write short stories: Walker personally believes that women are best suited to fiction of limited scope—David Bradley points out that this is "the kind of sexist comment a male critic would be pilloried for making"[27]—and she feels further that, as her career progresses, her writing has been "always moving toward more and more clarity and directness."[28] The often fragmentary and rambling tales of *You Can't Keep*, published eight years after the moving and tightly constructed *In Love & Trouble*, would suggest that this is not the case. At this point in her career as a short story writer, one wishes that Walker would acknowledge the validity of Katha Pollitt's appraisal of *You Can't Keep:* "Only the most coolly abstract and rigorously intellectual writer" can achieve what Walker attempts in this recent volume, but unfortunately that is not what she is like: "As a storyteller she is impassioned, sprawling, emotional, lushly evocative, steeped in place, in memory, in the compelling power of narrative itself. A lavishly gifted writer, in other words—but not of this sort of book."[29] What Alice Walker needs is to take a step backward: to return to the folk tale formats, the painful exploration of interpersonal relationships, the naturally graceful style that made her earlier collection of short stories, the durable *In Love & Trouble*, so very fine. Touch base, lady.

## NOTES

1. Alice Walker, *in Love & Trouble: Stories of Black Women* (New York: Harcourt Brace Jovanovich, n. d.), [i]. Henceforth, all page numbers will be indicated parenthetically in the body of the paper.

2. Barbara Christian discusses the significance of the agwu and its Western counterpart, "contrariness," in "A Study of *In Love and [sic] Trouble:* The Contrary Women of Alice Walker," *Black Scholar,* 12 (March–April, 1981), 21–30, 70–71.

3. Alice Walker, *You Can't Keep a Good Woman Down* (New York: Harcourt Brace Jovanovich, 1981), [i]. Henceforth, all page numbers will be indicated parenthetically in the body of the paper.

4. Barbara Christian, "Alice Walker: The Black Woman Artist as Wayward," in Mari Evans, ed., *Black Women Writers (1950–1980): A Critical Evaluation* (Garden City, New York: Anchor Press/Doubleday, 1984), p. 468.

5. Trudier Harris, "From Victimization to Free Enterprise: Alice Walker's *The Color Purple,*" *Studies in American Fiction,* 14 (Spring, 1986), 5.

6. In her review of *In Love & Trouble,* June Goodwin notes that "The title may hover on 'The Edge of Night,' but none of the rest of 'In Love and Trouble' has an inch of the soap opera about it" (*Christian Science Monitor,* 65 [September 19, 1973], 11).

7. Maria K. Mootry-Ikerionwu, ["Review of *The Color Purple*"], *College Language Association Journal,* 27 (March, 1984), 348.

8. The connection between Sarah Davis and Alice Walker is made by Martha J. McGowan, "Atonement and Release in Alice Walker's *Meridian,*" *Critique,* 23 (1981), 36; and Jacqueline Trescott, "A Child of the South, a Writer of the Heart," *The Washington Post* (August 8, 1976), G3.

9. "Advancing Luna—and Ida B. Wells," *Ms.,* 6 (July, 1977), 75; John O'Brien, "Alice Walker," in *Interviews With Black Writers* (New York: Liveright, 1973), p. 196.

10. Kristin Brewer, "Writing to Survive: An Interview with Alice Walker," *Southern Exposure,* 9 (Summer, 1981), 13.

11. McGowan [see note 8], 33.

12. Peter Erickson, "'Cast Out Alone/To Heal/and Re-Create/Ourselves': Family-Based Identity in The Work of Alice Walker," *College Language Association Journal,* 23 (September, 1979), 91.

13. "I have been influenced—especially in the poems in *Once*—by Zen epigrams and by Japanese haiku. I think my respect for short forms comes from this" (O'Brien [see note 9], pp. 193–94).

14. Barbara Christian points out the "almost cinematic rhythm" of the alternating points of view in "The Contrary Women" [see note 2], 26. The blues connection has been remarked by Mel Watkins in the *New York Times Book Review*

(March 17, 1974), 41; John F. Callahan, "The Higher Ground of Alice Walker," *New Republic*, 171 (September 14, 1974), 22; and Walker herself: "'I am trying to arrive at that place where black music already is; to arrive at that unselfconscious sense of collective oneness; that naturalness, that (even when anguished) grace'" (O'Brien, p. 204).

15. Walker discusses the genesis of "The Revenge of Hannah Kemhuff" in Mary Helen Washington, "An Essay on Alice Walker" in Roseann P. Bell, Bettye J. Parker, and Beverly Guy-Sheftall, eds., *Sturdy Black Bridges: Visions of Black Women in Literature* (Garden City, New York: Anchor Press/Doubleday, 1979), p. 136; and Claudia Tate, "Alice Walker," in *Black Women Writers at Work* (New York: Continuum, 1985), p. 186.

16. In the Winter, 1970–1971 issue of *American Scholar*, Mark Schorer reviewed both Didion's *Play It As It Lays* and Walker's *The Third Life of Grange Copeland*. Schorer argued that "One page of Didion's novel is enough to show us that she is the complete master of precisely those technical qualities in which Alice Walker is still deficient. One [may] read literally dozens of novels without encountering the kind of novelistic authority that she wields so coolly" (172). Perhaps Walker, taking her cue from Schorer, has been emulating Didion's example. Certainly this might help account for the Didionesque quality in so much of Walker's fiction.

17. Walker asserts that O'Connor "'is the best of the white southern writers, including Faulkner,'" and that she has been an important influence on her work (O'Brien, p. 200). See also Alice Walker's essay "Beyond the Peacock: The Reconstruction of Flannery O'Connor," *Ms.*, 4 (December, 1975), 77–79, 102–106.

18. Chester J. Fontenot, "Alice Walker: 'The Diary of an African Nun' and DuBois' Double Consciousness," in Bell, et al., eds., *Sturdy Black Bridges*, p. 151.

19. Katha Pollitt, "Stretching the Short Story," *New York Times Book Review*, (May 24, 1981), 9.

20. For a full discussion of the incest theme in this story, see Trudier Harris, "Tiptoeing through Taboo: Incest in 'The Child Who Favored Daughter,'" *Modern Fiction Studies*, 28 (Autumn, 1982), 495–505.

21. Walker explains the publishing history of "Coming Apart" in a disclaimer at the beginning of the story (*YCK*, pp. 41–42).

22. Watkins [see note 14], 41.

23. "A crazy-quilt story is one that can jump back and forth in time, work on many different levels, and one that can include myth. It is generally much more evocative of metaphor and symbolism than a novel that is chronological in structure, or one devoted, more or less, to rigorous realism . . . (quoted in Tate [see note 15], p. 176).

24. Quoted in Trescott [see note 8], G3.

25. Jerry H. Bryant, ["Review of *In Love & Trouble*"], *Nation*, 217 (November 12, 1973), 502; Alice Walker, "The Black Writer and the Southern Experience," *New South*, 25 (Fall, 1970), 24.

26. Carolyn Fowler, "Solid at the Core," *Freedomways*, 14 (First Quarter, 1974), 59.

27. David Bradley, "Telling the Black Woman's Story: Novelist Alice Walker," *New York Times Magazine* (January 8, 1984), 36.

28. Quoted in Brewer [see note 10], 15.

29. Pollitt, 15.

LYNN PIFER

# Coming to Voice in Alice Walker's Meridian: Speaking Out for the Revolution

In Alice Walker's second novel, *Meridian*, Meridian Hill has been conditioned by her community's patriarchal institutions to repress her individuality and, above all, not to speak out inappropriately. But when she finds that she cannot conform to authorized notions of appropriate speech (public repentance, patriotic school speeches, and the like), her only rebellious recourse is silence. Because of her refusal to participate in authorized discourse, Meridian fails to fit in with a succession of social groups—from her church congregation, to those at the elite college she attends, to a cadre of would-be violent revolutionaries. She begins a process of personal transformation when she sets out alone to fight her own battles, through personal struggle and Civil Rights work.

Walker posits Meridian's struggle for personal transformation as an alternative to the political movements of the 1960s, particularly those that merely reproduced existing power structures. As Karen Stein writes,

> . . . the novel points out that the Civil Rights Movement often reflected the oppressiveness of patriarchal capitalism. Activists merely turned political rhetoric to their own ends while continuing to repress spontaneous individuality. To overcome this destructiveness, Walker reaches for a new definition of revolution.

*African American Review*, Volume 26, Number 1, (1992) pp. 77–88. © 1992 Lynn Pifer

Her hope for a just society inheres not merely in political change,
but in personal transformation. (130)

Even the revolutionary cadre that Meridian tries to join insists that she perform an authorized speech, declaring that she would both die and kill for
the revolution. When she silently considers whether she could kill another
human being, the group becomes hostile towards her and finally excludes
her. Walker realizes that would-be revolutionaries must avoid reproducing
the power structures that they combat. Killing, for Meridian as well as for
Walker, is an act of tyranny, even if one kills in the fight against tyranny.

Meridian's life is shaped by those moments when she remains silent
although those around her demand that she speak. She could not publicly
repent, despite her mother's urgings; she could not utter the patriotic speech
she was assigned in high school; and she could not proclaim that she would
kill for the revolution when her comrades expected her to. She is tormented by
her peers' hissing, "'Why don't you say something?'" (28), and by the memory
of her mother pleading, "'Say it now, Meridian . . .'" (29). Meridian's silence
short-circuits the response expected by patriarchal discourse. Her refusal
to speak negates the existing order's ability to use her as a ventriloquist's
doll, a mindless vehicle that would spout the ideological line. But Meridian's
strategy does not prevent her from feeling guilt both for not conforming to
the standards of her family and friends, and for not being able to speak out
effectively against these standards.

Meridian lives on her own, separated from her family and the cadre that
has rejected her. Alone, she performs spontaneous and symbolic acts of rebellion,
such as carrying a drowned black child's corpse to the mayor's office to protest
the town officials' neglect of drainage ditches in black neighborhoods. She
accomplishes more than the would-be revolutionaries, who move on to live
yuppie lifestyles. Stein writes, "Walker's novel affirms that it is not by taking
life that true revolution will come about, but through respect for life and
authentic living of life . . . gained only through each individual's slow, painful
confrontation of self" (140). Only Meridian, who struggles with questions
that other characters gloss over, completes this personal transformation. Her
confrontations with her personal history, family history, and racial history
shape the way she chooses to live.

Meridian's struggle for personal transformation echoes June Jordan's
definition of her duties as a feminist:

I must undertake to love myself and to respect myself as though my
very life depends upon self-love and self-respect . . . and . . . I am
entering my soul into a struggle that will most certainly transform
the experience of all the peoples of the earth, as no other movement

can, . . . because the movement into self-love, self-respect, and self-determination is . . . now galvanizing . . . the unarguable majority of human beings everywhere. (qtd. in Hernton 58)

One of Meridian's most difficult struggles is to forgive herself for her perceived failings. If she can learn to love and respect herself, she can see her moments of silence as legitimate acts of rebellion against a system that would deny her individuality. Otherwise, she can only view her silences as examples of the times she has failed her family and friends.

In the course of the novel, Meridian learns to turn to folk traditions (stories, songs, May dances around The Sojourner) for expression and inspiration. Reluctant to depend on her own words, Meridian relies on stories of defiant actions by women who went before her. The large magnolia tree known as The Sojourner, located in the center of Meridian's college campus, is also central to many subversive tales. With The Sojourner's story, we receive a more thorough description of Saxon College and its goal of conferring "ladyhood" upon its students. On the property that had been a slave plantation, young black women learn "to make French food, English tea and German music" (39), and *are blessed to perpetuate / the Saxon name!* (93). These new Saxon women will spread the name, just as surely as the Saxon slave women were forced to increase Master Saxon's stock of slaves. But, irony of ironies, the new women are endowed with the elements of traditional white ladyhood, including its first requirement, virginity: "It was assumed that Saxon young ladies were, by definition, virgins. They were treated always as if they were thirteen years old" (94). And just as Saxon slaves were kept on the plantation, Saxon students are trapped within the campus's ornate fence.

The Sojourner is the only complex and meaningful centering point on this otherwise artificial campus. Generations of students have handed down stories and folk practices concerning The Sojourner. The first is the story of Louvinie, the slave woman who planted Sojourner. A skilled storyteller, she unintentionally frightened her master's young son to death with a tale he and his sisters had requested. As punishment, Master Saxon cut off her tongue at the root. Louvinie buried her tongue under Sojourner, and, as the story goes, the tree grew miraculously. "Other slaves believed it possessed magic. They claimed it could talk, make music. . . . Once in its branches, a hiding slave could not be seen" (44). According to the slaves' folk beliefs, Louvinie transferred her capacity for powerful speech onto The Sojourner. Susan Willis writes:

Named The Sojourner, the magnolia conjures up the presence of another leader of black women, who, like Louvinie, used language in the *struggle* for liberation. In this way, Walker builds a network of

women, some mythic like Louvinie, some real like Sojourner Truth,
as the context for Meridian's affirmation and radicalization. (114)

Louvinie and the conjured image of Sojourner Truth serve as positive examples of women who use their tongues as weapons in the struggle for liberation. Master Saxon's punishment, however, is an equally instructive example for Meridian. While it is possible to use your tongue to combat a racist patriarchy, that system will endeavor to silence such a tongue, even if it must cut it off at the root. At those moments when Meridian is expected to reproduce patriarchal discourse— in the form of public repentance during a church service, for instance, or a patriotic speech at her high school—, Meridian chooses to withhold her tongue as both a symbolic rupture of patriarchal ideology and as a means of preserving her tongue, preventing it from being cut out. Louvinie's burial of her severed tongue, and the subsequent creative transferral of her power, proves to be a more practical alternative for Meridian to follow than images of black women speaking out.

Early in *Meridian,* Walker links the contrasting strategies of silence (withholding one's tongue as opposed to having it forcibly removed) to the politics of racism and patriarchy. In the opening chapter, Walker crystallizes the oppression inherent in Southern segregation practices, as grown white men rush to prevent a group of black children from seeing what everyone acknowledges to be a worthless freak show, a ludicrous carnival attraction. She also examines patriarchy's ability to "kill" women, using the Marilene O'Shay exhibit as a visual reminder, as well as a parody of society's idolization of dead women as the perfect women (patriarchy's version of "The only good indian's a dead indian").

Chicokema is a town so segregated that even events as trivial as a carnival exhibit require separate days for white and black attendance. Chicokemans avoid labeling their customs as racially biased by basing their segregation on occupation: People who work in the guano plant must be sectioned off from the rest of the town. But the distinction is clearly racial, since the plant employs most of the black population and the segregation extends to their families: "'... the folks who don't work in the guano plant don't draw the line at the mamas and papas,'" explains a Chicokema resident, "'they throw in the childrens too. Claim the smell of guano don't wash off'" (20).

It is precisely this kind of unquestioned, all-pervasive discrimination that psychologist Kenneth Clark claimed has a detrimental effect on black children's self-perception. In 1939, Clark developed a doll test that was eventually used as evidence in *Brown vs. Board of Education*. He showed a group of black children two dolls, one black and one white, and asked them questions about the dolls. All children correctly identified which doll was white and which was black, but the majority of the children said they liked the white doll better and claimed that the black doll looked "bad." Clark recalls in an interview:

> The most disturbing question . . . was the final question: "Now show me the doll that's most like you." Many of the children became emotionally upset when they had to identify with the doll they had rejected. These children saw themselves as inferior, and they accepted the inferiority as part of reality. (Williams 20)

The children of Chicokema have been negatively socialized to believe that they are inferior to other children. And since the "smell of guano," or the color of their skin, does not "wash off," they cannot better their situation.

Meridian comes to Chicokema to help these children, not by making speeches or typing up flyers, but by silently lining them up to see the Marilene O'Shay exhibit on a "whites only" day. She places herself at the front of the line and marches across the square. With a style similar to Flannery O'Connor's, Walker demonstrates the ridiculousness of the white town's reaction to Meridian: "'This town's got a big old army tank,'" a young boy tells a Northern visitor, "'and now they going to have to aim it on the woman in the cap, 'cause she act like she don't even know they got it'" (18). Walker presents the entire situation in the absurd. The small town bought the tank to fight outside agitators, painted and decorated it, then smashed the leg of their Confederate Soldier Statue (an obligatory symbol of the Old South) in an attempt to park their latest weapon in the town square. Now they find themselves faced off against a hundred-pound woman leading an army of school children.

Meridian waits for the police to arrange themselves— "... two men were crawling into [the tank], and a phalanx of police, their rifles pointing upward, rushed to defend the circus wagon," (21)—before she steps in front of the tank and leads the children to see Marilene O'Shay. Not prepared to open fire on this woman and her band of children, the defenders of the Old South simply stare at Meridian in disbelief. Without speaking a word, Meridian succeeds in desegregating the O'Shay exhibit. The act of facing up to the town's white segregationalist army and entering the forbidden circus wagon will become a more important memory for the children than the exhibit itself—or its patriarchal message.

Three of the titles painted on the Marilene O'Shay trailer sum up the narrow possibilities for women in a patriarchal society: "Obedient Daughter," "Devoted Wife," and "Adoring Mother" (19). The fourth, "Gone Wrong," indicates the perceived tragedy involved when a woman rejects these roles: "Over the fourth a vertical line of progressively flickering light bulbs moved continually downward like a perpetually cascading tear" (19). Walker portrays, with maudlin kitsch, patriarchy's imperative that a woman accept her "place" (see Stein).

"The True Story of Marilene O'Shay" has been preserved for future generations on cheap mimeographed fliers which tell us how Henry O'Shay had lavishly provided for his lovely wife, Marilene, and how she had rebuked the role of Perfect Wife by having an affair with another man. An old black townsman's interpretation of Marilene O'Shay's story provides us with patriarchal society's view of the situation:

> Just because he caught her giving some away, he shot the man, strangled the wife. Throwed 'em both into Salt Lake. . . . everybody forgive him. Even her ma. 'Cause the bitch was doing him wrong, and that ain't right! . . . years later she washed up on shore, and he claimed he recognized her by her long red hair . . . Thought since she was so generous herself she wouldn't mind the notion of him sharing her with the Amurican public. (22)

As Stein writes, "A living woman may resist her husband's domination, but the mummy, static and reified, may be completely possessed. O'Shay, like the sinister Duke of Robert Browning's 'My Last Duchess,' has reduced his wife to permanent, if frigid, fidelity" (132). But Stein here reads only half the story: Not only has Henry O'Shay "mummified" his wife into a "frigid fidelity," he has also turned her body into a profitable specular commodity. According to this community's standards, her transgression was not simply adultery, but *thievery:* She was caught "giving some[one else's property] away." If Marilene O'Shay was objectified and privatized while alive, she is commodified and marketable once dead. A better analogy would be to the corpse of the Grimms Brothers' Snow White, displayed in her shining glass casket, with Prince Charming telling the dwarves he must have "it," no matter what the cost.[1]

Although Henry O'Shay shoots the man who cuckolds him, he does not turn the gun on his wife, choosing instead to strangle her with his own hands. In so doing, he dislodges her tongue and prevents her from speaking out while she dies. O'Shay's method avenges his pride and punishes his wife, literally choking off her voice. Conveniently for Mr. O'Shay, choking leaves Marilene's body intact and, therefore, more easily preserved for later viewing.

If Marilene O'Shay is patriarchy's perfect, petrified, and commodified woman, The Wild Child is nature's uncivilized answer. Barbara Christian writes that the main struggle in *Meridian* is the fight between a natural, life-driven spirit and society's deadly strictures:

. . . though the concept of One Life motivates Meridian in her quest toward physical and spiritual health, the societal evils that subordinate one class to another, one race to another, one sex to another, fragment and ultimately threaten life. The novel *Meridian* . . . is built on the tension between the African concept of animism, "that spirit that inhabits all life," and the societal forces that inhibit the growth of the living toward their natural state of freedom. (91)

The Wild Child, so removed from civilization that her language consists of swear words she picked up in the alleys, fits most closely the natural state of freedom Christian describes. Her pregnancy, however, arouses the neighborhood's concern, and demonstrates that she has been excluded from not only the negative restrictions of society, but the help and love of a community as well.

The first sight of this pregnant thirteen-year-old induces one of Meridian's corpse-like trances. Meridian feels compelled to try to help the wild girl, and sets out to trap her and take her back to her room at Saxon College. Unkempt, unpredictable, loud, and independent, The Wild Child embodies the opposite of every Saxon ideal and demonstrates the falseness of Saxon's social codes to Meridian: "Wile Chile shouted words that were never uttered in the honors house. Meridian, splattered with soap and mud, broke down and laughed" (36). In the midst of Saxon's tradition of proper attire and social etiquette, this wild pregnant girl protests in the only language she knows. And Meridian is delighted by the girl's free use of inappropriate language.

Unfortunately, no one else appreciates The Wild Child's natural state of freedom. A showdown between The Wild Child and the house mother becomes a life-and-death confrontation that death wins. The house mother, whose "marcel waves shone like real sea waves, and . . . light brown skin was pearly under a mask of powder" (37), is the only person in the honors house that Wile Chile trembles and cowers at. Like the Dean of Women (aptly nicknamed "The Dead of Women"), the house mother exemplifies proper behavior for a perfect lady: "'She must not stay here,'" the house mother tells Meridian. "'This is a school for young ladies'" (37). The Wild Child's display of natural manners cannot be tolerated at the honors house, no matter what moral responsibility Meridian may feel towards the girl. Frightened by the house mother, Wile Chile bolts from the unapproving house, only to be struck and killed by a speeding car.

There is no survival for the unrestrained independent female. It should come as no surprise, then, that the authorities of Saxon College will not allow its students to have a funeral service for The Wild Child. Saxon may treat its girls like thirteen-year-olds, but it has no use for real ones, especially if they are homeless and pregnant. The Wild Child is so dangerous to Saxon's reputation that she cannot be allowed on campus, even as a corpse. Saxon College's official reaction to the students' attempted funeral for The Wild Child confirms to Meridian and to the other students that the goal of this institution is the proper socialization of its young ladies, not the education of their minds. Although her fellow students are overwhelmed with the urge to rebel, they are already so far along the road to ladyhood that they do not know how to do it.

The fate of The Sojourner exemplifies the kind of destruction that can take place when this revolutionary anger has no effective outlet. The most beautiful and potentially subversive object on campus is destroyed by frustrated student rioters who would avenge The Wild Child. Their initial acts of rebellion seem childish and ineffectual: They throw their jewelry (symbols of ladyhood) on the ground and stick out their tongues (proof that they still *have* them). Their ultimate act of revolutionary violence, however, is directed towards their most beloved part of the campus: Despite Meridian's protests, they chop down The Sojourner.

Another piece of Sojourner folklore concerns the horrible effects of Saxon's demands on the outward appearance of its "girls." This gory tale tells of a Saxon student so ashamed by her unwanted pregnancy that she tries to hide it, and who later resorts to chopping her newborn to bits, which she flushes down the toilet. After being caught and severely punished—locked in a room with no windows—, Fast Mary hangs herself. She remains not just a grotesque warning to future Saxon students, but also a symbol that brings them together:

> There was only one Sojourner ceremony . . . that united all the students at Saxon—the rich and the poor, the very black skinned (few though they were) with the very fair, the stupid and the bright—and that was the Commemoration of Fast Mary of the Tower. . .
>
> Any girl who had ever prayed for her period to come was welcome to the commemoration, which was held in the guise of a slow May Day dance around the foot of The Sojourner. . . . It was the only time in all the many social activities at Saxon that every girl was considered equal. On that day, they held each other's hands tightly. (45)

The students' folklore allows them to form a community as they band together in a practice that subverts the conventional behavior at Saxon College. They relish the story of a girl forced to go to terrible lengths to maintain the college's demands regarding outward appearance, and it is clear that the unsympathetic authorities, not Fast Mary, are the villains of the story. Susan Willis writes: "Fast Mary's inability to call on her sister students and her final definitive isolation at the hands of her parents raise questions Meridian will also confront: Is there a community of support?" (113). Mary's story reveals the injustices of this "civilized" college, which seeks to separate its students from their folk community by forcing them to follow a notion of proper behavior that is merely a careful imitation of the white middle class.

Despite Saxon's training, favorite stories among its students feature heroines who dare to step out of line. Louvinie and Fast Mary received horrendously painful punishments for their deeds, but such penalties only reflect how intrepid they were; the more those in power tried to suppress them, the more popular they became with their peers. The folk tales and practices that surround The Sojourner work to subvert the strictures of the social systems that surround it. According to Willis, "As a natural metaphor, the tree is in opposition to the two social institutions—the plantation and the university" (114). The folk practices surrounding the tree allow the slaves, and later students, to oppose these institutions as well.

While images of women like Louvinie and Sojourner Truth provide Meridian with significant strategies for creative living, her own mother does not. Instead, Mrs. Hill carefully exhibits the attributes of the proper wife and mother in the eyes of her community. She has a clean house and attends church, but we learn that she is actually incapable of loving her children and will not forgive them for being born:

> It was for stealing her mother's serenity, for shattering her mother's emerging self, that Meridian felt guilty from the very first, though she was unable to understand how this could possibly be her fault. When her mother asked, without glancing at her, "Have you stolen anything?" a stillness fell over Meridian and for seconds she could not move. The question literally stopped her in her tracks. (51)

As far as we know, Meridian is the only child in the family who feels this guilt. Later she will resent her own pregnancies, and like her mother, she will also resent the fact that no one allows her to acknowledge her negative feelings. In this patriarchal community, the woman who would reject a pregnancy clearly does not know her place.

Although Mrs. Hill fulfills her duty as a religious woman and prays for her children's souls, she seems to have no understanding of her children or their struggles. Like Saxon College, Mrs. Hill only considers appearances. She devotes herself not just to the care of her children's bodies, but also to something even more superficial—the washing and ironing of their clothes: "Her children were spotless wherever they went. In their stiff, almost inflexible garments, they were enclosed in the starch of her anger, and had to keep their distance to avoid providing the soggy wrinkles of contact that would cause her distress" (79). Mrs. Hill's children grow up feeling "stiff, almost inflexible," and they learn not only to keep their distance from their distraught mother, but from other human contact as well.

Meridian, in fact, has been emotionally starched shut. Her mother has refused to tell her anything about sex, and Meridian only learns about it when she gets molested in a local funeral home. Meridian begins her relationship with Eddie mainly because she wants a boyfriend to protect her from all the other men around. And the demise of their relationship comes about when Eddie finally notices that Meridian does not enjoy having sex with him.

The chapter entitled "The Happy Mother" examines maternity's effects on Meridian. Now that she is a young wife and mother, everyone thinks of her as a "perfect woman." She is, in fact, nearly dead. Whereas they assume she is concentrating on her child, she is actually considering different ways to commit suicide. She spends her time at home, reading women's magazines: "According to these magazines, Woman was a mindless body, a sex creature, something to hang false hair and nails on" (71). Here Meridian's awareness of patriarchy's desire to "encase" her, to "process" her according to the specular code of the media, becomes most acute.

Walker's poem "On Stripping Bark from Myself" sums up Meridian's situation at this point in the novel: "I could not live / silent in my own lies / hearing their 'how *nice* she is!' / whose adoration of the retouched image / I so despise" *(Good Night* 23). Meridian rejects the "nice" role of the "happy" mother, recognizing that "happiness" is merely an empty sign that accompanies the equally empty role of young, pregnant wife. Happiness does not apply in any way to Meridian's emotional state, but the conventional (and therefore seemingly logical) association of "happiness" with "motherhood" precludes her ability to state otherwise.

In her essay "The Civil Rights Movement: What Good Was It?," Walker writes, "If knowledge of my condition is all the freedom I get from a 'freedom movement,' it is better than unawareness, forgottenness, and hopelessness, the existence that is like the existence of a beast" *(Gardens* 121). This, too, is the bottom line for Meridian. The knowledge of her condition, and of the condition of women in general, gives her hope. Perfect women in this community, as Meridian well knows, are perfectly mindless, nicely dressed, walking corpses.

At age seventeen, Meridian is left on her own to consider what to do with her life and her child's. When Meridian says no to motherhood, she offends and loses her own mother, her family, and her community. She feels guilty for leaving her baby, and cannot adequately explain why she must. But by shedding her prescribed "happy mother" role and standing up for her own needs, Meridian takes the first steps toward becoming a "revolutionary petunia."[2] She stops living by others' standards, learns to bloom for herself, as she must in order to survive, since her rebellious acts will alienate her from the rest of society.[3]

The battle fatigue Meridian encounters as a result of working in the Civil Rights Movement turns into emotional fatigue brought on by the endless guilt she feels for putting her child up for adoption. Even though she knows her child is better off without his seventeen-year-old mother, Meridian cannot forgive herself for giving him away. She feels that she has abandoned both her son and her own heritage:

> Meridian knew that enslaved women . . . had laid down their lives, gladly, for their children, that the daughters of these enslaved women had thought their greatest blessing from "Freedom" was that it meant they could keep their own children. And what had Meridian Hill done with *her* precious child? She had given him away. She thought . . . of herself as belonging to an unworthy minority, for which there was no precedent and of which she was, as far as she knew, the only member. (91)

Barbara Christian writes of the danger of the myth of Black Motherhood, noting that, according to this tradition, only stories of strong, successful mothers are passed on:

> . . . that tradition that is based on the monumental myth of black motherhood, a myth based on the true stories of sacrifice black mothers performed for their children . . . is . . . restrictive, for it imposes a stereotype of Black women, a stereotype of strength that denies them choice and hardly admits of the many who were destroyed. (89)

*Meridian* is full of victims of this tradition of Black Motherhood. Meridian's own mother, for instance, is an *unhappy* mother who manages to conform to the tradition only by suppressing her own emotions. She feels that she has been betrayed by other mothers because they never "warn[ed] her against children" (50); i.e., that there is no secret inner life or euphoria in motherhood, but a loss of one's independence. Meridian's girlhood friend Nelda is another victim: Nelda wanted to go to college, but since she became a mother at age fourteen, she never finished high school. Fast Mary's pregnancy leads to her suicide, and the heavy belly of the pregnant Wild Child limits her ability to move out of the path of the car that kills her. Meridian herself belongs to the "worthless minority" of mothers excluded by the tradition. Her own sacrifice—of giving up her child—is as painful and trying as any of the legendary sacrifices, but according to the code of the tradition, Meridian's is not a sacrifice but a case of willful neglect.

Meridian's attempts at personal growth through a love relationship also fail. Truman Held appears as Meridian's lover in a chapter that Walker aptly titles "The Conquering Prince." This clichéd role would be more appropriate in a fairy tale, but it is the role Truman would most like to play. True/man, called "True" by Lynne, is in fact, quite false: a black would-be revolutionary who loves to dress well and speak French. He paints strong black women, earth mothers, yet he finds himself attracted to white virgins. Meridian notes that, despite his revolutionary slogans and liberal education, Truman really wants a quiet little helper that would look good while hanging on his arm. Truman "did not want a woman who tried . . . to claim her own life. She knew Truman would have liked her better as she had been as Eddie's wife . . . an attractive woman, but asleep" (110). Meridian is too independent to be the clinging vine Truman desires.

With the failure of her romance, Meridian finds that she is haunted by a recurring dream: that ". . . she was a character in a novel and that her existence presented an insoluble problem, one that would be solved only by her death in the end" (117). Meridian's reflective moment creates, for the reader, a reflexive moment in the text. While Meridian's dream suggests a

truth that she can never "know" — that she actually is a character in a novel—, the significance of the dream lies in another, fictional direction. For Meridian, the problem of being a character in a novel is a problem of limitation and constraint, of definition and expectation bound to a clichéd way of reading and writing, one that privileges the *death* of a character as the most climactic (and therefore desired and inevitable) moment in a narrative. Death, however, solves nothing but the problem of how to end a plotline. Meridian's dream also reminds us that this "insoluble problem" is one that Walker herself must face in the creation of her narrative; having offered us a "revolutionary" character whose struggles have transgressed the boundaries of racism and sexism, Walker must find a way to end *Meridian* successfully without the expected end of its protagonist. If, as Walker states in an interview with Claudia Tate, *Meridian* is a novel "about living" (185), the conventional melodramatic death scene is out of the question. [4]

To her credit, Meridian has managed to escape the symbolic death of being killed by patriarchy's standards and petrified into a perfect woman—she leaves behind "Obedient Daughter," "Devoted Wife," and "Adoring Mother." She even goes a step further and escapes becoming "Enchanted Lover" to Truman's "Conquering Prince." But Meridian cannot be sure that she is not destined to die at the end of a novel, as someone's "Tragic Heroine." In order to avoid this unwanted role, she must accept the sacredness of her own life. Barbara Christian writes that Walker works with traditional and feminist perspectives on motherhood, attempting a compromise that would allow her protagonist to live:

> As many radical feminists blamed motherhood for the waste in women's lives and saw it as a dead end for a woman, Walker insisted on a deeper analysis: She did not present motherhood itself as restrictive. It is so because of the little value society places on children, especially black children, on mothers, especially black mothers, on life itself. In the novel, Walker acknowledged that a mother in this society is often "buried alive, walled away from her own life, brick by brick." Yet the novel is based on Meridian's insistence on the sacredness of life. (90)

Meridian does not object to children, or mothers bearing children, but to the role a woman is expected to play once she becomes a mother. According to this role, a mother, particularly The Mythical Black Mother, should sacrifice her individual personality and concerns in order to live for her children. Unfortunately, the only way Meridian can escape this unwanted role is to leave her child and family, accepting her own mother's disapprobation. And to do so she must first learn to shed the guilt this action produces.

Meridian's cumulative guilt becomes so great it prevents her from seeing or moving freely. She slips into a petrified trance, and it takes an act of sisterhood by Miss Winter to bring her out of it. Miss Winter had tried to help Meridian once before when Meridian found she could not utter the mindlessly patriotic speech at her high school graduation. (The capitalist/ patriarchal hegemony perpetuates itself when each year a high school girl recites this speech, providing ritual evidence of woman's position as subject to society's ideology, and all the other women participate by listening attentively and applauding the performance.) Miss Winter is the only member of the audience who truly understands Meridian's struggle against the hegemonic discourse of the speech:

> She told her not to worry about the speech. "It's the same one they made me learn when I was here," she told her, "and it's no more true now than it was then." She had never said anything of the sort to anyone before and was surprised at how good it felt. A blade of green grass blew briefly across her vision and a fresh breeze followed it. She realized the weather was too warm for mink and took off her coat. (122)

Miss Winter breaks the custom of accepting this speech by admitting to Meridian that, although she had once recited the words, she had not believed they were true. This is the first time that an older woman has given an honest, useful piece of advice to Meridian, and Miss Winter is rewarded immediately for her good act with a pleasing feeling that allows her, for a time, to shed a layer of woman's prescribed respectability, the heavy mink coat.

Miss Winter's first words of kindness, however, go unnoticed by Meridian, who at the time is obsessed with her mother's disappointment with her performance. Meridian feels completely weighed down by guilt for not living up to her mother's standards: "It seemed to Meridian that her legacy from her mother's endurance, her unerring knowledge of rightness and her pursuit of it through all distractions, was one she would never be able to match" (124). Miss Winter's second message comes through because she poses as that perfect (and perfectly dead) woman, and pulls Meridian out of her near-coma by saying "I forgive you" (125) at the right moment. Relieved of her guilt, Meridian recovers.

Gloria Steinem writes of the progress Walker has made for her heroines since she wrote her first story:

> Her first short story, unpublished, "The Suicide of an American Girl," describes a friendship between a young black American and an African student. Attracted and angered by her independence, he rapes her; as a kind of chosen sacrifice, she doesn't resist. But after he is gone, she quietly turns on the gas and waits for death. It's a conflict that Alice would no longer resolve by giving up. (93)

Meridian will not give up and resolve her problems by dying. As she tells Lynne, martyrs should walk away alive instead of acting out the melodramatic last scene: "'King should have refused. Malcolm, too, should have refused. All those characters in all those novels that require death to end the book should refuse. All saints should walk away. Do their bit, then— just walk away'" (151).

Earlier in the novel, Walker lists people assassinated for taking part in a "revolution": "MEDGAR EVERS/JOHN F. KENNEDY/ MALCOLM X/MARTIN LUTHER KING/ROBERT KENNEDY/ CHE GUEVARA/PATRICE LAMUMBA/GEORGE JACKSON/ CYNTHIA WESLEY/ADDIE MAY COLLINS/DENISE MCNAIR/ CAROLE ROBERTSON/ VIOLA LIUZZO" (33). To the names of famous political and spiritual leaders, Walker adds the names of lesser known Civil Rights workers such as Viola Liuzzo, a white housewife from Detroit killed by Klan members after participating in the Selma March, and Cynthia Wesley, one of four girls killed in the Sixteenth Street Baptist Church bombing. The placement of slashes and spaces makes the names slide into one another. "EVERS/ JOHN" seems more of a unit than "JOHN F. KENNEDY," and the entire list appears to meld together, blurring the identities of this group of martyrs who have become names mentioned on the nightly news. But the significance of the list, as Walker implies, involves the loss of modern people's ability to grieve collectively, as a community. And the agent of that loss is television, now *"the repository of memory"* (33).

In order to survive, Meridian must see through the mystique of martyrdom, learn to value her own life, and find a community to *live with*, rather than a company of names to be listed among. Meridian finally finds a living community in an unconventional church. Although Walker does not mention Truman and Lynne's daughter Camara in the section bearing her name, the image of this young victim of racial violence informs the chapter. In the middle of a church service, Meridian realizes she could kill to prevent a crime such as the brutal attack on Camara. This church, unlike the conventional Baptist church Meridian attended as a girl, has a stained-glass representation of B. B. King, a preacher who urges the congregation to stand up for their rights, and hymns with new lyrics that speak out to her: "'. . . the music, the form of worship that has always sustained us, the kind of ritual you share with us, these are the ways to transformation that we know'" (200). Listening to the congregation's hymn, Meridian finally achieves a spiritual release and transformation:

> In comprehending this, there was in Meridian's chest a breaking as if a tight string binding her lungs had given way, allowing her to breathe freely. For she understood, finally, that the respect she owed her life was to continue, against whatever obstacles, to live it, and not to give up any particle of it without a fight to the death, preferably *not* her own. . . . indeed she *would* kill, before she allowed anyone to murder [the guest speaker's] son again. (200)

Instead of adopting the murderous philosophy of the would-be revolutionary cadre, Meridian has transcended it. She will not kill, or die, "for the revolution" or any other abstract ideology. If forced to, she would kill to preserve life. And when unable to prevent a murder, she can gather together with other mourners to grieve that death publicly.

Thadious M. Davis writes that Meridian "divests herself of immediate blood relations—her child and her parents—in order to align herself completely with the larger racial and social generations of blacks" (49), and she seems to have achieved this alignment as she unites with the congregation. By the end of the novel her personal identity becomes part of their collective identity: "Meridian is born anew into a pluralistic cultural self, a 'we' that is and must be selfless and without ordinary prerequisites for personal identity" (Davis 49). As a collective group, this congregation can mourn and remember together. The repository of memory has returned to the community.

When Meridian opens her mouth to sing with the congregation, she at last finds her voice and moves beyond her method of strategic silences:

> ...perhaps it will be my part to walk behind the real revolutionaries— those who know they must spill blood in order to help the poor and the black . . .—and when they stop to wash off the blood and find their throats too choked with the smell of murdered flesh to sing, I will come forward and sing from memory songs they will need once more to hear. (201)

By turning to the songs and stories of her cultural heritage, she finds a way to serve her people. And, finally, she can speak out against racist patriarchal hegemony, rather than standing silent and alone in the margins.

## Notes

1. "Let me have the coffin, and I will give you whatever you like to ask for it" (Grimm 220).

2. I take this term from Walker's poem "The Nature of This Flower Is to Bloom": Rebellious. Living. / Against the Elemental Crush. / A Song of Color / Blooming / For Deserving Eyes. / Blooming Gloriously / For its Self. / *Revolutionary Petunia*" (*Petunias* 70).

3. In Walker's character Meridian, we are able to see her admiration for women such as Rebecca Jackson, of whose "remarkable general power" Walker writes: "a woman whose inner spirit directed her to live her own life, creating it from scratch, leaving husband, home, family, and friends, to do so" (*Gardens* 79).

4. "What happens when I write is that I try to make models for myself. I project other ways of seeing. Writing to me is not about audience actually. It's about living" (Tate 185).

## Works Cited

Christian, Barbara. *Black Feminist Criticism: Perspectives on Black Women Writers*. New York: Pergamon, 1985.

Davis, Thadious M. "Alice Walker's Celebration of Self in Southern Generations." *Southern Quarterly* 21.4 (1983): 39–53.

Grimm, Jacob, and Wilhelm Grimm. *Household Stories by the Brothers Grimm*. Trans. Lucy Crane. New York: Dover, 1963.

Hernton, Calvin C., *The Sexual Mountain and Black Women Writers: Adventures in Sex, Literature, and Real Life*. New York: Anchor, 1987.

Stein, Karen F., *"Meridian:* Alice Walker's Critique of Revolution." *Black American Literature Forum* 20 (1986); 129–41.

Steinem, Gloria. "Do You Know This Woman? She Knows You." *Ms.*, June1982: 36+.

Tate, Claudia. "Alice Walker." *Black Women Writers at Work*. New York: Continuum, 1983. 175–87.

Walker, Alice. *Good Night, Willie Lee, I'll See You in the Morning*. New York: Harcourt, 1979.

———. *In Search of Our Mothers' Gardens: Womanist Prose*. New York: Harcourt 1983.

———. *Meridian*. 1976. New York: Pocket, 1977.

———. *Revolutionary Petunias and Other Poems*. New York: Harcourt, 1971.

Williams, Juan. *Eyes on the Prize: America's Civil Rights Years, 1954-1965*. New York: Penguin, 1988.

Willis, Susan. *Specifying: Black Women Writing the American Experience*. Madison: University of Wisconsin Press, 1987.

FELIPE SMITH

# Alice Walker's Redemptive Art

The "saving" of lives is central to Alice Walker's art. This "redemptive" quality in her work goes beyond the thematic to the very heart of Walker's aesthetics, as she makes clear in her essay "Saving the Life That Is Your Own: The Importance of Models in the Artist's Life": "It is, in the end, the saving of lives that we writers are about. . . . We do it because we care. . . . We care because we know this: *the life we save is our own*" (*Gardens* 14). The urgency to "save lives" thus stems from Walker's acknowledgment of a spiritual bond connecting the writer to the lives she depicts: Artistic redemption "saves" the artist as well.

The most dramatic illustrations Walker provides of the saving power of art emphasize this mutual benefit to "saver" and "saved." In her essay "The Old Artist: Notes on Mr. Sweet," Walker tells how her career as a writer— her very life in fact— was "saved" by her art. She wrote her first published story "To Hell with Dying" instead of committing suicide. In the process, she saved for future generations the story of how the old guitar player Mr. Sweet "continued to share his troubles and insights [and] ... continued to sing." Simultaneously, through writing she gave herself the courage to "turn [her] back on the razor blade" (*Word* 39).

Mutual redemption is also the focus of Walker's discussion of her artistic debt to Zora Neale Hurston. In "Saving the Life That Is Your Own," she

*African American Review,* Volume 26, Number 3; Fall 1992: pp. 437–451. ©1992 Felipe Smith describes how crucial Hurston's *Mules and Men* (1935) was to her completion of a fictional version of her mother's remembrance from the Depression in a story called "The Revenge of Hannah Kemhuff." In this early Walker story, the narrator quotes a conjurer's curse directly from Hurston's book as part of her plan to secure justice for the wronged Hannah Kemhuff. Walker explains the effect of her "collaboration" with her esteemed literary ancestor this way:

> In that story I gathered up the historical and psychological threads of the life my ancestors lived, and in the writing of it I felt joy and strength and my own continuity. I had that wonderful feeling writers get sometimes, not very often, of being *with* a great many people, ancient spirits, all very happy to see me consulting and acknowledging them, and eager to let me know, through the joy of their presence, that, indeed, I am not alone. (*Gardens* 13)

The highly spiritualistic terms of this revelation are characteristic of Walker's discussions of the saving power of art. Walker secularizes such terms as *redemption* and *salvation* to encompass solutions to social problems such as racial and gender oppression. She models her redemptive strategy on writers such as Chopin, the Brontës, de Beauvoir, and Lessing, whom she describes as "well aware of their own oppression and search[ing] incessantly for a kind of salvation" (*Gardens* 251). One result of this is an implicit connection for Walker between "savers" and "saviors." She describes Anaïs Nin as "a recorder of everything, no matter how minute," a writer who "saves" in the sense of collecting and preserving. Tillie Olsen, though, "literally saves lives," in the sense of preventing danger or harm from befalling others. And by serving as a model for women, Virginia Woolf "has saved so many" from the terrible waste of unfulfilled lives (14).

Yet the key feature of Walker's redemptive art, in spite of the secular redemption that she envisions, is the feeling Walker gets from participating in the spiritual continuity of her people. At the heart of Walker's definition of the writer's social role is a cultivated awareness of the reciprocal saving potential of art, based on her sense of art as a means of keeping alive the connection between ancestral spirits and their living descendants. This multiple preservation of artist, subject, and communal spirit describes, I believe, the very core of Walker's artistic strategy.

In Walker's philosophy of redemptive art, *to save* means, first, to collect and thereby preserve the subject from loss by immortalizing it in art; by reclaiming the past the artist insures its availability to the future. The second meaning of *to save* involves providing the wisdom of the past both to ensure the continuity of the folk ethos and to serve as a blueprint for personal and communal survival for those who require artistic models. *To save* someone, in Walker's eyes, includes the obligation to liberate her/him from an oppressive cycle of violence. *To be saved* means to have achieved an "unself-conscious sense of collective oneness; that naturalness, that (even when anguished) grace" (*Gardens* 264).

# I

In certain ways, Walker's belief in the redemptive power of writing recalls Mark C. Taylor's description of textual interpretation as a form of "radical Christology." Taylor poses a theory of the text that views the act of interpretation as a reenactment of ritual sacrifice. For Taylor, the critic produces a text by victimizing the "host" text, dismembering and incorporating it in the process (63–69). The antecedent text, a victim of sacrifice, is for Taylor a "victimizer" as well because it cannot fulfill itself without the critic's participation. Like Christ, the text *requires* victimization in order to fulfill its destiny of becoming dismembered and disseminated to the multitudes. Identifying the central paradox that links textual and Christological functions, Taylor quotes Jeffrey Mehlman's assertion that "in order to be preserved the text must be interpreted, opened up, violated." Thus Taylor finds that textual interpretation is a process not unlike the commemoration of the crucifixion of Christ by the consumption of the Holy Eucharist in the Catholic mass: "Dismembering is, paradoxically, a condition of remembering, death the genesis of life." Taylor stresses that "incorporation is not mere destruction but is also reembodiment, reincarnation" (67).

Alice Walker has similarly iterated a theory of textual production that follows the process of incorporation, reembodiment, and reincarnation of anterior texts in the newly (re)created text. The spiritualistic terms in which Walker discusses her intertextual strategy show that she considers her approach not simply a form of rhetorical play, indirect critique, or homage to her literary ancestors (what Henry Louis Gates has termed "motivated and unmotivated Signification" [94, 121, 124, 255]). Walker, in summoning ancestral voices, seems to have bi-directional "salvation" in mind—redemptive "reincarnation." The process involves much more than acknowledging Zora Neale Hurston, to cite one example, as a literary "foremother"; it suggests instead a determined effort "literally" to reincarnate and redeem her as text-within-text.

Rather than focus on the "parasitic" relationship between host text and interpretive text that grounds Taylor's analysis, Walker sees her texts as eucharistic hosts in their ternary conjunction of spirit, word, and flesh. Simply put, Walker envisions her texts as redemptive sites which host the spiritual infusion of words, reincarnating actual flesh-and-blood martyrs, saints, and sinners. Embodied in words, spirits "take flesh" in her texts. Her redemptive art, broadly imagined, is akin to the "radical Christology" which Taylor envisions the interpretive act to be. In Taylor's figuration, textuality is the state common to both the material and the immaterial. Everything nameable is a text: author and subject, body and spirit, the living and the dead. If living flesh can be converted into Word (text), then so can the dead. If existence within a text provides a kind of "life," then, by analogy, the generation of a text is a form of "transubstantiation," giving life to that which may in fact have no material existence. Textual inscription re-calls, reincarnates, and reembodies ancestral spirits.

Here we can compare Taylor's "Embodied Word" to Alice Walker's description of the process by which the novel *The Color Purple* came into being. Walker explicitly addresses that novel's "invocation" "*To the Spirit:* / Without whose assistance / Neither this book / Nor I / Would have been / Written.*" Assuming the "I" here is Walker herself, how do we account for her description of both the novel *and herself* as written texts? As Taylor points out, "When Incarnation is understood as Inscription, we discover Word. Embodied Word is Script(ure), the writing *in which we are inscribed and which we inscribe*" (71; emphasis added).[1]

Similarly, the novel's envoi ("I thank everybody in this book for coming. / A. W., author and medium") conceives the novel's characters as autonomous entities inhabiting Walker's newly created text, participating in the moral drama there enacted.[2] But as they are, like her, "written" by the "Spirit," their claim to autonomy rests upon their priority as "texts." Walker acknowledges the anteriority and autonomy of these in-dwelling "texts" by describing her role as that of "author and medium." As "author," she participates in the inscription of ancestral voices into written text. As "medium," she invokes and "channels" the wisdom of ancestral "texts." Walker's own description of textual production relegates to herself a priestly role in the continuity of the textual chain, the site of gathering among ancestral presences, the living, and the unborn. Her strategy makes a place for the reader, too, conceiving the reader as a past, present, future potentiality whose presence and participation fulfill the text (and therefore part of the "everybody" thanked "for coming"). Despite the many interesting lines of inquiry that such a formulation raises, the importance of this collectivity of presences within the text to Walker's quest for a redemptive art has not been examined heretofore.[3]

Beyond thematic and structural considerations, Walker's "Signifyin'" gestures (in Gates's usage) signal her concern with rhetorical aspects of textual "salvation." To see clearly how the writer's power to "save lives" resides in rhetorical practices, we can look to Walker's description of the character Grange Copeland in her 1973 self-interview. Walker explains that Grange's reason for killing his son Brownfield in *The Third Life of Grange Copeland* (1970) and his subsequent death at the hands of the police are based on his desire to preserve what he valued in life: "To [Grange], the greatest value a person can attain is full humanity, which is a state of oneness with all things, and a willingness to die (or to live) so that the best that has been produced can continue to live in someone else." Grange does not acknowledge a spiritual authority, making his self-sacrifice an even greater gesture. For him, material continuity replaces spiritual value, giving urgency to his desire that "the best" continue in his absence. His act is a gesture of revolutionary theological revision, a skepticism comparable to Walker's added claim that she doesn't believe in "a God beyond nature. The world is God. Man is God. So is a leaf or a snake" (*Gardens* 265).

Walker's interest in communal continuity as an alternative to spiritual transcendence continues in *Meridian* (1976). Meridian Hill decides that, in the absence of spiritual value, existence itself should be revered above all: "'All those characters in all those novels that require death to end the book should refuse. All saints should walk away. Do their bit, then—just walk away'" (151). To her the only reason for self-sacrifice should be, as in the case of Grange, the preserving of another life: ". . . she understood, finally, that the respect she owed her life was to continue, against whatever obstacles, to live it, and not to give up any particle of it without a fight to the death, preferably *not* her own." This heightened sense of existence extends "beyond herself to those around her because, in fact, the years in America had created them One Life" (204). Thus, the murder of the Civil Rights worker whose memorial she attends is essentially a killing of herself, and Meridian finds herself "approach[ing] the concept of retaliatory murder" (205) as a recognition of the need to preserve "the best that has been produced."[4]

But it is during the memorial ceremony that Meridian discovers the notion of preserving ancestral "spirits" as an extension of her obligation to One Life. The commemorative statement of the surviving parent of the slain worker provides a moment of existential clarity and economy: "'My son died'" (202). The response of the community is qualitatively different, however. In their ritual remembrance of the youth, they attempt to keep him "alive" by preserving in their memories the text of his liberation and reform philosophy. Meridian "hears" their covenant with the martyr as an unspoken communal "voice" addressing the aggrieved parent:

> ". . . we are gathering ourselves to fight for and protect what your son fought for on behalf of us. If you will let us weave your story and your son's life and death into what we already know—into the songs, the sermons, the 'brother and sister'—we will soon

be so angry we cannot help but move. . . . the church . . . , the music, the form of worship that has always sustained us, the kind of ritual you share with us, these are the ways to transformation that we know. We want to take this with us as far as we can." (*Meridian* 204)

Not only is the youth's idealism textualized for communal preservation, but his "life and death" are also "woven" into that text—it is he who is repeatedly revived and sacrificed for the community. In order to see this "radical Christology" in its full rhetorical dimensions, we should recall Barthes's reminder that a text (from the Latin *textus*) is always "woven" from pre-existing materials (76). The unspoken "voice" of the communal One Life practices a distinct form of intertextuality ("'let us weave your story and your son's life and death into what we already know'") as a method of spiritual continuity and as a "way to transformation." That the text of the dead man does transform the community can be seen in the distinct departures in tone, content, and iconography of the church: The songs have a "martial" cadence and different, less conciliatory words; the church mission has been redefined as social activism; in the liturgy, God has been reduced to a "reference"; and the Lamb of God depiction of Christ has been replaced with a painting of a surrealistic, sword-wielding avenger (*Meridian* 199–203).

To the extent that she is certainly registering a critique through repetition and revision, Walker's "reformed" black church "Signifies" on traditional Christian ritual and doctrine. Further, Walker specifies through the unvoiced "voice" that the community is aware of "Signifyin' " as one of the primary "ways to transformation that [they] know" by highlighting the rhetorical nature of their attempt to keep the text of the worker "alive." His "life and death," as texts, are "woven" into the "songs," "sermons," and forms of address ("'brother and sister'") by which they identify themselves as a community. Walker underscores the significance of the process by describing another, more famous martyr being kept "alive" by the congregation:

> The minister—in his thirties, dressed in a neat black suit and striped tie of an earlier fashion— spoke in a voice so dramatically like that of Martin Luther King's that at first Meridian thought his intention was to dupe or to mock. She glanced about to see if anyone else showed signs of astonishment or derision. (199)

Since signifying typically connotes disapproval, Meridian is immediately suspicious about the minister's intention and looks for clues in the reactions of the others to see if mockery is really the "message." The minister's youth and dress likewise semiotically "Signify" on Martin Luther King; the "text" of King—youth, voice, dress, sermon—has been "woven" into the ritual as one of the church's "ways of transformation," to enable the church to keep the past alive and to prepare for the future:

> It struck Meridian that he was deliberately imitating King, that he and all of his congregation *knew* he was consciously keeping that voice alive. It was like a *play*. This startled Meridian; and the preacher's voice—not his own voice at all, but rather the voice of millions who could no longer speak—wound on and on. . . . (200)

The preacher's voice is "not his own voice at all" because it is a "text" woven of many other texts, the ancestral "millions who could no longer speak." Mark Taylor notes the difficulty of ascribing authorship to any text: "Rather than *an author*, we discover a seemingly endless chain, an infinite proliferation of authors. Authors within authors, or as [Kierkegaard] puts it, 'one author seems to be enclosed in another, like the parts in a Chinese puzzle box'" (61). Meridian's discovery that the preacher's voice is a compendium of ancestral voices makes clear to her that the perpetuation of the "Signifyin' chain" of ancestral voices is the chief responsibility she owes to One Life: The "circle is unbroken" as long as someone remains alive to "speak" the texts. Her decision to kill before letting that "voice" become silent would not be possible except for her awareness that, beyond its implementation as a form of critique, "Signifyin' " is a culturally recognized vehicle of reincarnation and redemption—a "way of transformation." Significantly, Walker wrote "Saving the Life That Is Your Own" the same year that she wrote *Meridian*.

Thus the invocation to the "Spirit" writer with which Walker foregrounds *The Color Purple* (combined with Stevie Wonder's *"Show me how to do like you / Show me how to do it,"* as an epigraph) follows the question of authority to one of its several conclusions. While there is no one "author" of the text of ancestral voices, the collectivity of authority may itself be named "the Spirit." Walker acknowledges that this authority "writes" her since its texts shape her (*"show [her] how to do it"*) and, through her, shape her texts. In *The Temple of My Familiar* (1989) Walker's idea of the corporeal text ("Embodied Word") is best exemplified in the character Lissie, " " "the one who remembers everything" " " (*Temple* 52). Lissie, whose spiritual reincarnations allow her to thumb through the texts of her lives back to the dawn of human history, achieves godhead through the saving of all of her "selves," even those which have been inimical to One Life. As Embodied Word she becomes a paradigm of redemptive intertextuality:

She is Walker's spirit made text, many times over, each successive text a "repetition and revision" of past selves. Her authority derives from the unbroken chain of revisionary texts like Chinese puzzle boxes within her, herself the compendium of black female, of world experience.

## II

*We are a people. A people do not throw their geniuses away.* And if they are thrown away, it is our duty *as artists and as witnesses for the future* to collect them again for the sake of our children, and, if necessary, bone by bone. (*Gardens* 92)

I will focus now on Walker's critique of the Christological model as a specific aspect of her redemptive art. Shug Avery's assertion in *The Color Purple* that "you have to git man off your eyeball, before you can see anything a'tall" (168) is an initial step in her ultimately successful campaign to teach Celie (and the reader) that religious observance is a matter of social convention. Since the characterization of Christ as male agent of salvation without whom the passive and powerless female cannot be saved serves, in Shug's estimation, to reinforce patriarchal and hierarchical social formations which perpetuate female oppression, that characterization is an obstacle to spiritual growth.[5] The notion of self-sacrifice and martyrdom runs counter to Walker's reformist impulses, since it valorizes victimhood as an index of spiritual progress. Walker's alternative to the Christ model, the result of many years of struggle with the implications of the entirely submissive role of the female and the otherwise oppressed, is a collective female agency (so-called "woman-bonding") that stresses self-help and group support.[6]

The supplanting of the Christ model by the collective redemption model in Walker's work, I will argue, is part of a complex intertextual strategy of redemptive art that involves Walker's two most cherished literary ancestors—Jean Toomer and Zora Neale Hurston. "*Cane* and *Their Eyes Were Watching God* are probably my favorite books by black American writers," Walker said in her 1973 self-interview, referring to the best known works by Toomer and Hurston, respectively. "*I love* [Cane] *passionately;* could not possibly exist without it" (*Gardens* 259). Her reverence for Hurston has also been well established. Through essays like "Looking for Zora," which recounts how Walker literally claimed kinship with Hurston in order to locate the writer's burial place, Walker herself became very instrumental in the "rescue" of Hurston from neglect by readers and scholars. Yet Walker's expressed reservations about each of these authors indicates that she would change things about their lives and about their writing, too, if it were in her power.

As the epigraph to this section clearly demonstrates, Walker feels it is not only within her power, but it is her duty as a writer, to reclaim and restore ancestral geniuses.

Because Walker sees her texts as redemptive sites, the rehabilitation and preservation of her adopted ancestors, Toomer and Hurston, have been part of her creative practice almost from the start. Yet there is a clear distinction in the manner of Walker's textual reincarnations of the pair. Interestingly, while she strongly associates the Christological model with Toomer-like figures in her texts, Walker inscribes Hurston-like characters in her texts as innovators of the collective uplift model. Insofar as Walker characteristically associates Toomer with the discredited ideal of masculine agency, she must not simply reclaim him; she must (ironically) "redeem" him from his role as failed Christ. Walker must reclaim Hurston, on the other hand, in a fashion that compensates for the destitution and desperation that marked the writer's last years. In the process, Walker has become the catalyst for the current Hurston revival, "an act of literary bonding quite unlike anything that has ever happened within the Afro-American tradition" (Gates 244).

Walker's fascination with Toomer may be attributed in part to the fact that the site of his famous trip to the South immortalized in *Cane* is approximately an hour's drive from Walker's own hometown of Eatonton, Georgia. The women whose lives he sketched were women of Walker's own mother's time and circumstances. In "In Search of Our Mothers' Gardens," Walker describes Toomer's women as "our mothers and grandmothers, some of them: moving to music not yet written" (*Gardens* 232). Yet in explaining her attachment to Toomer, Walker acknowledges that her feelings for *Cane* come from a "perilous direction" (86). Despite her claim that she "could not possibly exist without" *Cane*, Walker says that she could indeed learn to do without Toomer himself: "I think Jean Toomer would want us to keep [the] beauty [of *Cane*], but let *him* go" (65; emphasis added). Apparently she allows Toomer to "go" based upon his choice "to live his own life as a white man," a "choice [which] undermined Toomer's moral judgment: there were things in American life [racism] and in his own [racial opportunism] that he simply refused to see" (62).

Examining Walker's valediction carefully shows it to be a more profound critique of Toomer than it might appear at first glance, for she lifts the phrasing of her dismissal of Toomer from Toomer himself. In "Theater," a sketch in the middle section of *Cane*, the story's central character, John, becomes transfixed by the earthy beauty and physical immediacy of the dancer Dorris as she performs on the stage before him. John, however, decides against emotional or even physical involvement with the purple-stockinged chorine. He "desires her," but "holds off." This is but one instance in a pattern of ironized, self-conscious desire and denial that typifies Toomer's educated males (as well as some of his middle-class women), throwing into relief Toomer's own speculative relationship with black culture. Ultimately John's ambivalence about a black beauty whose vitality frightens him evolves into a passive aesthetic appropriation that provides him with the emotional distance he requires (and, in the process, produces the line that echoes in Walker's emotional separation from Toomer: "Keep her loveliness," he tells himself, but "let her go" [*Cane* 51]).

John, as the author's stand-in, embodies Toomer's tenuous relationship to *his* subject, "the rich dusk beauty" of black folk culture (*Cane* xvi). The aesthetic resolution to John's emotional dilemma is emphasized with a chiasmatic refrain, recalling the versification of Toomer's "Song of the Son": "Let her go," he repeats. "And keep her loveliness" (52). Walker's appropriation of Toomer's language is a classic example of "Signifyin'," identifying implicitly the aspects of Toomer's biography which most trouble her: his rejection of black women, compounded by his objectification and scopic appropriation of their pain and their beauty. In many of the sketches in *Cane,* the various Toomer surrogates, faced with the possibility of union with black women of the South, almost always choose to take the women's loveliness with them, but let their bodies go (or, rather, *stay*).

In "Fern," for example, the would-be savior who narrates the story is overcome by Fern's physical proximity, and, moving to exploit her vulnerability, he precipitates in her a fit of madness. Guiltily, he plans to do "some fine unnamed thing for her" (17)—something short, that is, of taking her with him as he leaves on the train. The narrator of "Avey" tries to interest Avey in an art that would articulate the black female soul, but as narrator and interpreter of the woman's life, it is *his* art, not hers, that he recites to her, putting her to sleep in the process. His art—in effect, the text of *Cane* writ small—repeats the pattern of the male observer who objectifies female existence, extracts its beauty, but leaves the woman herself behind. Ironically, the narrator's final comment on Avey—"Orphan-woman" (47)—certifies this emotional abandonment.

In fact, Toomer's men are themselves the orphans—cultural orphans dislodged from the saving womb of their maternal culture by the stronger pull of a supersessive patriarchal embrace. Like Kabnis, they are figuratively Antaean, "suspended a few feet above the [culture] whose touch would resurrect [them]" (96). Like Dan Moore in "Box Seat" and Paul in "Bona and Paul," they are haunted by visions of earth mothers who would nurture them toward fulfillment of their potential destinies as "new-world Christs." Strikingly, Toomer's textual surrogates conjure a "new-world Christ" who is not a savior, but simply a martyr or, as Dan Moore puts it, "a slave of a woman who is a slave" (63). Committing themselves to black women signifies commitment to a black identity, a closing off of options that neither Toomer nor his surrogates seem willing to abide: "'God Almighty, dear God, dear Jesus, do not torture me with beauty,'" cries Kabnis. "'Take it away. . . . Dear Jesus, do not chain me to myself . . .'" (83). Despite his prayer for deliverance, Kabnis becomes, however, a martyr—a Christ figuratively chained to the slow, tortuous wheel of racial antagonism in the South. When we read this event in light of Toomer's later disaffiliation with black culture and identity, it leaves the impression that Kabnis, who alone among Toomer's surrogates achieves physical union with the women and the soil of the South, exemplifies Toomer's horror at the prospect of "saving" the South's suffering black women at the expense of his own freedom.

The failure of the "new-world Christ" figures in Toomer's work is significant, given Toomer's professed desire to "save" the "plum" of black culture which had been "saved" for him in the folksongs he heard.[7] Unable to move beyond a model of redemption that requires their cultural "deaths" to "end the book," Toomer and his surrogates flee the South in tacit admission that those who stand apart from both the community and its culture cannot "redeem" either. What Toomer actually preserves is not the Southern black folk culture he set out to document, but the fact of his ambivalence toward it.

For her part, Walker not only critiques the proclivity of Christ figures to victimize those they have come to save, but she typically characterizes them as cultural voyeurs in the Toomer mold. Walker effectively encodes the "text" of Toomer as would-be savior into her fiction, and there forces him to atone for the crimes of theft and abandonment. Toomer's appropriation of the stories of the women of the South, the real substance of *Cane*, followed by his abandonment of the race (and its women), is the "crime" which Walker redresses by her reappropriation of their lives and texts. She "redeems" the women of *Cane* in her own works—takes *back* their beauty, and lets the Toomer/Christ figure go. But she doesn't let him "off."

Among the earliest of the "Toomer archetypes" incarnated in Walker's fiction is Mordecai Rich, in the short story "Really, Doesn't Crime Pay?" The "crime" of the title is that of creative theft, a crime which Rich commits against a woman, Myrna, whose "madness" links her clearly to the women of Toomer's *Cane*. A Northern black man who goes to the South in search of literary material upon which to launch his career, Rich describes himself as an aesthete and a Romantic in the Toomer mold: "'A cold eye. An eye looking for Beauty. An eye looking for Truth.'" Myrna's suspicion of him stems from her belief that "nobody ought to look on other people's confusion with that cold an eye" (*In Love* 14), yet in the end, he seduces her and steals her stories—tales, fittingly, of women victimized by men. His praise of her creative power masks his parasitical intent: "'You could be another Zora Hurston,'" he says archly (18). Sure—and *he* could be another Jean Toomer, for he appropriates Myrna's life and works and uses them to become a celebrated writer. To compound his crime, he replaces the black matriarch of Myrna's story "with a white cracker, with little slit-blue eyes" (21)—a commentary, perhaps on Toomer's aesthetic/romantic preferences—and announces his intention to write a book called "'The Black Woman's Resistance to Creativity in the Arts.'" Like the teller of "Avey," Rich becomes an "authority" on the inability of black women to appreciate "an art that would open the way for women the likes of her" (*Cane* 46), a trickster masked as savior.

Another such trickster/savior of Walker's is Truman Held in *Meridian*. Held, too, is a Northern black man who goes to the South during the Civil Rights Movement; leaves a local Southern girl (Meridian) behind physically, psychically, and emotionally violated; returns to the North to embark upon an artistic career built upon the representation of the black women of the South; and there marries, as Toomer did, a white woman. Similarly, Held's pretense of internationalism in clothing (African) and speech (French) "Signifies" upon Toomer's retreat into pan-culturalism to escape the onus of his black American identity. In naming Held, Walker also "Signifies" on Toomer's narrator in "Fern," who is "held" by Fern's eyes: "Her eyes, unusually weird and open, held me. Held God" (*Cane* 17).[8] Beyond these details, the interesting coincidence of Walker's heroine's having the same name as a favorite retreat of the young Toomer in Washington, D.C.—Meridian Hill—points to Walker's strategy of intertextual reference. It is on Meridian Hill that the Toomer surrogate in "Avey" tries to teach Avey the meaning of her life with a high-blown poetry also intended to seduce. If Truman Held stands in for Toomer in *Meridian*, Meridian certainly fills the role of the Aveys that have become "trapped in an evil honey" of Toomer's art (*Gardens* 232).[9]

In the end it is the very image which he exploits for profit, that of the Southern black earth mother, which "holds" Truman: "It was as if the voluptuous black bodies, with breasts like melons and hair like a crown of thorns, reached out—creatures of his own creation—and silenced his tongue. They began to claim him" (*Meridian* 170). Just as Fern haunts the would-be seducer who abandons her, Meridian ("'The woman I should have married and didn't'") becomes "a constant reproach, in [Truman's] thoughts" (138, 141). Since Truman surrounds himself with pictures of Meridian and with paintings and sculptures of the black women of the South, his torment poetically stems from the nature and source of his crime—the sin of reducing people to Art (128). Significantly, Truman, haunted by the image of the mother culture against which he has transgressed, must expiate his crimes by working as the "servant" to women who are "servants" in the South. Under Meridian's direction, he works out his "salvation" as a freelance Civil Rights activist, assuming Meridian's role as communal sufferer after she decides to "just walk away."[10]

Male characters such as these and the white rock star Traynor in Walker's short story "Nineteen Fifty-five" share attributes which separate them from other victimizers of women in her works. Unlike the more typical male antagonist, they do not commit their crimes as a result of ignorance or simply as rough embodiments of a brutal patriarchy, but see themselves as saviors and liberators of women from emotional and physical violence, as men more sensitive to the plight of women due to their artistic temperaments. This Toomer-inspired figure of the "new-world Christ" who participates in the oppression of those he comes to liberate, and for whom "martyrdom" constitutes lifelong union with the culture and women of the black South, forms the core of Walker's "text" of the Christ model. The racial and cultural ambiguity of the figure, his outsider status to the culture, his "racial opportunism," and his career-defining cultural voyeurism and aesthetic banditry round out the cluster of discrete signifiers which typify this enduring Walker paradigm.

The fact that this violator suffers psychically from his crime echoes Toomer's summation of Fern's history of victimization: "When she was young, a few men took her, but got no joy from it. And then, once done, they felt bound to her" (*Cane* 14). Not only do these transgressors typically get no joy from their crimes in Walker's stories, but the very image of the violated "black madonna" (the nurturer in Toomer's work of the "new-world Christ") becomes the avenging ghost who drives the transgressor on a path toward purgation. Walker's textual appropriation of Toomer serves a purgatorial function then, becoming the theater for the passion, fall, and redemption of a particular, gender-focused Christology.

While Walker's redemptive efforts at textually reincarnating Toomer center on rehabilitating his history of racial and female exploitation, her effort at textual resuscitation of Zora Neale Hurston is redemptive in the sense that Walker attempts to reverse the catastrophic effects of poverty, isolation, and critical neglect. Noting Langston Hughes's description of Hurston as "a perfect book of entertainment in herself," Henry Louis Gates has also discovered the "presence" of Hurston in Walker's *The Color Purple*, but he attributes it to Walker's revisionary reconsideration of Hurston's heroine, Janie Woods, in *Their Eyes Were Watching God* (245). Gates compares Walker's description of a picture of Hurston which she owns to the picture of Shug Avery standing beside a motor car that Celie describes (Gates 254). He interprets this "Signifyin' " gesture as evidence that Shug is a revision of Janie, a "letter of love to [Walker's] authority

figure" (244). I think, however, that Walker's depiction of Shug Avery
is meant to "Signify" on Hurston herself, especially since the picture of
Hurston metamorphoses into the picture of Shug. Just as Walker "saves"
the text of *Mules and Men* by transcribing it into "The Revenge of Hannah
Kemhuff," Walker "saves" Hurston herself in *The Color Purple*. Shug Avery
is Zora Neale Hurston reincarnated as "a perfect book of entertainment in
herself."

Further, this inscription of Hurston serves the strategic purpose of
"redeeming" the Christological model previously associated with Toomer.
Toomer's outsider view of black women in the South falls just short, in
Walker's estimation, of Hurston's insider view: *"There is no book more important
to me than this one,"* says Walker of *Their Eyes Were Watching God,* "(including
Toomer's *Cane,* which comes close, but from what I recognize is a more
perilous direction)" (*Gardens* 86). The "ghost" of Hurston which dwells in
Walker's works takes precedence over the "ghost" of Toomer, just as Hurston's
text of black womanhood in the South authoritatively and chronologically
supersedes Toomer's. Gates is correct, I think, to see *The Color Purple* as
revisionary of both *Cane* and *Their Eyes* (194, 249). But Walker's novel seems,
more appropriately, an attempt to "redeem" both parent texts by ensuring
that "the best that has been produced" in *both* "can continue to live" in *The
Color Purple.*

Not only does *The Color Purple* revise key tropes in Toomer's *Cane,* it
owes its very title to the urgent chromatic display of Toomer's work, where
we find the "purple haze" of dusk, the "purple" skin of the "Face" at sundown,
lavender-tinted houses, and "pale purple shadows" contrasting with the
"deep purple" of a woman's hair. Dusk tinges men with "purple pallor." The
purple glow of the "Crimson Garden" signifies its transition from Eden to
Gethsemane in "Bona and Paul," while women dress in "silk stockings and
purple dresses" in the South and "silk purple stockings" in the East. Nettie's
discovery of the near-purple (i.e., "blue-black") skin of the Africans in *The
Color Purple* tips off a further meaning of "the color purple" for Walker as
well as Toomer: "the colored people." Toomer's memorable poem in *Cane,*
"Song of the Son," shows his most striking use of the color in a figuration
that captures the essence of *Cane:*

O Negro slaves, dark purple ripened plums,
Squeezed, and bursting in the pine-wood air,
Passing, before they stripped the old tree bare
One plum was saved for me, one seed becomes

An everlasting song, a singing tree,
Caroling softly souls of slavery,

What they were, and what they are to me,
Caroling softly souls of slavery (12)

For Toomer, the "saved" plum is the essence of the slavery experience captured in the folksongs of the South which he believed were doomed to extinction. His text, then, has the redemptive purpose of preserving the souls of black folk, immortalizing them in "everlasting song"—but as *written*, not spoken, texts. As such, Toomer's saving gesture, a figurative "singing tree," represents the prototype of Walker's redemptive art.

"When reading Toomer's 'Song of the Sun' [sic] it is not unusual to comprehend—in a flash—what a dozen books on black people's history fail to illuminate," Walker has said. "I have embarrassed my classes occasionally by standing in front of them in tears as Toomer's poem about 'some genius from the South' [i.e., 'Georgia Dusk'] flew through my body like a swarm of golden butterflies on their way toward a destructive sun. Like Du Bois, Toomer was capable of comprehending the black soul" (*Gardens* 258). Walker's particularly emotional response to this poem indicates her awareness of Toomer's characterization of "the colored people" as "the color purple" ("O Negro slaves, dark purple ripened plums"), and her depiction of Shug Avery in *The Color Purple* involves a redemptive gesture built on that figuration. Shug's nickname is an abbreviation for "Sugar," significantly, the chief product of the cane crop. On first seeing Shug, Celie notes, "Under all that powder her face black. . . . She got a long pointed nose and big fleshy mouth. Lips look like black plum" (42). Later, Celie views Shug's disease-racked body in the tub: ". . . Shug Avery long black body with it black plum nipples, look like her mouth . . ." (45). In an interesting "Signifyin' " gesture, Walker transforms Toomer's "saved" plum into a real "singer" (and worshipper of trees). And, more importantly for Walker's redemptive strategy, by "saving" Shug, Celie performs the enabling action toward her own redemption, for the kiss of those very black plum lips opens up to Celie her own sexuality, spirituality, and ultimately (through Shug's "saving" of Nettie's letters) her very identity.

In her most recent collection of essays, *Living By the Word* (1988), Walker claims that "there is no story more moving to me personally than one in which one woman saves the life of another, and saves herself . . .," a feat that "black women wish they were able to do all the time" (19). In effect, what we see in *The Color Purple* is Walker's inscription of that very mutual saving gesture between herself and her literary ancestor, Hurston. Walker appropriates Toomer's figure of the "saved plum," which becomes the seed of the "singing tree" of his art. But significantly, the "voice" which comes through clearest is Hurston's, not Toomer's, and the song she sings is not of ineffectual male saviors who end up exploiting those they would redeem, but of women individually and collectively working toward their own and each other's salvation.

Moving Toomer "off her eyeball" allows Walker to see beyond the hierarchical Christological path, just as Shug opens up for Celie the route of mutual salvation. Toomer's singing tree is figuratively incorporated into Hurston's chorus of Nature. When, in *Their Eyes*, Janie's grandmother saves "de text" of her slave experience for Janie, the moment strikingly parallels Toomer's "saved plum" of the black slave experience. But Janie learns, as Walker does too, that saved "texts" are meant to be rewritten through the vantage of new experience. Janie revises, and therefore redeems, her grandmother's "text" of male-agent salvation (i.e., respectable marriage), passing on to Pheoby her own text of transformation from unvoiced cultural orphan to voiced and participating (yet determinedly autonomous) member of the folk community, a paradigm of redemptive agency which Walker appropriates and expands upon. Toomer's text of male-agent redemption—cognate with Nanny's, and therefore implicitly critiqued by Janie's experience in *Their Eyes*—becomes entirely obsolete in light of the manifold saving gestures of the women of *The Color Purple*.

At the heart of *The Color Purple* lies a complex redemptive artistry that encompasses saving gestures of various types. For example, Walker has acknowledged her grandmother as her source for Celie ("Characters" 67). Walker has also made much of the tale of the shared underwear as an influence (*Gardens* 355–56). But the un-text of the redemptive fantasy at the heart of the novel appears in Walker's 1979 essay "Zora Neale Hurston," which concludes with the definitive statement of Walker's redemptive art that serves as the epigraph to this section of my essay: "*We are a people. A people do not throw their geniuses away.* And if they are thrown away, it is our duty *as artists and as witnesses for the future* to collect them again for the sake of our children, and, if necessary, bone by bone" (*Gardens* 92). In this concluding statement to an article on the cautionary aspects of Hurston's life and career, Walker signals her intent to reassemble the "text" of Hurston, "if necessary, bone by bone," and to reincarnate her as "Embodied Word." Equally revealing is what immediately precedes this declaration in the essay, a fantasy of mutually assisted salvation which includes not only Hurston but, significantly, the singers Billie Holiday and Bessie Smith too:

> In my mind, Zora Neale Hurston, Billie Holiday, and Bessie Smith form a sort of unholy trinity. Zora *belongs* in the tradition of black women singers, rather than among "the literati," at least to me. . . . Like Billie and Bessie she followed her own road, believed in her own gods, pursued her own dreams, and refused to separate herself from the "common" people. *It would have been nice if the*

*three of them had had one another to turn to, in times of need. I close my*
*eyes and imagine them* [my emphasis]: Bessie would be in charge of
all the money; Zora would keep Billie's masochistic tendencies in
check and prevent her from singing embarrassing anything-for-a-
man songs, thereby preventing Billie's heroin addiction. In return,
Billie could be, along with Bessie, the family that Zora felt she
never had. (*Gardens* 91–92)

Does this fantasy not represent the core of *The Color Purple*? Walker's
assertion that Hurston *"belongs"* more among the singers than the writers
grounds Shug Avery's incarnation as blues singer. Further, in Mary Agnes
(Squeak), we can hear not only the words but also the "sort of meowing"
voice of Billie Holiday. Both her drug use and tragic history with men relate
her to Holiday, and the fact that she, like Celie (Hurston), benefits from an
extended network of female strivers fulfills the fantasy's intent of rewriting
and redeeming the lives of the ancestral voices Walker acknowledges.
Physically and temperamentally, Sophia suggests Bessie Smith, the one who
would keep the money. Walker's redemptive strategy works to empower each
historical figure in a way that fictionally reverses the putative cause of her
life's suffering. As Walker explains of her step grandmother's reincarnation
in the novel as Celie: "I liberated her from her own history. . . . I wanted her
to be happy" ("Characters" 67).

Walker's various statements indicate her belief in the *actual, not
figurative,* saving power of art—the ability of the artist to liberate people
from their tragic histories—if necessary, to make them happy. In her
poem "Each One, Pull One," Walker elevates this ability to an obligation.
Addressing all who "write, paint, sculpt, dance / or sing" as sharers in the
"fate / of all our peoples" (i.e., One Life), she exhorts those standing with
her on "the rim / of the grave" of the ancestors (including King, Malcolm X,
Lorraine Hansberry, Hurston, Nella Larsen, and Toomer) to stop helping
their enemies to "bury us":

Look, I, temporarily on the rim of the grave
have grasped my mother's hand my father's leg.
There is the hand of Robeson Langston's thigh
Zora's arm and hair . . .
Each one, pull one back into the sun
We who have stood over
so many graves
know that
all of us must live
or none. (*Horses* 50–53)

## III

The story of Walker's redemptive effort on behalf of Toomer and Hurston has one additional chapter. In Walker's recent novel *The Temple of My Familiar,* he Toomer archetype reappears as the folk/pop singer Arveyda, a man of multiracial background like Toomer. Arveyda's fame as a musician derives from his ability to "sing" the souls of his largely female audience, and as in Toomer's case, this talent feeds off his exploitative relationship with the women in his life. At the novel's end, Arveyda meets Fanny, the genetic descendant of Celie (through Olivia) and the spiritual descendent of Shug, having been raised in the household of the two women. The sexual union of these two, then, marks the "textual" bonding of the Toomer and Hurston archetypes in Walker's work. Their orgasm (in Shug's theology, the ecstatic achievement of god's presence) returns us to the key tropological refiguration in *The Color Purple:* Arveyda feels as if he has rushed to meet all the ancestors and they have welcomed him with joy" (407). During this ancestral communion, they also share a vision which hints at their textual origins:

> She is fearful of asking him what she must. Timidly she says: "And did you also see the yellow plum tree and all the little creatures, even the fish, in its branches? . . ."
> But Arveyda says simply, "Yes. . . . But best of all . . . was the plum tree and everything and everybody in it, and the warmth of your breath and the taste in my mouth of the sweet yellow plums."
> (407–408)

This scene represents, I believe, Walker's reconciliation with the Toomer archetype—her attempt to lay to rest this ghost that has roamed her works in search of atonement. The yellow plums perhaps result from the cross-pollination of the two trees of Walker's ancestral *Gardens*—Janie's pear and Toomer's plum. The sexual positioning of Fanny above Arveyda reflects the Toomer surrogate's abandonment of hierarchical sexual politics, while his achieved physical union with Fanny (a "space Cadet" in the mold of Toomer's Fern) indicates a fulfillment of both Toomer's quest for physical union with the spirit-maddened women of the race and the women's parallel discovery of a spiritual anchor. Thus their final salutes to each other attest to their success in mutually-assisted salvation:

> "My . . . *spirit,*" says Fanny . . . .
> "My . . . *flesh,*" says Arveyda . . . . (408)

## Notes

1. Wendy Wall (85) suggests that Walker ascribes a similar power to Celie, since Celie too is the author of a self which has only a textual existence.

2. See Walker's essay "Writing *The Color Purple*" (*Gardens* 355–60), in which she describes the "visitations" by the book's characters as crucial to the production of her text.

3. Henry Louis Gates (239–58) and Michael Awkward (135–64) have pursued other possibilities in interpreting Walker's spiritualistic stance, also with reference to Hurston and Toomer as literary ancestors.

4. In my forthcoming essay "Survival *Whole*: Redemptive Vengeance and Forbearance in Alice Walker's Novels," I consider Walker's continued interest in retaliatory violence as an alternative method of redemption.

5. Mary Daly points out that the Christological model leads inevitably toward sexism: "The underlying—and often explicit—assumption in the minds of theologians down through the centuries has been that divinity could not have deigned to 'become incarnate' in the 'inferior' sex, and the 'fact' that 'he' did not do so of course confirms male superiority" (70). Daly goes on to insist that even the reform theologians who interpret Christ as a symbol miss the point that the historical use of the "symbol" to oppress indicates "some inherent deficiency in the symbol itself" (72).

6. Mary Daly's chapter The Bonds of Freedom: Sisterhood as Antichurch" explains the rationale for such a reformist gesture: The development of sisterhood is a unique threat, for it is directed against the basic social and psychic model of hierarchy and dominion upon which authoritarian religion *as authoritarian* depends for survival" (133).

7. See Darwin T. Turner's "Introduction" to *Cane* xxii–xxiii. For other aspects of Toomer's messianic self-image, see page xi of the "Introduction."

8. The eyes of Truman Held's own "judge," Meridian Hill, have a similar effect upon Truman: "There was something dark, Truman thought, a shadow that seemed to swing, like the pendulum of a dock, or like a blade, behind her open, candid eyes, that made one feel condemned. That made one think of the guillotine" (*Meridian* 139).

9. See Kerman and Eldridge (74) on Meridian Hill. When we consider the implications of the name Meridian, we should also note the central importance of the poem "Blue Meridian" as Toomer's attempt at racial and cultural self-definition. See Kerman and Eldridge (80–81) for a discussion of "Blue Meridian" (originally titled "The First American").

10. Martha J. McGowan points out that the working title for *Meridian* was *Atonement and Release* (29).

## Works Cited

Awkward, Michael. *Inspiriting Influences: Tradition, Revision, and Afro-American Women's Novels*. New York: Columbia University Press, 1989.

Barthes, Roland. "From Work to Text." *Textual Strategies: Perspectives in Post-Structuralist Criticism*. Ed. Joshué V. Harari. Ithaca: Cornell University Press, 1979: 73–81.

"Characters in Search of a Book." *Newsweek* 21 June 1982: 67.

Daly, Mary. *Beyond God the Father: Toward a Philosophy of Women's Liberation.* Boston: Beacon, 1973.

Gates, Henry Louis, Jr. *The Signifying Monkey: A Theory of Afro-American Literary Criticism.* New York: Oxford University Press, 1988.

Kerman, Cynthia Earl, and Richard Eldridge. *The Lives of Jean Toomer: A Hunger for Wholeness.* Baton Rouge: Louisiana State University Press, 1987.

McGowan, Martha J. "Atonement and Release in Alice Walker's *Meridian*." *Critique: Studies in Modern Fiction* 23.1 (1981): 25–36.

Taylor, Mark C. "Text as Victim." *Deconstruction and Theology.* Ed. Thomas J. J. Altizer. New York: Crossroad, 1982: 58–78.

Toomer, Jean. *Cane.* 1923. New York: Liveright, 1975.

Walker, Alice. *The Color Purple.* New York: Harcourt, 1982.

———. *Horses Make a Landscape Look More Beautiful: Poems.* San Diego: Harcourt, 1986.

———. *In Love & Trouble: Stories of Black Women.* New York: Harcourt, 1973.

———. *In Search of Our Mothers' Gardens: Womanist Prose.* San Diego: Harcourt, 1983.

———. *Living By the Word: Selected Writings, 1973–1987.* San Diego: Harcourt, 1988.

———. *Meridian.* 1976. New York: Harcourt, 1976.

———. *The Temple of My Familiar.* San Diego: Harcourt, 1989.

Wall, Wendy. "Lettered Bodies and Corporeal Texts in *The Color Purple*." *Studies in American Fiction* 16 (1988): 83–97.

ROBERT JAMES BUTLER

# Alice Walker's Vision of the South in The Third Life of Grange Copeland

Two-heading was dying out, he lamented. "Folks what can look at things
in more than one way is done got rare."

(*Third Life* 129)

In "The Black Writer and the Southern Experience," Alice Walker defines
her response to the South in a richly ambivalent way.[1] Although she stresses
that she does not intend to "romanticize Southern black country life" and
is quick to point out that she "hated" the South, "generally," when growing
up in rural Georgia, she nevertheless emphasizes that Southern black writers have "enormous richness and beauty to draw from" (*In Search* 21). This
"double vision" (19) of the South is at the center of most of her fiction and
is given extremely complex treatment in her best work. While Walker can
remember with considerable resentment the larger white world composed of
"evil greedy men" who paid her sharecropper father three hundred dollars
for twelve months of labor while working him "to death" (21), she can also
call vividly to mind the "sense of *community*" (17) which gave blacks a way
of coping with and sometimes transcending the hardships of such a racist
society. Although she emphatically states that she is not "nostalgic. . . for
lost poverty" (17), she can also lyrically recall the beauties of the Southern
land, "loving the earth so much that one longs to taste it and sometimes
does" (21). Even the Southern black religious traditions, which she con-

*African American Review*, Volume 27 (2), Summer 1993: pp. 195–204. © 1993 Robert
James Butler

sciously rejected as a college student because she saw them with one part of her mind as "a white man's palliative," she values in another way because her people "had made [religion] into something at once simple and noble" (18), an "antidote against bitterness" (16).

Walker's ambivalence, therefore, is a rich and complex mode of vision, a way of seeing her Southern background which prevents her from either naïvely romanticizing the South or inducing it to an oversimplified vision of despair and resentment. Ambivalence, or what Grange Copeland might call "two-heading" (*Third Life* 129), allows Walker to tell the full truth about her experience in the South. Avoiding the "blindness" created by her awareness of the injustices done to blacks in the South, she is able to draw "a great deal of positive material" from her outwardly "'underprivileged'" (*In Search* 20) background. Indeed, she stresses that her status as a black Southern writer endows her with special advantages:

> No one could wish for a more advantageous heritage than that bequeathed to the black writer in the South: a compassion for the earth, a trust in humanity beyond our knowledge of evil, and an abiding sense of justice. We inherit a great responsibility as well, for we must give voice to centuries not only of silent bitterness and hate but also of neighborly kindness and sustaining love. (*In Search* 21)

Walker's sense of herself as both a black and a Southern writer, then, enables her to participate in a literary tradition containing a richness of vision which she finds missing in the mainstream of American literature. In "Saving the Life That Is Your Own: The Importance of Models in the Artist's Life," she expresses a distaste for the overall pessimism of modern American literature. She claims that "the gloom of defeat is thick" in twentieth-century American literature because "American writers tended to end their books and their characters' lives as if there were no better existence for which to struggle." But because Southern black experience is rooted in both "struggle" and "some kind of larger freedom" resulting from such struggle, the black writer is able to overcome the despair which enervates so much modern literature (*In Search* 5). African American writers, therefore, participate in a literary tradition which is distinctive for both its lucid criticism of modern life and its special ability to recover human value and thus make important affirmations which give black American literature a unique vitality and resonance.

The single work which best expresses Walker's powerful ambivalence toward Southern life is her first novel, *The Third Life of Grange Copeland*, a book notable for its vitality and its resonance. Walker's complex vision of the South can be seen in her development of the novel's three main characters—

Brownfield, Ruth, and Grange Copeland. While Brownfield is a terrifying example of how the South can physically enslave and spiritually cripple black people, Ruth's story offers considerable hope because she is able to leave the South, rejecting the racist world which destroys Brownfield and, in so doing, move toward a larger, freer world which offers her fresh possibilities. Grange Copeland's narrative points out some of the positive features of Southern black life. He returns to Georgia after an unsuccessful journey north to find the things he needs for his identity—a sense of place and a feeling of family and community, what Michael Cooke has called "intimacy" (x). Although the narratives, taken in isolation, do not express the author's whole vision of Southern life, together they offer a series of interrelated perspectives which capture Walker's richly ambivalent vision of the South. While Grange's story in isolation might suggest a glib romanticizing of the black South and while the stories of Ruth and Brownfield might suggest an equally simplistic debunking of black Southern life, all three narratives constitute what Walker has called "the richness of the black writer's experience in the South" (*In Search* 18).

Brownfield's narrative concentrates all that is negative about Southern culture: He is cruelly victimized by the extreme racism and poverty of the Georgia backwoods world in which he is born and raised. As his name clearly suggests, his is a case of blighted growth; he is a person who has been physically and emotionally withered by the nearly pathological environment which surrounds him. By the end of the novel, he is portrayed as "a human being . . . completely destroyed" (225) by the worst features of rural Southern life—ignorance, poverty, racism, and violence. Appropriately, one of the earliest images of him in the novel describes him as undernourished and diseased, his head covered with tatter sores, his legs afflicted with tomato sores, and his armpits filled with boils running with pus. As his narrative develops, these images of disease coalesce into a frightening metaphor which dramatizes how Brownfield is infected and eventually destroyed by a racist world which systematically deprives him of human nourishment.

This is particularly true of the way in which the system of Southern sharecropping destroys his family by enslaving them to the land which would otherwise nourish them. Because Brownfield's father Grange cannot make an adequate living for his family, his ego is gradually eroded, until he comes to see himself as a "stone," a "robot," and a "cipher" (8). He therefore fails as a husband and a father, driving his wife to suicide and withdrawing emotionally from his son. The net effect on Brownfield is to engrave deep emotional scars into his character which ultimately stunt his growth. After being abandoned by Grange and losing his mother shortly afterwards, Brownfield is frozen into a condition of Southern servitude. His efforts to establish a new life fail to materialize because his loss of family and the destruction of self-esteem caused by a racist environment trap him in a kind of moral vacuum:

> He was expected to raise himself up on air, which was all that was left after his work for others. Others who were always within their rights to pay practically nothing for his labor. He was never able to do more than exist on air; he was never able to build on it, and was never able to have any land of his own; and was never able to set his woman up in style, which more than anything else was what he wanted to do. (54–55)

Literally cheated out of land and morally dispossessed of a human foundation for his life, Brownfield is ironically condemned to repeat his father's failures. As he realizes not long after being abandoned by Grange, ". . . his own life was becoming a repetition of his father's" (54). His efforts to go north result in "weeks of indecisive wandering" (31), eventually bringing him to a small Georgia town where he forms a debilitating relationship with Josie, one of his father's discarded lovers. When he does discover a fruitful relationship with Mem, their marriage is ruined by the same factors which destroyed his parents' marriage. The "warm, life-giving circle" of their life together is gradually dissolved by "the shadow of eternal bondage" (49) which eroded his father's self-esteem. Bound like his father by "the chain that held him to the land" (50), Brownfield too becomes neurotically jealous of his wife and degrades her to the point where he can recover part of his ego by feeling superior to her. Like his father, who pushed his wife into suicide because he could not bear loving her and could not adequately support her, Brownfield murders Mem because a social environment that strips him of manhood cancels out his love for her. Forced by an oppressively racist society to "plow a furrow his father had laid" (45), Brownfield is indeed a "brown field," a crop that has failed to mature and bear fruit because his life has been deprived of necessary nutrients.

Like his five-year-old daughter, who is slowly poisoned by the arsenic she uses to dust the cotton crop in order to protect it from boll weevils, he is gradually victimized by a uniquely Southern system of segregation and sharecropping which infects his life. He eventually becomes exactly what his social environment wants him to be—an extension of its most pathological impulses. Indeed, Brownfield not only comes to accept the South but develops a perverse love of the world which dehumanizes him. Thus, he blankly accepts the impoverished roles extended to him by his Southern environment and makes no attempt either to rebel against these roles or to seek a better world:

He had no faith that any other place would be better. He fitted himself into the slot in which he found himself; for fun he poured oil into the streams to kill the fish and tickled his own vanity by drowning cats. (59)

A normal boy early in the novel, Brownfield becomes the book's most degraded character, for in accepting his "place" in Southern society, he degenerates into a killer of families and a poisoner of innocent life.

If Brownfield's narrative dramatizes Walker's most severe criticisms of the South, the story of his daughter Ruth qualifies this pessimistic vision by providing an alternative to the meaninglessness of Brownfield's life. Even though Ruth spends her formative years in the same environment which poisoned her father, she is able to protect herself with a number of antidotes because she develops a consciousness of Southern life which makes her aware of both its strengths and dangers. She is thus able to empower herself with some of the strengths of black folk culture in the Deep South and is also able to imagine her life in terms which transcend the South, ultimately leaving it for a larger world which offers her new possibilities. Whereas Brownfield's life travels a deterministic circle of futility (all his efforts to gain physical and emotional distance from the racist South fail), Ruth's story is existential in outlook. It involves a process of awakening and liberation. Like the slave narratives, which Walker has described as a part of a literary tradition where "escape for the body and freedom for the soul went together" (*In Search* 5), Ruth's story is a flight from twentieth-century forms of Southern bondage. Her consciousness distills all that is good in her Southern black traditions and allows her to imagine a broader world beyond the South. As a result, she is able to create "a way out of no way" (iii). Like the Biblical Ruth, she finds herself an alien in a strange land, but, unlike Ruth, she can find her way to a kind of promised land, a new space offering fresh possibilities.

A crucial part of her liberation is contained in the fact that she does not grow up in the kind of spiritual and emotional vacuum which blighted Brownfield's life. Although she has had to face the physical poverty and racism which characterize her father's existence, she gains the benefit of the family life he was deprived of, and this puts her in contact with nourishing cultural and personal values. In contrast to Brownfield, who spins in futile circles because he "was expected to raise himself up on air" (54), Ruth is raised by a mother whom she comes to regard as "a saint" (126), someone who makes heroic efforts to meet her human needs. Although Mem literally gives up her life opposing Brownfield's acceptance of his "place" in Southern society, she succeeds in moving the family to a town where Ruth, for a time at least, has the benefit of a real house and formal schooling. More importantly, Mem provides Ruth with a powerful role model, for she is a woman who maintains her human dignity in a dehumanizing environment. Like the women whom Walker describes in *In Search of Our Mothers' Gardens* who provided her with role models, Mem is an "exquisite butterfly trapped in an evil honey" (232). By "inheriting" her mother's "vibrant, creative spirit" (*In Search* 239), Ruth comes to transcend the limitations which white society seeks to impose on black women.

After Mem is murdered—literally by Brownfield and symbolically by the Southern society he comes to love and represent—Ruth is taken in by Grange, who becomes her surrogate father. From the moment of her birth, Grange sees Ruth as unique and beautiful, someone who almost magically appears in the midst of an environment which is harsh and ugly. Marveling at Ruth as a newborn child, he exclaims, "Out of all kinds of shit comes something soft, clean, and sweet smellin'" (71). From this point on, Grange dedicates himself to protecting Ruth from the foulness of the Southern environment into which she was born, and he commits himself to nurturing that which is "sweet" and "clean" in her. He provides her with a "snug house" (69) in which to live and also gives her for the first time in her life an adequate supply of nourishing food.

More importantly, he nourishes her mind and soul. He forbids her to work in the cotton fields which have helped to destroy Brownfield's life, telling her, "You not some kind of field hand!" (125), and he arranges for her to attend school. But in an important way he also becomes her teacher, instructing her in "the realities of life" (139), drawing material from his own wide experience and his extensive knowledge of black folklore. His retelling of folktales from the black South provides her with a vivid sense of a mythic hero—the trickster "who could talk himself out of any situation" (128). She thus learns from an early age a lesson which her father never acquired— that words and intelligence, not raw violence, have the power to transform experience by creating understanding and control over life. When listening to Grange sing blues music, she likewise feels "kin to something very old" (133), a musical tradition arising out of the black South which transforms suffering into a kind of human triumph rooted in what Ralph Ellison has called a "near tragic, near comic lyricism" (90).

By connecting Ruth to the life-giving tradition of the black folk art of the South, Grange provides her with the time-tested values which will help her to survive and even triumph over the racist world which destroys so many other people in the novel. His recounting episodes from black history reinforces in her mind the crucial idea that black people established a strong and viable culture in the South, despite the efforts of the dominant society to destroy that culture. His accounts of his personal past, especially from his boyhood, also bring to life in Ruth's consciousness "all sorts of encounters with dead folks and spirits and occasionally the Holy Ghost" (129). In other words, his stories give her vital access to an imaginatively rich, emotionally potent world—precisely the kind of world which the psychologically underdeveloped Brownfield never becomes aware of. As Ruth grows older, Grange also teaches her about the world beyond the South. He steals books from the white library which open her mind and stimulate her imagination—books about mythology, geography, Africa, and romantic rebellion. He also reads her episodes from the Bible, especially the story of Exodus, again empowering her with the compelling myth of an oppressed people who triumph over circumstance through the strength of their will and spirit.

Although he twice offers her his farm, which would root her deeply to the South he has come to accept as his home, Grange loves Ruth enough to prepare her for the most dramatic action of her life, her flight from the South. Late in the novel, when Ruth asks him about her future, he tells her, "'We got this farm. We can stay here till kingdom come.'" But by this point in her life she feels stifled by the segregated South and tells him, "'I'm not going to be a hermit. I want to get away from here someday'" (193). The same fences which provide Grange with a sense of security Ruth perceives as encroachments.

The final third of the novel, therefore, deals with Ruth's increasing dissatisfaction with the rural South and her desire to move toward a larger, broader world which her protean identity needs. This struggle finally takes the form of her gaining independence from Brownfield and everything he represents about the South. A man who "had enslaved his own family" (227), as well as himself, he is intent on taking Ruth back after he has been released from prison. When he encounters Ruth late in the novel as she walks to school, he shouts at her, "'You belongs to me, just like my chickens or my hogs.'" "'You need shooting,'" she defiantly replies (220). Rejecting the crippling roles imposed on her mother and grandmother by Southern society, she observes that "'I'm not yours'" (219).

As the novel draws to its close, Ruth, with Grange's help, achieves her independence from her father and Southern life in general. It becomes increasingly clear to Grange that the only way to protect Ruth from Brownfield is to encourage her to leave the South, for the full weight of Southern law is in favor of returning her to Brownfield, whom Judge Harry regards as her "'*real* daddy'" (244). Grange, therefore, centers his life on helping "to prepare Ruth for some great and herculean task" (198)—her emancipation from Southern slavery and her pursuit of a new life. He buys her an automobile on her sixteenth birthday and begins saving money which she will use for college. He ultimately sacrifices his own life to save her from Brownfield, for he is killed by the police after shooting Brownfield when the court takes Ruth away from him.

The novel ends on a painful note of ambivalence. Southern injustice erupts in violence which takes Grange's life, yet his death frees Ruth for a new life of expanded possibilities. By the conclusion of the book, Ruth is poised for flight into a fast-changing world which will transform her. Observing the nightly television news, she becomes fascinated by "pictures of students marching" (232) as they work toward a more open and fluid society. Even the Georgia backwater in which she has been raised shows dramatic evidence of real change—voter registration campaigns, interracial marriage, and the beginnings of integration.

But the novel strongly implies that Ruth will not stay long in the South because her own protean self requires more space and possibility than the South at this point in its history can provide. Eager to "'rise up'" (196) in life, she dreams of going north. As she tells Grange, "'I want to get away from here someday. . . . I think maybe I'll go North, like you did . . .'" (193). Later she thinks vaguely of journeying to Africa. The exact physical direction of her life is not made clear, nor could it be. Like many African American heroic figures such as Frederick Douglass and the persona of Richard Wright's *Black Boy*, she has a lucid notion of the Southern places she must leave but keeps an indeterminate vision of the open space to which she will move. Like the Jews in Exodus, whose story Grange has told her "for perhaps the hundredth time" (209), she must leave an all-too-real Egypt in order to quest for a mythic "Promised Land."

The third major narrative in the novel incorporates the visions of the South implicit in the other two narratives and offers one more critically important perspective on the South. Whereas Grange Copeland's "first" life powerfully reinforces the bleakly pessimistic view of the South implicit in Brownfield's narrative, and his "second" life is very similar in certain ways to Ruth's story, because it is a flight from the slavery of the segregated South, Grange's "third" life contains an important element missing in the other two narratives—his remarkable return to the South, which regenerates him as a human being. It is this return, like Celie's return to Georgia at the end of *The Color Purple*, which underscores Walker's most affirmative vision of the South. In returning to Baker County, Grange achieves "his total triumph over life's failures" (136), creating a new place for himself by transforming the racist society which has withered Brownfield into a genuine "home" (141) which nurtures Ruth and also causes him to be "a reborn man" (157). Like the hero described in Joseph Campbell's *Hero with a Thousand Faces*, Grange attains truly heroic status by a three-part journey involving the leaving of a settled, known world; the experiencing of tests in an unknown world; and the returning home with a new mode of consciousness which transforms his life and the lives of others (246).

Walker, who knew the most brutal features of the rural South firsthand, is careful not to romanticize the South to which Grange returns. She emphasizes that Grange goes back to Georgia not because of a sudden nostalgia for magnolias and wisteria but simply because the circumstances of his life have made him a Southerner, for better or for worse: ". . . though he hated it as much as any place else, where he was born would always be home for him. Georgia would be home for him, and every other place foreign" (141). Crucial to Grange's creation of a new home for himself in the South is his securing of land. Using the money he obtained in various devious ways in the North and the money he gets from Josie's sale of the Dew Drop Inn, he builds a farm which constitutes "a sanctuary" (155) from the white world which has victimized him economically and poisoned him with hatred. As his name suggests, he is able to "cope" with his "land" so that he can build a "grange" or farm which will nourish himself and others. This "refuge" (156) not only provides him with food from his garden and a livelihood from his sale of crops but, more importantly, gives him the independence and freedom he needs to assume meaningful roles which his earlier life lacked: ". . . he had come back to Baker County, because it was home, and to Josie, because she was the only person in the world who loved him. . . " (155–56).

Accepting the love from Josie which he had earlier rejected because he found it "possessive" (144), he marries her shortly after returning from the North, thus embracing the role of husband. In this way he transforms her Dew Drop Inn from the whorehouse which was a grotesque parody of a human community into a real place of love between a man and a woman. Not long after this he begins to assume the role of father when he assists Mem in the delivery of Ruth on Christmas Day, a time when Brownfield is too drunk to be of much use to his family. After Brownfield murders Mem, Grange fully undertakes the role of father, providing Ruth with the love and care which he was unable to extend to Brownfield in his "first" life. In all these ways Grange is able to create a small but vital black community separated from the larger white world intent on destroying the black family.

Grange's journey north failed him because it poisoned him with the same kind of hatred which damaged his previous life in the South. His Northern experiences are revealed in the terrifying epiphany when he gloats over stealing a white woman's money while watching her drown in Central Park Lake. The whole experience becomes a grotesque inversion of a religious conversion, very much like Bigger Thomas's killing of Mary Dalton in *Native Son*. Like Bigger, who feels a grisly sort of "new life" (101) when he savors the death of Mary Dalton, Grange feels "alive and liberated for the first time in his life" (153) as he contemplates the image of withdrawing his hand from the drowning woman. He thus commits in a different form the same sin which brought his "first" life in the

South to such a disturbing close. Just as Grange is partly responsible for the deaths of his wife and stepchild, whom he abandons when he is no longer able to cope with the societally induced hatred which poisons all of his human relationships, so too does he abandon the pregnant white woman when societally induced hatred causes her to call him a "nigger" (152). Withdrawing his hand from her also echoes an earlier gesture of withdrawing his hand from his son shortly before he abandons him. Just as his hand "nearly touche[s]" (152) the woman's in Central Park, his hand has earlier "stopped just before it reached [Brownfield's] cheek" (21). In both cases his withdrawal of human sympathy from people is a clear index of how Grange has been emotionally damaged by the racist society in which he lives.

The South and North, therefore, are portrayed in Grange's first two lives as dehumanized and dehumanizing environments. But whereas the South has turned him into a "stone" and a "robot" (8), the North converts him into the kind of invisible man classically described in African American literature by Du Bois and Ellison:

> He was, perhaps, no longer regarded merely as a "thing"; what was even more cruel to him was that to the people he met and passed daily he was not even in existence! The South had made him miserable, with nerve endings raw from continual surveillance from contemptuous eyes, but they *knew he was there.* Their very disdain proved it. The North put him into solitary confinement where he had to manufacture his own hostile stares in order to see himself. . . . Each day he had to say his name to himself over and over again to shut out the silence. (144–45)

Although both environments pose severe threats to his humanity, Grange finally chooses the South over the North because he is humanly visible to Southerners, whereas Northern society is completely blind to him. Although Southern whites regard blacks with "contemptuous eyes" (145) which distort their vision, they at least focus upon blacks as human beings; the white Northerners Grange meets would reduce blacks to complete anonymity. Thus, Grange experiences a condition of "solitary confinement" in the North but in the South is given the opportunity to feel the "sense of *community*" (*In Search* 17) which Walker has extolled in her essays as a particularly important feature of Southern black life.

It is Grange's achievement of a "home" in Georgia which provides him with a genuine human conversion. He returns to Baker County with disturbing vestiges of his first two lives, fits of depression which lead him to contemplate suicide and express an "impersonal cruelty" (137) which frightens Ruth. But his recovery of the meaningful roles of husband, father, and farmer lead to his regeneration, providing him with a "third" life. Josie's love, though flawed, is deeply experienced for a while, and Ruth is able, with "the magic of her hugs and kisses" (124), to bring him out of his bouts of suicidal depression. As the novel develops, he admits to Ruth that she has "'thaw[ed]'" the "'numbness'" (233) in him. Whereas early in the book Grange seems "devoid of any emotion . . . except that of bewilderment" (13) and whereas in the middle of the book he is blinded by a nearly demonic hatred of whites, he finally becomes a fully developed, even heroic, person because of his recovery of a "home" in the black South.

Walker, however, consciously avoids idealizing Grange's Southern home. As the novel's ending makes clear, it is a small oasis of human love surrounded by the same kind of Southern racism which has blighted the lives of scores of black people in the novel. Southern courts continue to mete out injustice, and Southern violence continues to take the lives of innocent people, most notably Fred Hill, who is murdered when his son attempts to integrate a previously all-white school. And as Ruth's narrative demonstrates, even Grange's home has its restrictive features. Although such a pastoral "refuge" satisfies Grange with a sense of place and continuity with the past, Walker clearly endorses Ruth's desire to leave it for the open space which her young spirit desires. Grange's story may contradict Thomas Wolfe's notion that you can't go home again, but Ruth's story emphasizes the fact that staying home or returning home for good can stifle certain kinds of people. Although Grange's Southern home provides Ruth with an essential foundation for human growth, ultimately she must leave that home if she is to continue to grow.

As Alice Walker has observed in *In Search of Our Mothers' Gardens,* her sense of reality is inherently dialectical:

> "I believe that the truth of any subject comes out when all sides of the story are put together, and all their different meanings make one new one. Each writer writes the missing parts of the other writer's story. And the whole story is what I'm after." (49)

*The Third Life of Grange Copeland* succeeds as a novel because it consciously avoids an oversimplified vision which expresses only one "side" of Southern life. Artfully mixing its three main narratives in order to include the "missing parts" absent from any single narrative, the novel suggests a "whole truth" about the South which is complex and many-sided. The book thus remains true to its author's deepest promptings and her most profound sense of her Southern black heritage.

## Note

1. *In Search of Our Mothers' Gardens* contains other essays about Walker's view of the South, and each of them expresses a similarly ambivalent vision. For example, in "Choosing to Stay Home: Ten Years after the March on Washington," Walker observes that she felt like "an exile in [her] own town, and grew to despise its white citizens almost as much as I loved the Georgia countryside where I fished and swam and walked through fields of black-eyed Susans . . . (162). In the same essay she remarks that she is attracted to the "continuity of place" (163–64) the South offers but also is intent on leaving Mississippi for the North because she feels bored by its "pervasive football culture" and is appalled by its "proliferation of Kentucky Fried Chicken stands" (170). In "Coretta King Revisited," she praises Martin Luther King for exposing "the hidden beauty of black people in the South" and for showing blacks that "the North is not for us" (156). But in subsequent essays she speaks of greatly enjoying her life in Northern cities such as New York and Boston. Her observations on Zora Neale Hurston also reflect a powerfully split view of the South. Although she claims that ". . . Zora grew up in a community of black people who had enormous respect for themselves . . ." (85), she also is painfully aware that Hurston had to leave the rural South to become a writer and that she was shunned by the community when she returned to Florida in her later years, eventually dying a pauper and suffering the indignity of being buried in an unmarked grave.

## Works Cited

Campbell, Joseph. *The Hero with a Thousand Faces.* Princeton: Princeton University Press, 1968.

Cooke, Michael. *Afro-American Literature in the Twentieth Century: The Achievement of Intimacy.* New Haven: Yale University Press, 1984.

Ellison, Ralph. *Shadow and Act.* 1964. New York: NAL, 1966.

Walker, Alice. *In Search of Our Mothers' Gardens: Womanist Prose.* New York: Harcourt, 1983.

———. *The Third Life of Grange Copeland.* New York: Harcourt, 1970.

Wright, Richard. *Native Son.* 1940. New York: Harper, 1966.

GAIL KEATING

# Alice Walker: In Praise of Maternal Heritage

In her autobiographical essay, "In Search of Our Mothers' Gardens", Alice Walker looks at the tremendous burden black women have had to carry from a historical perspective and analyzes the overwhelming odds they have had to overcome to express their creativity. All too often women's accomplishments have been viewed as inferior since, traditionally, they have been judged according to male standards. Walker, however, acknowledges the great contributions women have made to our culture and traces the power of women through her own matrilineage.

In looking at the folklore, which Walker notes very often reveals a person's status in society, she found that very often black women are referred to as "the mule of the world" ("In Search of Our Mothers' Gardens" 2378) since they have, traditionally, been forced to do what no one else wanted to. She acknowledges how difficult it is to be both a black woman and an artist but urges women today to find strength in their heritage and "to look at and identify with our lives the living creativity some of our great-grandmothers were not allowed to know" ("In Search of Our Mothers' Gardens" 2378).

Nina Auerbach has written a very interesting book focusing on female bonding entitled *Communities of Women* in which she compares male and female communities, discovering a basic and very significant difference between them. Auerbach discovered that male communities possess a

*The Literary Griot: International Journal of Black Expressive Cultural Studies*, 6 (1); Spring 1994: pp. 26–37. ©1994 Gail Keating.

grandeur and a magnitude that female communities do not. The typical quest novel is a fine example. Males are out to conquer the world and leave their imprint on it in a significant way. They are interested in obtaining power and symbols are an important and integral part of their lives. They refer to one another as "King," "Captain" and "Master" (7).

Communities of women, however, have no such lofty aspirations: "In almost all instances, the male quest is exchanged for rootedness—a school, a village, a city of their own" (Auerbach 8). Very often a woman's activities center around the home. But, because of the awesome number of daily responsibilities a woman must deal with, her creative spirit rarely has time to develop in traditional ways. A woman, in order to be successful, must remove herself from the distractions that prohibit her having the time to create. Ellen Moers agrees that a woman's life is far from easy: "A woman's life is hard in its own way, as women have always known and men have rarely understood" (3). These same feelings are expressed by Virginia Woolf in *A Room of One's Own*. Woolf points out that the reason why so many women writers are not successful is because they allow unimportant, unnecessary, irrelevant distractions to take precedence over their work. According to Woolf, having money and the privacy to write makes it easier for a woman to be successful: "Genius needs freedom; it cannot flower if it is encumbered by fear, or rancor, or dependency, and without money freedom is impossible" (viii). Thus, for Woolf, freedom and success are functions of class. Is it any wonder so few women have become successful artists? How many have actually had the freedom, the time, the money to pursue their interests? In Woolf's analysis of the difficulties women face in their attempts at writing, she notes the enormous obstacles they must overcome. In the Introduction to *A Room of One's Own*, Gordon summarizes Woolf's belief that women

> . . . were uneducated; they had no privacy; even Jane Austen had to write in the common sitting room and hide her work under blotting paper so as not to be discovered. Yet even when they were freed from the practical impediments imposed upon their sex, they could not write, because they had no tradition to follow. No sentence had been shaped, by long labor, to express the experience of women. "It is useless to go to the great men writers for help, however much one may go to them for pleasure . . . [they] never helped a women yet, though she may have learnt a few tricks of them and adapted them to her use." (x)

What Walker suggests, however, is that we must broaden our perspective on what constitutes art, thereby allowing us to see creativity expressed in areas available and readily used by women. If we continue to insist on defining creativity and success in grand male terms, for instance, if one need be a poet, a novelist, an essayist, a short story writer to be considered an artist, then these women are not. But there are other ways.

Using her own mother as an example, Walker shares with us the very difficult life her mother led, raising eight children, working beside her husband all day—and she emphasizes beside, not behind—doing her chores at home all night, and never having a minute to think of her own needs, never having time to even think about creativity. Walker muses: "But when, you will ask, did my overworked mother have time to know or care about feeding the creative spirit?" ("In Search of Our Mothers' Gardens" 2379). Walker's answer is that women, and black women in particular, needed to find an outlet for their creative spirit in order to survive and find it they did in ways that have for too long been overlooked by society.

In "In Search of Our Mothers' Gardens" Walker gives several examples of the types of creativity these women used to express their innerselves. One is a quilt that hangs in the Smithsonian Institution in Washington, D.C. According to Walker:

> In fanciful, inspired and yet simple and identifiable figures, it portrays the story of the Crucifixion. It is considered rare, beyond price. Though it follows no known pattern of quilt-making, and though it is made of bits and pieces of worthless rags, it is obviously the work of a person of powerful imagination and deep spiritual feeling. Below this quilt I saw a note that says it was made by "an anonymous Black woman in Alabama, a hundred years ago."

> If we could locate this "anonymous" black woman from Alabama, she would turn out to be one of our grandmothers–an artist who left her mark in the only materials she could afford, and in the only medium her position in society allowed her to use. (2379)

This same idea is conveyed by Walker in "Everyday Use," a short story about a mother and two daughters, Maggie & Dee. Maggie is the poor, self-conscious backward daughter who has remained on the farm with her mother, a large, masculine, hard-working woman. Dee, however, who is quite self-assured and worldly and has left her rural surroundings, returns home for a visit with the rather pretentious-sounding name of Wangero. In a very condescending way, Dee (Wangero), now that she has made her way in the world, appreciates the beauty of the "art" of her maternal heritage. And once again Walker uses quilt-making as an example of the creativity these women expressed:

After dinner Dee (Wangero) went to the trunk at the foot of my bed and started rifling through it. Maggie hung back in the kitchen over the dishpan. Out came Wangero with two quilts. They had been pieced by Grandma Dee and then Big Dee and me had hung them on the quilt frames on the front porch and quilted them. One was in the Lone Star pattern. The other was Walk Around the Mountain. In both of them were scraps of dresses Grandma Dee had worn fifty and more years ago. Bits and pieces of Grandpa Farrell's Paisley shirts. And one teeny faded blue piece, about the size of a penny matchbox, that was from Great Grandpa Ezra's uniform that he wore in the Civil War. (2372)

Realizing the value of these quilts, Dee (Wangero) asks her mother if she can have them. When her mother tells her they have been promised to Maggie, Wangero is astonished: "'Maggie can't appreciate these quilts!' she said. 'She'd probably be backward enough to put them to everyday use'" (2372). The mother admits she hopes Maggie will do just that and recalls how, when she offered them to Dee (Wangero) when she went away to college, Dee refused finding them "old-fashioned, out of style" (2373). But her understanding and appreciation of what constitutes art has changed; it has been broadened to include common everyday things women put their hearts and souls into. Desperate to have the quilts, Dee (Wangero) cries out, "But they're 'priceless!' Maggie would put them on the bed and in five years they'd be in rags. Less than that!" (2373). But the mother understands what Dee (Wangero), even though she feels superior to Maggie, will never be able to understand: Maggie, backward as she is, has found a way to express her creative spirit in the same way generations of women before her have done. Very simply, the mother says, "She can always make some more . . . Maggie knows how to quilt" (2373). As Dee (Wangero) prepares to leave–without the quilts–she reveals what little understanding she has of her mother and sister:

"You just don't understand," she said, as Maggie and I came out to the car.

"What don't I understand?" I wanted to know.

"Your heritage," she said. And then she turned to Maggie, kissed her, and said, "You ought to try to make something of yourself, too, Maggie. It's really a new day for us. But from the way you and Mama live you'd never know it." (2373)

What Dee (Wangero) doesn't realize is that her mother and sister are doing just fine. They are not dissatisfied with their lifestyle; rather they are quite happy and content. They have their very simple, plain little home on their tiny piece of land. They have each other. And, perhaps unknown to them, they have found a very natural outlet for their creativity which society has just begun to appreciate, but is not a part of. It is Maggie, not Dee (Wangero), who has bonded with generations of women past, who is in touch with her matrilineage.

The message Walker wishes to convey to us is that women have always expressed themselves, whether it be through quilting, sewing, cooking, canning or gardening. According to Nagel:

> Gardens play an important role throughout the development of American literature. From the Puritans, who saw their mission as the establishment of a new Eden or New Earth in the American wilderness, to those who came later and saw the potential for an American New World, North America represented a distillation of the Biblical and classical pastoral ideals. (43)

And gardens have traditionally been a woman's domain. Granted, male strength may have been needed to dig the beds and till the soil but the garden itself has always been feminine territory. Nagel goes on to note the close association between gardening and one's maternal heritage:

> Instead of destroying gardens, girls must become "worthy successors" to their grandmothers, preservers of nature and, specifically, their gardens. Since women had authority in their gardens and had been entrusted with their guardianship, they must bear the responsibility for their neglect or disappearance and the way of life associated with them. Modern women who neglect the garden and its concomitant values axe, by extension, just as guilty as the destructive child in her grandmother's Edenic garden. (48)

These same ideas can be seen in the fiction of Willa Cather. Transplanted so to speak from conservative, settled, orderly, safe Virginia to the rough, unsettled prairielands of Nebraska, Cather desperately needed to discover her roots, to find some link with the past that would sustain her and give her the strength and courage she would need to survive in this frontier land. Most young girls, of course, would have looked to their mothers for this support. Cather's mother, however, unable to adapt to the new environment herself, was not the female figure a young girl could rely on for strength. Looking back to the previous century, Annette Kolodney's interesting study of women's imaginative responses to the frontier reveals that the kinds of apprehensions Cather's mother experienced were, in fact, quite common. However, there were many women, transplanted from the East, who adapted, if not easily, at least quite well. Kolodney discovered that one means these women found of accommodating themselves to the new landscape was by creating "a garden that reflected back images of their own deepest dreams and aspirations" (8). And, as Sharon O'Brien acknowledges:

> [Cather] chose to see herself as the adopted daughter of these pioneer mothers–professionally as well as personally. Recognizing the creativity rural women channeled unobtrusively into the garden, the quilt, and the meal, she reestablished continuity . . . with Nebraska's farm women . . . . (73)

Cather's link with this female tradition provided her with an important emotional support system and a sense of cultural continuity. She used her own experiences in the kitchens and gardens of her immigrant neighbors as a foundation upon which to build her image of herself as a person, as a woman:

> Cather had personal grounds for praising woman's role in preserving life from one home to another. The rituals of domesticity— preserving, cooking, gardening, housekeeping—are the bearers of culture in her fiction, where establishing a home signifies the human ability to transform an empty world into an inhabited one. (O'Brien 74)

Alice Walker has these same personal grounds to call upon. In "In Search of Mothers' Gardens" Walker recalls her own mother's green thumb:

> . . . my mother adorned with flowers whatever shabby house we were forced to live in. And not just your typical straggly country strand of zinnias, either. She planted ambitious gardens–and still does–with over fifty different varieties of plants that bloom profusely from early March until late November. (2380)

Morning and night, no matter how exhausted she was, she labored–a labor of love–in her garden. And it gave comfort and great pleasure to her family: "Because of her creativity with her flowers, even my memories of poverty are seen through a screen of blooms–sunflowers, petunias, roses, dahlias, forsythia, spirea, delphiniums, verbena . . . and on and on" (2381). What greater praise could be given any work of art?

And her mother's gift was not lost on the community at large either. People came to her for cuttings, praising her ability to turn even the poorest, rockiest soil into a garden and enjoying a "garden so brilliant with colors, so original in its design, so magnificent with life and creativity" (2381). But most of all, Walker emphasizes the creativity expressed by her mother when she says:

> I notice that it is only when my mother is working in her flowers that she is radiant, almost to the point of being invisible—except as Creator: hand and eye. She is involved in work her soul must have. Ordering the universe in the image of her personal conception of Beauty.

> Her face, as she prepared the Art that is her gift, is a legacy of respect she leaves to me, for all that illuminates and cherishes life. She has handed down respect for the possibilities—and the will to grasp them.

> For her, so hindered and intruded upon in so many ways, being an artist has still been a daily part of her life. This ability to hold on, even in very simple ways, is work black women have done for a very long time. (2381)

More than that we do not ask from those artists, primarily males, who have been the novelists, the essayists, the short story writers and the poets. Walker makes us realize that the time has come to acknowledge the tremendous burden so many women have been forced to carry, especially those born black; time to pay tribute to what they have managed to accomplish given so little to work with and so much opposition; time to expand our vision of what constitutes art; time to become aware of our maternal heritage, to be proud of it and do our best to carry on the tradition.

We can also see women's creativity expressed through quilt-making and sewing in Walker's widely-acclaimed novel, *The Color Purple*. Celie, the narrator, leads a wretched life. Sexually abused as a child by a man she believes to be her father, she is forced to marry a man she doesn't love who doesn't love her. He not only makes her work like a dog, which she does without daring to say a word, but he also abuses her sexually and beats her whenever he feels like it. Celle is thin and dark and ugly. She has so little going for her in life except for her natural ability and creativity displayed in her quilt-making and sewing. In the beginning expressing her talent in this way serves almost as an escape from her downtrodden, painful, dull, daily existence but, in the end, it becomes her salvation, giving meaning to her life and enabling her to become a fulfilled, independent women. Not only does her self-image change drastically but it becomes possible for her to interact with others as a mature adult woman because of her creative ability.

In the beginning of the story we see Celie's ability to endure her suffering with a sense of humor. When her stepson's wife, Sofia, is angry with Celie and returns the curtains Celie had made for the newlywed's house, the two women fight and then talk. Reconciled, Sofia says, "Let's make quilt pieces out of these messed up curtains" (44). Delighted, Celie runs off to get her "pattern book" and later reveals that in contrast to the many sleepless nights she has experienced, "I sleeps like a baby now" (44). The women have argued, made up and finally sat together as friends, doing what they do best, sewing a quilt which will be both beautiful and useful and, even more importantly, an expression of themselves.

Another instance of the bonding quilt-making makes possible for women occurs when Celie's brother-in-law, Tobias, comes to visit. Once again Sofia and Celie use their time both productively and creatively: "Me and Sofia piecing another quilt together. I got about five squares pieced, spread out on the table by my knee. My basket full of scrapes on the floor" (58). Tobias appreciates Celie's industriousness, wishing his own lazy wife could be more like her. "Always busy, always busy, he say. I wish Margaret was more like you. Save me a bundle of money" (58). Even though Celie's husband is so abusive to her and rarely, if ever, does any work either around the house or on the land, she never gives up. She is strong and courageous, a much more capable person than he could ever hope to be.

And she is understanding and patient, almost saint-like in her acceptance of the woman her husband has always loved and hoped to marry, the woman of very questionable reputation, Shug Avery. Aware of the attraction between the two of them—they've had three children together—she nonetheless welcomes Shug into their home when Shug becomes deathly ill. In fact, Celie is so awed by this glamorous, irreverent singer who is such a contrast to her own ugly, pitiful self that she, too, falls in love with Shug. But even these two women, who have so little in common, find a bond in quilt-making:

Me and Mr — both look up at her. Both move to help her sit down. She don't look at him. She pull up a chair next to me.

She pick up a random piece of cloth out of the basket. Hold it up to the light. Frown. How you sew this damn thing? She say.

I hand her the square I'm working on, start another one. She sew long crooked stitches, remind me of that little crooked tune she sing.

That real good, for first try, I say. That just fine and dandy. She look at me and snort. Everything I do is fine and dandy to you, Miss Celie, she say. But you ain't got good sense. (59)

But Celie does have good sense; in fact, more than the rest of them put together. Once again, Tobias recognizes her worth, saying: "She got a heap more than Margaret . . . Margaret take that needle and sew your nostrils together" (59). And, in addition to her good sense, Celie has a worthwhile skill, a skill that will enable her to rise above her deplorable condition, a skill that must be passed on to others. Possessing this talent that others admire will, in time, raise Celie in the others' eyes and, at the same time, raise her own self-esteem. Celie's skill now brings not only she and Sofia together, but Shug as well. We now see three women bonding:

> Me and Sofia work on the quilt. Got it frame up on the porch. Shug Avery donate her old yellow dress for scrap, and I work in a piece every chance I get. It a nice pattern called Sister's Choice. If the quilt turn out perfect, maybe I give it to her, if it not perfect, maybe I keep. I want it for myself, just for the little yellow pieces, look like stars, but not. (61)

Celie wants her "art" to be perfect just as any artist would. But she also wants to share it with others, for it to be put to good use as we saw in "Everyday Use." Art for a woman like Celie is not a luxury to be admired and enjoyed. Art is an integral part of daily life. And, being the kind, generous, self-sacrificing woman she is, she gives the quilt she would love to keep for herself, since a part of Shug is in it, to Sofia who needs it more than she does: "At the last minute I decide to give Sofia the quilt. I don't know what her sister place be like, but we been having right smart cold weather long in now. For all I know, she and the children have to sleep on the floor" (71).

Years later, in a letter Celie finally receives from her sister, Nettie, who she has been separated from since the early days of her marriage, we again see how quilts represent the daily lives of women. Nettie has been living in Africa with a wonderful missionary couple, Corrine and Samuel, and Celie's two children who were taken from her at birth. When Corrine is dying, she reveals that she believes the children, who look so much like their aunt, are Nettie and Samuel's. Nettie tries desperately to convince her that she is wrong and tells her the true story. Corrine had once met Celie at a dry goods store in town and Nettie is determined to help her recall their meeting. The only way she is able to do this is by showing her the quilts Corrine had made many years ago:

Then I remember her quilts. The Olinka men make beautiful quilts which are full of animals and birds and people. And as soon as Corrine saw them, she began to make a quilt that alternated one square of appliqued figures with one nine-patch block, using the clothes the children had outgrown, and some of her old dresses.

I went to her trunk and started hauling out quilts . . . .

I held up first one and then another to the light, trying to find the first one I remembered her making. And trying to remember, at the same time, the dresses she and Olivia were wearing the first months I lived with them.

Aha, I said, when I found what I was looking for, and laid the quilt across the bed.

Do you remember buying this cloth? I asked pointing to a flowered square. And what about this checkered bird?

She traced the patterns with her finger, and slowly her eyes filled with tears. (192–193)

She remembers, not just the day but, more importantly, how much the little girl, Olivia, looked like Celie and how afraid Corrine was that Celie would want Olivia back. And, because of this, she admits, "I forgot her as soon as I could" (193). But now that she remembers, she forgives both Nettie and Samuel and dies in peace. Quilts have enabled three more women to bond, to understand what each woman has been forced to endure. Dying, Corrine turns to her husband Samuel and says, "I believe" (194).

When Celie finally decides to leave Mr. — after learning that he has hidden Nettie's letters from her for years, she goes to Memphis with Shug to begin a new life. And, because she has a talent, a skill, and a sincere desire to understand what each person wants, she finally makes a life for herself: "I am so happy, I got love, I got work, I got money, friends and time" (222). What else could any person want? All this is made possible through Celie's ability to sew:

I sit in the dining room making pants after pants. I got pants now in every color and size under the sun. Since us started making pants down home, I ain't been able to stop. I change the cloth, I change the print, I change the waist, I change the pocket. I change the hem, I change the fullness of the leg. I make so many pants Shug tease me. (218)

Celie, like any artist, seeks perfection. She is not satisfied with anything less, so she experiments until she can say: "Then finally one day I made the perfect pair of pants"(219). Her greatest desire is to make others happy so, in making each pair of pants, she carefully considers each individual's specific needs. She understands who and what Shug is when she creates pants for her:

> They soft dark blue jersey with teeny patches of red. But what make them so good is, they totally comfortable. Cause Shug eat a lot of junk on the road, and drink, her stomach bloat. So the pants can be let out without messing up the shape. Because she have to pack her stuff and fight wrinkles, these pants are soft, hardly wrinkle at all, and the little figures in the cloth always look perky and bright. And they full round the ankle so if she want to sing in 'em and wear 'em sort of like a long dress, she can. Plus, once Shug put them on, she knock your eyes out. (219)

This admiration is mutual. Not only is Celie awed by Shug's appearance, but Shug is awed by Celie's talent, "Miss Celie, she say, you is a wonder to behold" (219). How good it feels to be appreciated for one's worth, to have one's creativity acknowledged and respected.

Just as we saw people coming to Walker's mother for advice on gardening in, "In Search of Our Mothers' Gardens," word now spreads about Celie's ability to make "the perfect pants" and people begin coming to her. Shug brags to Grady and Squeak about her pants and "By now Squeak see a pair 'she' like. Oh, Miss Celie, she say. Can I try on those?" (219). And she looks so good in them that "Grady look at her like he could eat her up" (219). Is it any wonder Celie's creations are in demand? "Next thing I hear Odessa want a pair. Then Shug want two more like the first. Then everybody in the band want some. Then orders start to come in from everywhere Shug sing. Pretty soon I'm swamp" (220).

But Celie's art has matured. Her pants weren't always the beautiful, comfortable creations they have become. Through trial and error she has reached perfection: "Shug finger the pieces of cloth I got hanging on everything. It all soft, flowing, rich and catch the light. This is a far cry from that stiff army shit us started with, she say" (219). Shug says "us started with" because it is her money that has made Celie's endeavor possible. Without Shug's financial support, Celie would not have had the money to buy the material. There is a mutuality here: Celie taught Shug how to sew and Shug enables Celie to start a business.

Up to this point Celie's art has been given to others as a gift, as when Shug suggests she make a special pair for Jack, Sofia's brother-in-law, who helped raise Sofia's children. And, as Celie did when she made Shug's pants, she thoughtfully considers how to best fashion the pants to meet Jack's needs:

> I sit looking out cross the yard trying to see in my mind what a pair of pants for Jack would look like. . . . Love children. . . .

> I start to make pants for Jack. They have to be camel. And soft and strong. And they have to have big pockets so he can keep a lot of children's things. Marbles and string and pennies and rocks. And they have to be washable and they have to fit closer round the leg than Shug's so he can run if he need to snatch a child out the way of something. And they have to be something he can lay back in when he hold Odessa in front of the fire. And . . . .

> I dream and dream and dream over Jack's pants. And cut and sew. And finish them. And send them off. (220)

Celie's creations are a labor of love. She designs these pants with the same precision and diligence and inspiration an architect would use in designing a building, a painter in painting a landscape, a composer in writing an opera, a writer in writing a novel. Her means of expression is no less significant than theirs. It is a woman's way of expressing her creativity, using the talent, skill and material she has at hand.

By now, however, Celie realizes that she must begin earning her own living. What she doesn't understand is that she has the means at her fingertips: "One day, when Shug come home, I say, you know I love doing this, but I got to git out and make a living pretty soon. Look like this just holding me back" (220). Shug just laughs for she knows that Celie is already on her way:

> Let's us put a few advertisements in the paper, she say. And let's raise your prices a hefty notch. And let's us just go ahead and give you this dining room for your factory and get you some more women in here to cut and sew, while you sit back and design. You making your living, Celie, she say. Girl, you on your way. (220–221)

The love she expresses in every pair of pants she makes, she sends to Nettie in Africa. They have been separated for years, but Celie has never forgotten her and understands her needs even though they are continents apart. She writes to her sister:

> Nettie, I am making some pants for you to beat the heat in Africa. Soft, white, thin. Drawstring waist. You won't ever have to feel too hot and overdress again. I plan to make them by hand. Every stitch I sew will be a kiss. (221)

Years later, as Mr. — and Celie, "two old fools left over from love" (278), console each other over Shug's running off with a nineteen-year-old named Germaine, he asks her why her pants are so special. She understands what his masculinity and macho perspective have prevented him from seeing: "Anybody can wear them, I said. Men and women not suppose to wear the same thing, he said. Men spose to wear the pants" (278). But she explains to him that in places like Africa people dress for comfort, regardless of their sex, and it is not uncommon for men to sew. He makes a confession to her: "When I was growing up, he said, I use to try to sew along with mama cause that's what she was always doing. But everybody laughed at me. But you know I liked It" (279). So Celie decides to teach him. She becomes his mentor:

> Well, nobody gon laugh at you now, I said. Here, help me stitch in these pockets.
> But, I don't know how, he say.
> I'll show you, I said. And I did. (279)

She teaches him so well that they spend hours together sewing. Mr. — enjoys designing shirts to go with Celie's pants:

> Mr. — is busy patterning a shirt for folks to wear with my pants. Got to have pockets, he say. Got to have loose sleeves. And definitely you not spose to wear it with no tie. Folks wearing ties look like they being lynch. (290)

After all the years of hurt, abuse and misunderstanding between these two human beings, they finally sit together, united through a lifetime of shared experience, "Now we sit sewing and talking and smoking our pipes" (279). He will never again be able to take advantage of her. Carrying on a tradition of generations of women before her sewing, Celie has turned her art into a business which has enabled her to rise above her deplorable situation. She is a free, independent and happy woman. When Shug returns, as Mr. — and Celie know she will, she asks what they have been up to. Celie replies, "Nothing much" (291) but Shug knows better. Pressed for more information, Celie expresses the contentment she has found in life at last, "Us sew, I say. Make idle conversation" (291). And just like the black women Walker refers to in "In Search of Our Mothers' Gardens," Celie has managed "to hold on" (2381), carrying forth the legacy of so many generations of black women before her, and setting an example for those to follow.

## Works Cited

Auerbach, Nina. *Communities of Women: An Idea in Fiction*. Cambridge, Mass.: Harvard University Press, 1978.

Kolodney, Annette. *The Land Before Her: Fantasy, and Experience of the American Frontiers, 1630–1860*. Chapel Hill: University of North Carolina Press, 1984.

Moers, Ellen. *Literary Women*. Garden City, N.Y.: Anchor, 1977.

Nagel, Gwen. "This Prim Corner of Land Where She Was Queen: Sarah Orne Jewett's New England Gardens." *Colby Library Quarterly* 22.1 (1986): 43–62.

O'Brien, Sharen. *Willa Cather: The Emerging Voice*. New York: Fawcett, 1987.

Walker, Alice. *The Color Purple*. New York: Simon & Schuster, 1982.

Walker, Alice. "Everyday Use". *The Norton Anthology of Literature by Women*. Ed. S. Gilbert & S. Gubar. New York: Norton & Company, 1985.

Walker, Alice, "In Search of Our Mothers' Gardens". *The Norton Anthology of Literature by Women*. Ed. S. Gilbert & S. Gubar. New York: Norton & Company, 1985.

Woolf, Virginia. *A Room of One's Own*. New York: Harcourt, Brace, Jovanovich, Inc., 1929.

BONNIE BRAENDLIN

# "Alice Walker's The Temple of My Familiar as Pastiche"

[Claudia Dreifus]: Your new novel . . . has been published to mixed
reviews. You spent eight years writing it. Surely, this must hurt.

Alice Walker: Yes, you would like to be understood by people. But I
*do* understand that my worldview is different from that of most of the
critics. . . . [T]hey are defending a way of life, a patriarchal system, which
I do not worship.

— Interview, *The Progressive*, 1989

Reviewers generally applauded Alice Walker's 1989 novel, *The Temple of
My Familiar,* for its development of ideas and themes introduced in her earlier fiction and essays—its castigation of white and male oppression, its valorization of African American and female identity, and its emphasis on the
importance of community and female friendship. At the same time, however, they were perplexed by the novel's conglomeration of narrative techniques and styles. Joyce Maynard, for example, labeled *The Temple* "a radical
feminist Harlequin romance written under the influence of hallucinogenic
mushrooms. . . . There's a little black history here, a little crystal healing
there, with a hot tub and some acupressure thrown in for good measure";[1]
James Wolcott, complaining that the text "doesn't gel at any junction," abandoned critical analysis in alliterative mock despair: "Pantheistic plea, lesbian

*American Literature: A Journal of Literary History, Criticism, and Bibliography*, Volume 68,
Number 1, March 1996: pp. 47–67. Copyright © 1996 by Duke University Press.

115

propaganda, past-lives chronicle, black-pride panorama, *The Temple of My Familiar* [is] the nuttiest novel I've ever read."[2] Even a sympathetic reader like J. M. Coetzee, who praised *Temple* as "a fable of recovered origins . . . long on inspirational message," complained about Walker's "cliché-ridden prose" and the novel's lack of "narrative tension."[3] Doris Davenport affirmed Walker's womanist world view but found the novel flawed by "awkward, corny and embarrassing" language in "nauseating and contrived" sex scenes.[4] Clearly, *Temple* disconcerted reviewers who expected Walker to be in control of language and narrative form, their responses perhaps implying that in this novel she had failed as an artist. Scholarly articles have focused upon Walker's idealism, maternalism, and spirituality, following the lines established by Coetzee and Davenport but largely ignoring—or sometimes excusing—her problematic style and narrative strategy.[5]

All of Alice Walker's novels are polemical in their opposition to "racism, sexism, classism, and colorism" and their plea for universal equality. Even *The Color Purple*, which was critically acclaimed and established Walker as a major American novelist, occasioned accusations of divisiveness, reverse racism, and male-bashing. As a self-proclaimed "revolutionary" author, Alice Walker has never been intimidated by the negative criticism her polemical fiction invites. Throughout her essay collections, *In Search of Our Mothers' Gardens* and *Living by the Word*, and in numerous interviews, she articulates her political and aesthetic vision as a "womanist" committed "to survival and wholeness of entire people, male *and* female," beginning with "my people" and "black women," extending to "the multiplicity of oppression—and of struggle,"[6] and ultimately to "human life" and the polluted earth.[7] Her authorial mission of salvation depends upon consciousness raising: "We must begin to develop the consciousness that everything has equal rights because existence itself is equal" (*LBW*, 148). From the beginning of her writing career in the early 1970s, Walker defied public criticism with a radical stance: "The writer—like the musician or painter—must be free to explore, otherwise she or he will never discover what is needed (by everyone) to be known. This means, very often, finding oneself considered 'unacceptable' by masses of people who think that the writer's obligation is not to explore or to challenge, but to second the masses' motions, whatever they are. Yet the gift of loneliness is sometimes a radical vision of society or one's people that has not previously been taken into account."[8] Undaunted by adverse criticism, perhaps even encouraged by it to persist in pursuing her messianic goal, Walker continues to defend her vision. In an interview with Paula Giddings about her controversial and overtly political *Possessing the Secret of Joy* (1992), Walker connects the African practice of clitoridectomy with broader issues that have figured prominently in her life and writings, including AIDS, "a healthy continent," slavery, "our mothers' collaboration," "organized religion," "heterosexist culture," "a male-dominant tradition," connectedness, "community," and "multiracial, multiethnic, multisexual, multieverything." Again, she articulates her revolutionary goal: "What I'm hoping is that this book will invite whatever movement there is to converge with all of the people who may now be aware of it, and together we may be able to do something."[9]

Walker's artistic and political vision also informs *The Temple of My Familiar,* novel wider in scope and more experimentally audacious than her other works that may signal a more extreme position in her oeuvre. I wish to offer here some ways of reading the novel as a polyvocal text in a postmodern context, an approach usually reserved for white male authors. I propose that although the opposition of womanism to patriarchy may be thematically central to the text, Walker's stylistic strategies decenter any propagandistic focus, creating what Catherine Belsey calls an "interrogative text," that is, one in which style functions as an alienating device to urge readers toward disengaged reflection upon self and society and to "invite [them] to produce answers to the questions [the text] implicitly or explicitly raises."[10] Experimental novels, as Raymond Federman laments, are often misunderstood and unappreciated because they lack a reassuring "readability," that is, continuity and clarity that reinforce "our own knowledge . . . our own culture"; they destabilize the security of our ideological positions, prompting us to ask, "how total, how coherent, continuous, rational, how whole, how secure we are in our culture."[11] Experimental fiction disconcerts readers with the unexpected, the incoherent, the irrational, with repressed and suppressed ideologies that often run counter to those of the dominant culture and canon. Walker's interrogatory text works to alienate us from our cultural and ideological complacencies; through a clash of ideologies and literary styles that risks scorn and rejection, *Temple* urges us to reflect upon our cherished beliefs and to consider other, countercultural responses to contemporary personal, communal, and global issues.

> As long as we expect a nectarine to taste like either a peach or a plum we are bound to be disappointed. But once we assimilate this new category—nectarine—we begin to know what we are dealing with and how to react to it. We can judge and appreciate.—Robert Scholes

The title of *The Temple of My Familiar* directs our attention to Walker's description of an ancient priestess's familiar: "a small, incredibly beautiful creature that was part bird, for it was feathered, part fish, for it could swim and had a somewhat fish/bird shape, and part reptile, for it scooted about like geckoes do, and it was all over the place. . . . Its movements were graceful and clever, its expression mischievous and full of humor. It was *alive!* It slithered and skidded here and there."[12] This hybrid creature offers a clue to Walker's narrative strategy in *Temple,* which mixes tones and styles with abandon; at times Walker's language is serious and beautifully lyrical, at other times comic and clichéd. An unconventional, non-narrative text, the novel may be read as pastiche—a juxtaposing of the profound and the mundane not intended to "gel at any junction."

In our postmodern era pastiche belongs to what Ihab Hassan calls "the mutation of genres . . . promiscuous or equivocal forms: paracriticism, paraliterature, happening, mixed media, the nonfiction novel, the new journalism. Cliché, pop, and kitsch mingle to blur boundaries. . . . Throughout culture, a jumbling or syncretism of styles."[13] A traditional handbook to literature defines pastiche texts as "literary patchworks,"[14] calling attention both to their mixing of styles and their imitation of previous works, authors, or genres in their attempts to ridicule or to flatter. As a form of parody not necessarily satirical, contemporary literary pastiche reinvents genres, perpetuating established conventions and initiating changes, thus insuring generic continuity with variation.[15] By expressing alternate visions of the world and the self, contemporary writers transform, transgress, and perhaps subvert established genres. More specifically, pastiche may provide women and ethnic authors with a means of appropriating genres to represent individual and group beliefs, values, and versions of reality in conflict with those of the dominant culture and the traditional canon, both of which marginalize Otherness.[16] In pastiche, where, as Henry Louis Gates Jr. explains, "[w]riters Signify upon each other's texts by rewriting the received textual tradition,"[17] African American writers emulate and revise both the white and the black literary canons. In general, Paul Gilroy contends, "[t]he clutch of recent African-American novels which deal explicitly with history, historiography, slavery, and remembrance all exhibit an intense and ambivalent negotiation of the novel form that is associated with their various critiques of modernity and enlightenment."[18] In *The Temple of My Familiar,* read as pastiche, the clash of traditional and contemporary ideas and ideologies revises a particular genre, namely, the bildungsroman.

> I believe in change: change personal, and change in society.
> —Alice Walker, *In Search of Our Mothers' Gardens*

Many twentieth-century novels, including *The Temple of My Familiar,* perpetuate with variation the bildungsroman, a novel of the formation of personality or identity, of an individual (often adolescent) coming to consciousness, shaping and being shaped by social and cultural ideologies as expressed in such discourses as those of education, religion, the law, and the media. *Bildung* constructs a subject as the end product of a process of choosing among various roles defined by these discourses and thus privileges ideologies of individualism and autonomy. The term *Bildung* traditionally denotes both the self-development journey, a formation of individual personality or coming-to-consciousness, and the goal of that journey, variously seen as harmonious, well-rounded development of talents and abilities, self-knowledge, communal/social responsibility, or a combination thereof. Franco Moretti argues that the goal of *Bildung* in its bourgeois capitalist historical context is, for Anglo-European society, the integration of its sons and daughters into their designated societal spheres, the workplace and the home respectively, and, for the developing individual, a happy state of harmony dominated by "the feeling that the world is *his* [or *her*] world."[19] But *Bildung* is not necessarily a mindless adherence to social dictates; David H. Miles defines it as a more positive developmental process characterized by three stages—observing without action or thought, "seeing and feeling," and "thinking and *reflecting*"—a process that integrates emotions with reason, although privileging the latter.[20] Alice Walker's earlier novels contribute to the appropriation and adaptation of the bildungsroman by authors outside the American mainstream, a strategy that enables them to inscribe the values of the margins in texts that challenge constructions of identity as exclusively white male. *The Third Life of Grange Copeland* (1970), *Meridian* (1976), and *The Color Purple* (1982) construct an individual identity directed and supported by African American communal values and expounded by the female voice. On one level *Temple* narrativizes *Bildung* as a midlife awakening by both men and women to the stultifying life occasioned by erroneous choices made in adolescence, as a movement from inactive, unenlightened paralysis of will to an educated, perceptive determination to change, a progression roughly approximating Miles's three stages. Walker's interest in an ideal of mutual and reciprocal nurturance and support between the individual and the community is derived from her African heritage but resembles a goal of the classical European bildungsroman obscured or lost over the years of postromanticism in the white male canon, namely, the *Humanitätsideal*, the cultivation of individual talents and abilities in service of the communal good. Walker's re-emphasis on community, in addition to being a way of improving bourgeois society (as it was in the German ideal of *Humanität*) is also a means of positioning her protagonists in protective and creative environments in order to nourish individual growth, a strategy which indicts contemporary racism and sexism and ultimately suggests social and ecological cooperation.

*Temple* reshapes the bildungsroman midlife coming-to-consciousness narrative by positioning the identity stories of five young intellectuals in several contexts—race, sex, and class prejudice; the 1980s preoccupation with sex, rock music, and New Age beliefs; African myth and diaspora history; and the African American woman's faith in matriarchal power and wisdom. Walker's novel opens by introducing, in omniscient narration, four main characters in midlife crises. The co-opted, antifeminist Suwelo, enamored of the dominant-culture history he teaches, is discouraged by his failures as a husband and lover. His wife Fanny, disillusioned by marriage, mainstream vocation, and academic feminism, has left the college where she taught women's studies to work in a massage parlor. The Latina Carlotta feels betrayed by her husband's infidelity and by her academic colleagues' racial and sexual biases. Her husband Arveyda, an African/Native American rock star, has both caused and suffered from dissension and separation between women by having an affair with Carlotta's mother Zedé. Fanny, Carlotta, Arveyda and Suwelo are self-absorbed and frustrated by the animosity they harbor toward others. Fanny's anger is directed against white racism but displaced onto Suwelo; Suweb's is displaced from his parents onto Fanny and her attempts to raise his consciousness through feminist and black texts; Arveyda's anger is disguised as sexual desire for Zedé but finally explained as desire for unity with his own mother, who neglected him in childhood; and Carlotta's ire is aroused by and aimed at her husband's and mother's sexual betrayal. Driven apart by bitterness, these four characters engage in affairs, leave their jobs, and languish in debilitating unhappiness. Claiming the reader's attention through several chapters of part 1 (of six divisions), their stories constitute the primary plot line of *Temple*. A fifth story, that of Mary Jane Haverstock, the radical Caucasian commando-turned-humanitarian, is told later and piecemeal by Mary herself and by various characters who knew her; it is removed from the narrative of the other journeys but linked to them thematically. Only Miss Lissie, the reincarnated storyteller, does not develop, for she is already self-aware and socially conscious, burning with a righteous anger that is more social than personal.

The protagonists' preoccupation with the present reflects postmodernism's "one major theme," defined by Fredric Jameson as "the disappearance of a sense of history, the way in which our entire contemporary social system has little by little begun to lose its capacity to retain its own past, has begun to live in a perpetual present and in a perpetual change that obliterates traditions of the kind which all earlier social formations have had in one way or another to preserve."[21] More specifically, *Temple* represents this problem as a separation of African Americans from their heritage, a state that replicates the plight of earlier slaves but one for which African Americans now share responsibility: "Our new masters [Miss Lissie notes] had a genius for turning us viciously— in ways that shamed and degraded even themselves, if only they'd had sense enough to know it—against anything that once we loved" (*T*, 64). In *The Temple of My Familiar* Walker voices her concern that in the eighties the ideals valorized in her earlier fiction are endangered as contemporary women and people of color who have earned a prominent place in the mainstream forget their history and its lesson of concerned community, a lesson more crucial than ever in the face of threats of human and global extinction.

> The fantastic traces the unsaid and the unseen of culture: that which has been silenced, made invisible, covered over and made "absent."
>
> —Rosemary Jackson

The bildungsroman plot of *Temple* is interrupted almost immediately by accounts of nearly forgotten South American and African slavery in the recent past and by stories of female power from the lost "dream memory" of "the very ancient past" (*T*, 83, 53). Walker's montage of historical and mythic images from various speakers interspersed with narrative action creates plot discontinuity, but the tales of ancient matriarchies in the jungles of Africa and South America—both usurped by patriarchal religions and the violent wrenching of natives from their homelands— offer a thematic continuity. Her retelling of the past exposes the dark underbelly of white colonial history—the privileged and privileging narrative that scapegoats Others. Through horrific recollections of slavery in Zedé's tales of her youth in South America and through Miss Lissie's stories of the African slave trade and the diaspora, *Temple* offers eyewitness accounts of the deliberate and relentless enslavement and extermination of peoples of color. It also reintroduces myths and legends antedating the Greco-Roman and Judeo-Christian traditions, which have through force and exclusion exerted their claim to power in Western culture. In counterpoint to the protagonists' modern lives of dissension and divorce, Walker constructs fantastic tales of a utopian prehistory when men and women lived apart in respect for one another's privacy and uniqueness but cooperatively and in harmony with one another, as well as with their cousins, the jungle beasts. Her motive is to reconnect past to present in order to renew eclipsed values; as she says in an earlier essay, "[if] we kill off the *sound* of our ancestors, the major portion of us, all that is past, that is history, that is human being is lost, and we become historically and spiritually thin, a mere shadow of who we were, on the earth" (*LBW*, 62). She has said of *Temple*, "[w]hat I'm doing is literarily trying to reconnect us to our ancestors. All of us. I'm really trying to do that because I see that ancient past as the future, that the connection that was original is a connection; if we can affirm it in the present, it will make a different future."[22]

The loss of familial and communal values is depicted in *Temple* as affecting—even effecting—the plight of contemporary sons and daughters whose maturation processes have been crippled by their relationships with parents, especially by a mother's rejection. The task of re-educating them belongs to African American women who recover not only the immediate past but also a prehistorical, largely matriarchal heritage. Unlike Walker's earlier novels, in which motherhood is rejected (*Meridian*) or thwarted by oppression (*The Color Purple*), *Temple* valorizes motherhood; Miss Lissie and Zedé, who remember and teach lost ideals of harmony and nurturing, are biological mothers, and Celie and Shug nurture Fanny as surrogate mothers. Mothers thus are given voice and allowed to speak the discourses that have been suppressed through male-authored history.[23]

Together with the Afracentric wisdom of both Zedé and Miss Lissie, The Gospel According to Shug—carried over from *The Color Purple* and interpolated into *Temple* as a series of beatitudes—may be seen as constructing the concept of *Bildung* as process and goal: people must strive to admire and love "the entire cosmos" and "the Earth, their mother," to live in harmony with "Creation" and all "the citizens of the world," to "receive only to give" in the spirit of "generosity," to pray "for harmony in the Universe," to "give up their anger," and to "forgive . . . every evil done to them" (*T*, 287–89). The last two injunctions articulate Walker's most pressing concerns, the ones that prepare people to achieve the other, more remote goals. Personal and social anger is understandable, especially when motivated by abusive parents, unfaithful spouses, or racists and sexists, but Shug's gospel calls for the rejection of personal anger because it causes the separation and dissension that thwart global communal harmony. In *Temple* the journey toward harmony involves consciousness raising rather than just individual coming-to-consciousness.

Exoneration of the mother, frequently blamed by adult children for their faults and failures, becomes a key to self-knowledge and cultural awareness in *Temple*, as Walker's characters, guided by matriarchal wisdom, exorcise their personal anger through painful reassessments of their relationships with their mothers and grandmothers. This process occurs consciously, combining the seeing, feeling stage of *Bildung* with that of thinking and reflecting, but it is realized in epiphanies. Release of anger occurs in moments when the conscious mind relaxes its defensive censoring of memory: "Suwelo is suddenly too tired to keep watch over the door of his heart. It swings open on its own" (*T*, 403). The men forgive the mothers who neglected them after recognizing the reasons for their neglect: Suwelo blames his father and then forgives his abusiveness, while Arveyda comes to respect his mother's spirituality, which absorbed the attention he craved as a child. Recalling their mothers, the women rediscover and reclaim lost ties with their female heritage: As a "bell chimist" (*T*, 372), Carlotta replicates her grandmother's "magical" artistic talent; when Fanny recalls her early upbringing in the warm communality of Celie and Shug's house, she allows herself to bond with the others in friendships and a marriage that respect individuality in community. The dissipation of anger releases the mothers from personal blame and responsibility for adult children's problems and affirms female love and nurturance—the lessons of matriarchal prehistory.

The goal of *Bildung* in the mainstream novel is a maturity rewarded by a profitable vocation and a loving spouse, indeed a valorization of bourgeois marriage. Communal *Bildung* in Walker's fiction is a function of "maternal eros," which Jean Wyatt sees in women's fiction as replacing "the patriarchal family system, where one mother is burdened with meeting everyone's needs while neglecting her own," with "a circle of mothering persons . . . each nurturing the others."[24] Walker thus substitutes for the nuclear family—in which a mother is forced to sacrifice her sexuality and pleasure to maternal love and devotion—a community that fosters and satisfies the desires of all, including the mothers. The novel of awakening, a subgenre of the female bildungsroman to which *Temple* also belongs, depicts a nostalgic inward journey toward "self-discovery," defined by Rita Felski as "an abrupt and visionary apprehension of underlying unity which leads to an overcoming of ironic and alienated self-consciousness" and a "conceptualization of female identity as an essence to be recovered rather than a goal to be worked toward."[25] In place of a lost personal self, Walker envisions a suppressed and silenced prelapsarian unity and a respect for life that, once recovered by self-absorbed people, may stem the tide of racial and sexual disharmony and of ecological destruction.

By recreating "the speaking black voice in writing"[26] in homage to Zora Neale Hurston, Walker continues to signify on the black literary tradition; by revising the process of *Bildung* from self-individuation to social consciousness raising and by replacing the phallocratic narratives of individualism and autonomy that underwrite the traditional bildungsroman with philosophies of maternality and community, she signifies upon the dominant-culture canon. *Temple* responds not only to the conventional but also to the parodic bildungsroman, in which, according to Miles, protagonists are "guilt-laden pilgrims who can make no progress" because they are incapable of "recogniz[ing} or confess [ing] their pasts." The challenging by authors like Franz Kafka and Günter Grass of the Judeo-Christian belief that "knowledge. . . leads to virtue" results in what Miles terms "merely new anti-values, new anti-novels, new revolts against the literary past." A dialectical return to the past is necessary if the bildungsroman is to survive; yet the past must be "transform[ed] and transcend[ed]."[27] By moving beyond parody, by imitating but transvaluing self-development in the contexts of female spirituality, alternate versions of history, and countercultural stances, *The Temple of My Familiar* may be hailed as an anti-anti-bildungsroman, though perhaps not of the sort that Miles predicted would "transform" the genre.

> You only have to look at the Medusa straight on to see her. And she's not deadly. She's beautiful and she's laughing.
> —Hélène Cixous

When *Temple* collapses the distinctions between realism and romance, between past and present, it confirms Walker's womanist "world view," which, she maintains, opposes phallogocentrism. Davenport speculates that while Walker's previous novels may be described as "realistic-natural-istic fiction," *Temple* "certainly could be seen as 'mystical,' or even as a new form of Fantasy/Science Fiction."[28] Cast as "a romance of the past 500,000 years" (*T*, dust jacket), Walker's novel participates in Feminist Romanticism, described by Felski as positing "mythic and nonrational consciousness" as an "appropriate modality for a 'feminine' identity [offered by Walker also to men] which has been excluded from public history."[29] In our culture, the postmodern breakdown of the great narratives of Western culture (*Les Grands Récits*), those totalizing discourses that, according to Jean-Francois Lyotard, underwrite and thus privilege certain cultural and political practices to the exclusion or marginalization of others, has generally occasioned widespread nostalgia for certainty, which Dana Polan sees expressed in "the Reagan moment" (the era in which *Temple* appeared) as a "reinvestment in great myths." In contrast to establishment nostalgia, however, which "lead[s] to certain attempts to make the large corporation mythic and inspiring,"[30] Walker's Afracentric nostalgia for a lost harmony in *The Temple of My Familiar* positions matriarchal communal spiritualism against Western white-male corporate mythologizing. In this respect the novel may be defined as a transgressive modernist text.

As a multilevel, polyvocal text, however, *Temple* opens itself to a number of readings, offering a postmodern multivalency of meaning, even to the extent of risking alienating readers by problematizing the nature of meaning itself. How we as readers respond to pastiche may depend upon our political and artistic orientations, which condition us to denounce or defend postmodernism and its art forms as either "retrograde or progressive, regressive or transgressive."[31] I want at this point to open my own text to various ways of reading Walker's pastiche, acknowledging multiple and even contradictory interpretations, suggesting, I hope, that the novel is more interrogatory than propagandistic.

Reading an experimental, interrogatory text, as Belsey notes, can be both "frustrating and exhilarating."[32] Politically committed readers of *Temple* may agree that group collaboration is better for social reform than self-individuation, yet they may question the pacifism inherent in the advice offered to Fanny by her African father Ola: "Make peace with those you love and that love you or with those you wish to love. These are your companeros, as the Latin Americans say" (*T,* 317). One problem with this advice, especially coupled with Shug's gospel, is that it rejects resistance to racism through overt political action. While Ola admits, "I have been responsible for the deaths of whites" in retaliation for racist brutality, he maintains, "It did not 'liberate' me psychologically, as Fanon suggested it might. It did not oppress me either. I was simply freeing myself from the jail that they had become for me, and making a space in the world, also, for my children" (*T,* 316). Walker's novel suggests that political violence was a necessary but regrettable stage of liberation for African Americans, one that Meridian passed through during the Civil Rights Movement; now, however, a new stage of resistance and transformation is in the offing, one in which forgiveness and love replace anger as weapons against racism. Whereas in *The Color Purple* the characters "learn to channel anger into creativity,"[33] here anger gives way to sensuality and eroticism: both the artistic and the sexual counter phallocratic oppression and control exercised upon Americans through the Puritan ethic. Love becomes problematic, though, when it is equated in the novel with nontraditional expressions of sexuality by a community depicted as a "new age clan," oiling one another's bodies as they "walk slowly, their arms loosely around each other, back and forth, up and down the . . . beach . . . . always talking and listening to each other intensely, as if whole worlds hang on their words . . . all . . . perfectly beautiful" (*T,* 405), their sexual couplings occurring in and around a hot tub, a sauna, and a massage mat, standard trappings of California hedonism. Read satirically, this clan may be seen as ironic exemplars of contemporary *Bildung,* although they may also be seen as nostalgic reminders of the 1960s, when "Eros appeared capable of undermining the civilization of oppression,"[34] and many believed that "everything was possible . . . [in] a moment of universal liberation, a global unbinding of energies."[35] The clan's erotic play expresses a longing for prelapsarian innocence that characterizes contemporary romanticism and permeates Walker's mythologizing in *Temple.* "Free love" in this novel is not just nostalgia for the 1960s (although it might be partly that) but also an expression of the desire to return to the freedom and unity of the ancient "dream memory" time when, as Miss Lissie remembers it, "[l]ovemaking was considered one of the very best things in life, by women and men; of course it would have to be free" (*T,* 358). That is why "Arveyda feels [in orgasm] as if he has rushed to meet all the ancestors and they have welcomed him with joy" (*T,* 407). While Jameson views nostalgic pastiche as an "indictment of consumer capitalism" because it is "an alarming and pathological symptom of a society that has become incapable of dealing with time and history,"[36]

Walker's pastiche reclaims a repressed history, an alternative tradition of matrilineal ancestral wisdom that embodies the values of caring, love, and harmony our society needs to remember to overcome the narcissism, waste, and pollution of contemporary consumerism. The reunited protagonists may be read as her own "indictment of consumer capitalism," their preference for the simple life, attuned to nature and to one another's needs, countering and condemning yuppie consumerism and the desire for upward mobility.

Readers will undoubtedly also note resemblances between the female wisdom embodied in Shug's gospel and New Age beliefs. Shug's key words and phrases—"circular energy," "a new age on Earth," "love the entire cosmos," "love the Earth, their mother," "harmony in the Universe," "love all the colors of all the human beings," "lose their fear of death," "love and actively support the diversity of life"—are also those of New Agers, who, according to a 1987 *Time* magazine article, exhibit "a lack of faith in the orthodoxies of rationalism, high technology, routine living, spiritual law-and-order." *Time* characterized the era's New Age philosophy as "a combination of spirituality and superstition, fad and farce, about which the only thing certain is that it is not new . . . . [M]any elements of the New Age, like faith healing, fortune-telling and transmigration of souls, go back for centuries."[37] In this respect Walker's counterculturalism, while problematic for some readers, may be seen by others as a recovery of lost or repressed arts, sciences, and religions formerly practiced and believed by women and others outside the mainstream. Her characters' countercultural activities, presented as vestiges of ancient medicine concentrated in the hands of women before the domination of science and technology, attest to their connections to the ancestors: Fanny's massage, for instance, is not only sexual foreplay but also a healing art, as she seeks out and relieves bodily pain and its underlying mental and psychological stress. Although Arveyda has been commercialized as a rock musician, he is also a healer: "Arveyda and his music were medicine, and, seeing or hearing him, people knew it. They flocked to him as once they might have to priests. He did not disappoint them" (*T*, 24). A soulmate to Carlotta, Arveyda is a reincarnation of the Indians and priests of her mother's South American background and embodies the spirituality of the dream memory time: "It was his Indianness that she saw, not his blackness. She saw it in the way he really looked at her, really saw her. With the calm, detached concentration of a shaman" (*T*, 7).

Walker's interest in the New Age culture may also be seen more positively in light of its resemblances to goddess theology, expressed in Shug's gospel as a desire for universal harmony. The "concept of a Black/Brown African Goddess," as Davenport points out, reinforces Walker's belief in a "connection between spiritual and physical empowerment."[38] It also reflects a movement among feminists to celebrate female spirituality as a counterforce to the restrictive and debasing position accorded women in male religions. Carol Christ notes that images of the goddess in female-authored literature oppose and seek to undermine "the power of the symbolism of God the Father," which has excluded women from affirming their identity "in the image and likeness of God." Christ suggests that various meanings attach to the goddess symbol, including "the acknowledgement of the legitimacy of female power as a beneficent and independent power" rather than an "inferior and dangerous" one, the reclamation of the female body and its life cycles, and new connections between women and nature.[39] Walker's protagonists resemble characters in current feminist science fiction, who, according to Phyllis J. Day, "are integral to and often protectresses of Earth and ecology. [These characters] are part of an organic whole, a return to our premechanistic past, and they represent a force against man in his assumption of the right to dominate either women or Earth/Nature."[40] Following Christ's contentions that "[t]he Goddess as symbol of the revaluation of the body and nature thus also undergirds the human potential and ecology movements," and that both movements reflect an "affirmation, awe, and respect for the body and nature . . . the teachings of the body and the rights of all living things,"[41] ecofeminists may read Walker's goddess as an affirmation of the potential for both human and environmental improvement.

The preoccupation with matriarchal wisdom in *Temple* foregrounds the maternal not in the restrictive sense of individual mothering but in the wider contexts of social nurturing and pre-oedipal development. The new community established at the end of this novel is comprised of individuals whose enlightened awareness appears to be both unconscious and conscious and to express itself both in their unabashed sensuality and in their concerned caring for one another's needs and desires. Their uninhibited sexuality may represent an eroticism that, like the "maternal erotics" Wyatt sees replacing "a masculine erotics of dominance" in *The Color Purple*, "fosters personal growth" because sex "involve[s] liberating each other's powers of self-expression rather than trying to suppress them."[42] A celebration of *jouissance* is inherent in this replication of pre-oedipal, undifferentiated energy and relational, nonsexist identity, where legally married couples—Arveyda and Carlotta, Suwelo and Fanny—remain in their now transformed marriages while flaunting infidelity, paradoxically participating in and defying patriarchal law and custom. At the same time, Walker's reinscription of sixties' counterculturalism in an eighties' milieu historicizes her promulgation of matriarchal myth and legend.

The somber tone of Walker's earlier fiction has perhaps conditioned readers to expect in *The Temple of My Familiar* tragic realism rather than comic pastiche. In this novel, however, laughter seems essential to *Bildung*; its absence marks the self-absorption of contemporary life, as Suwelo realizes when he reminisces about his Uncle Rafe's ability to amuse everyone: "And the *depth* of the laughter! The way it seemed to go so far down inside it scraped the inside bottoms of the feet. No one laughed like that any more" (*T*, 36). And surely lines like those describing Fanny's sexual freedom—"She was soon meditating and masturbating and finding herself dissolved into the cosmic All" (*T*, 385)—or Arveyda's embarrassed reaction to Fanny's lovemaking—"'I'm afraid,' he groans, 'you have lit a little candle'" (*T*, 407)— are funny even to readers who are surprised to find Walker writing comedy. One of Shug's beatitudes reads "HELPED are those who laugh with a pure heart; theirs will be the company of the jolly righteous" (*T*, 289). By the end of the novel, self-deprecating and playful laughter becomes one way of mitigating the sarcasm that has divided people throughout history. Walker is often tongue-in-cheek, and her readers are invited to laugh also.

Walker's preoccupation with language, analyzed in a recent article as a recognition by African American authors of the power of the word "to prevent or foster the development of authentic selves,"[43] extends to *Temple*, which mixes "high" and "low" language, perhaps to disconcert readers and suggest revolutionary possibilities for dismantling hegemonic discourses at the level of the individual narrative text. Walker's clichés, trite expressions, profanity, and jokes—"A woman without a man is like a fish without a bicycle" (*T*, 383), the linking of "motherworshipers" and "motherfucker" (*T*, 64), and Suwelo's pun, "Talking . . . is the very afro-disiac of love" (*T*, 322) are salient examples—offend linguistic proprieties, calling attention to a potentially subversive discourse. This language, by calling attention to itself, contributes to Walker's experimental alienation effect, resembling the pastiche strategy, described by E. Ann Kaplan, of employing a "semi-comic, self-conscious stance" toward content, a ploy which keeps audiences off balance, doubting, and never sure of any fixed ideological stance.[44]

Like the priestess's familiar, Walker's techniques in *The Temple of My Familiar* slither and skid between modernist epistemological concerns with the kinds and limits of knowledge and postmodernist ontological concerns with being and becoming. The most obvious and most important instances of this shifting occur when Walker blurs the lines between past and present, life and death—particularly when Miss Lissie moves via reincarnation in and out of various historical periods and between history and the "dream memory" of myth and legend—or the lines between fiction and fact—as when Fanny meets the real-life novelist Bessie Head. The conflation of historical time and prehistorical memory, coupled with the juxtaposing of official and alternative histories and of fiction and history creates what Brian McHale terms "an ontological flicker" through which distinctions between truth and falsehood, bible and apocrypha, insider and outsider are called into question. By crossing ontological boundaries, postmodern pastiche simulates death in ways that demystify it and, McHale argues, "models not only the ontological limit of death, but also the dream of a return."[45] Walker's pastiche, especially in its depiction of reincarnation, implies that fear of death may be mitigated by viewing it as a "part of life" (*LBW,* 74.) She unites the living with the dead in order to employ the dead's wisdom in creating a better future for the living.

While reconstructing neglected matriarchal values, Walker's pastiche also recognizes the ambiguity of contemporary vestiges and manifestations of sexual spirituality, of female power, and of vital but obscured links between humans and animals and the rest of nature. Rather than privileging her philosophy through one spokeswoman, Walker problematizes it by distributing wisdom among several male and female storytellers, some of whom are still searching for self and knowledge. Furthermore, while Miss Lissie appears close to being a goddess, having survived eons of oppression, she is not presented as a transcendent, unified self. She displays herself in numerous photographs that not only document and present various nameless and forgotten African identities but also fragment her character, dispersing it across time and space. The fragility and possibly ephemeral nature of goddess identity is suggested also by her life story, written in invisible ink, a text that Suwelo discovers can be read only once before it disappears forever. At the end of the novel even Miss Lissie has departed this life and text, leaving readers to interpret her portrait, with its lion and a "very gay, elegant, and shiny red high-heeled slipper" (*T,* 416). These images remind readers that in the postmodern moment meaning is decentered, multivalent, problematic, and accessible only through parable and pastiche. Recognizing this, we are at liberty to enjoy this experimental novel as a text that, like the temple familiar, is mercurial and chameleonic, "graceful and clever, its expression mischievous and full of humor . . . and *alive!*" even as we are cajoled into speculation: Is Miss Lissie transformed into a bestial familiar, waiting to assume her human shape at a later stage, or has she disappeared forever, leaving the slipper as a souvenir? Are there other possible interpretations of the portrait? Or of *The Temple of My Familiar?*

## NOTES

1. Joyce Maynard, "The Almost All-American Girls," review of *The Temple of My Familiar, Mademoiselle,* July 1989, 72.

2. James Wolcott, "Party of Animals," review of *The Temple of My Familiar, New Republic,* 29 May 1989, 29–30.

3. J. M. Coetzee, "The Beginnings of (Wo)man in Africa," review of *The Temple of My Familiar, New York Times Book Review,* 30 April 1989, 7.

4. Doris Davenport, "Afracentric Visions," review of *The Temple of My Familiar, Women's Review of Books,* September 1989, 13–14.

5. See, for example, Madelyn Jablon, "Rememory, Dream History, and Revision in Toni Morrison's *Beloved* and Alice Walker's *The Temple of My Familiar*," *CLA Journal* 37 (1993): 136–44; Felipe Smith, "Alice Walker's Redemptive Art," *African American Review* 26 (1992): 437–51; Ikenna Dieke, "Toward a Monastic Idealism: The Thematics of Alice Walker's *The Temple of My Familiar*," *African American Review* 26 (1992): 507–14; and Maureen T. Reddy, "Maternal Reading: Lazarre and Walker," in *Narrating Mothers: Theorizing Maternal Subjectivities*, ed. Brenda O. Daly and Maureen T. Reddy (Knoxville: University of Tennessee Press, 1991), 222–38.

6. Alice Walker, *In Search of Our Mothers' Gardens: Womanist Prose* (San Diego: Harcourt Brace Jovanovich, 1983), xi, 250, 311.

7. Alice Walker, *Living By the Word: Selected Writings 1973–1987* (San Diego: Harcourt Brace Jovanovich, 1988), 147; hereafter this work is cited parenthetically as *LBW.*

8. Alice Walker, interview with John O'Brien, in *Alice Walker: Critical Perspectives Past and Present*, ed. Henry Louis Gates Jr. and K. A. Appiah (New York: Amistad, 1993), 340.

9. Alice Walker, interview with Paula Giddings, *Essence*, July 1992, 60, 61, 102. A recent critique of *Possessing the Secret of Joy* by Margaret Kent Bass, (*CLA Journal* 38 [1994]: 1–10) accuses Walker of "cultural condescension," "smugness," and Western imperialism in her attempt to rescue African women from their "ignorance and misery" (4, 9), as exemplified by the continuance of female circumcision today. Bass, however, recognizes Walker's invitation to polyvocality in *Possessing*, where "she includes all arguments against her position and attitude in the narrative" (4) and again fragments, hence decenters, the authorial and authoritative female subject (2). Bass's admission "that I have no quarrel with what Walker attempts to do, but rather with the way she does it" (3) typifies many reactions to Walker's oeuvre.

10. Catherine Belsey, *Critical Practice* (London: Methuen, 1980), 91.

11. Raymond Federman, "What Are Experimental Novels and Why Are There So Many Left Unread?" *Genre* 14 (1981): 27.

12. Alice Walker, *The Temple of My Familiar* (San Diego: Harcourt Brace Jovanovich, 1989), 118–19; hereafter this work is cited parenthetically as *T.*

13. Ihab Hassan, "Making Sense: The Trials of Postmodern Discourse," *New Literary History* 18 (1987): 446.

14. C. Hugh Holman, *A Handbook to Literature, 4th ed.* (Indianapolis: Odyssey, 1972), 381.

15. See Linda Hutcheon, *A Theory of Parody: The Teachings of Twentieth-Century Art Forms* (New York: Methuen, 1985).

16. Pastiche finds a special place in the liberated and liberating spaces created by the postmodern moment, a time, as Edward Said reminds us, of "opening the culture to experiences of the Other which have remained 'outside' (and have been repressed or framed in a context of confrontational hostility) the norms manufactured by 'insiders' ("Opponents, Audiences, Constituencies and Community," in *The Anti-Aesthetic: Essays on Postmodern Culture*, ed. Hal Foster [Port Townsend, Wash.: Bay Press, 1983], 158).

17. Henry Louis Gates Jr., *The Signifying Monkey: A Theory of African-American Literary Criticism* (New York: Oxford University Press, 1988), 124.

18. Paul Gilroy, *The Black Atlantic: Modernity and Double Consciousness* (Cambridge: Harvard University Press, 1993), 218.

19. Franco Moretti, *The Way of the World: The Bildungsroman in European Culture* (London: Verso, 1987), 68.

20. David H. Miles, "The Picaro's Journey to the Confessional: The Changing Image of the Hero in the German *Bildungsroman*," *PMLA* 89 (1974): 984.

21. Fredric Jameson, "Postmodernism and Consumer Society," in *The Anti-Aesthetic*, 125.

22. Alice Walker, interview with Claudia Dreifus, *The Progressive*, August 1989, 31.

23. See Marianne Hirsch, *The Mother/Daughter Plot: Narrative, Psychoanalysis, Feminism* (Bloomington: Indiana University Press, 1989), for discussions of silenced mothers.

24. Jean Wyatt, *Reconstructing Desire* (Chapel Hill: University of North Carolina Press, 1990), 19. In Walker's earlier novels, as Patricia Waugh has demonstrated, the "women characters discover a personal strength through the revalidation of family connection," and homely, communal activities like quilting, gardening and cooking create a "*functional* art" that "implies that culture must not be elevated above the community, that artistic expression should be a voicing of the establishment of human identity in relationships and connections between equals" (*Feminine Fictions: Revisiting the Postmodern* [London: Routledge, 1989], 213–14). In *Temple*, activities such as bread baking, massage, and music help to unite people in a similar communal relationship, emphasizing their similarities while respecting their differences, a utopian vision akin to that of *The Color Purple*, a novel in which, as Susan Willis observes, "extended family" members "are bound up in a network of care that is . . . sustaining and open" (*Specifying: Black Women Writing the American Experience* [Madison: University of Wisconsin Press, 1987], 160).

25. Rita Felski, *Beyond Feminist Aesthetics: Feminist Literature and Social Change* (Cambridge: Harvard University Press, 1989), 142.

26. Gates, xxv.

27. David H. Miles, "Kafka's Hapless Pilgrims and Grass's Scurrilous Dwarf: Notes on Representative Figures in the Anti-Bildungsroman," *Monatshefte* 65 (1973): 344, 348.

28. Davenport, 14.

29. Felski, 147.

30. Dana Polan, "Postmodernism and Cultural Analysis Today," in *Postmodernism and Its Discontents: Theories, Practices*, ed. E. Ann Kaplan (London: Verso, 1988), 55.

31. E. A. Grosz, "Introduction," *Futur*Fall: Excursions into Post-Modernity*, ed. Grosz, et al. (Sydney, Australia: Power Institute of Fine Arts, University of Sydney, and Futur*Fall, 1986), 10.

32. Belsey, 106.

33. King-Kok Cheung, "'Don't Tell': Imposed Silences in *The Color Purple* and *The Woman Warrior*," *PMLA* 103 (1988): 169.

34. Julian Henriques, Wendy Hollway, Cathy Urwin, Couze Venn, Valerie Walkerdine, *Changing the Subject: Psychology, Social Regulation, and Subjectivity* (London: Methuen, 1984), 4.

35. Fredric Jameson, "Periodizing the 60s" (1984), in *The Syntax of History*, vol. 2 of *The Ideologies of Theory: Essays 1971–1986*, 2 vols. (Minneapolis: University of Minnesota Press, 1988), 207.

36. Jameson, "Postmodernism and Consumer Society," 117.

37. "New Age Harmonies," *Time*, 7 Dec. 1987, 64, 62.

38. Davenport, 13.

39. Carol P. Christ, "Why Women Need the Goddess: Phenomenological, Psychological, and Political Reflections," in *Womenspirit Rising: A Feminist Reader on Religion*, ed. Carol P. Christ and Judith Plaskow (New York: Harper and Row, 1979), 274–75; 271–81.

40. Phyllis J. Day, "Earthmother/Witchmother: Feminism and Ecology Renewed," *Extrapolation* 23 (1982): 14.

41. Christ, 282.

42. Wyatt, 164, 167.

43. Keith Gilyard, "Genopsycholinguisticide and the Language Theme in African-American Fiction," *College English* 52 (1990): 776.

44. E. Ann Kaplan. "Feminism/Oedipus/Postmodernism: The Case of MTV," in *Postmodernism and Its Discontents*, 37.

45. Brian McHale, *Postmodernist Fiction* (New York: Methuen, 1987), 90, 235.

DEBORAH E. BARKER

# Visual Markers: Art and Mass Media in *Alice Walker's* Meridian

The most powerful form of media representation is that which creates not just an obtainable demand for a particular product or style, but one that creates an unobtainable desire in the audience, a sense that there is something missing in one's life that can only be found in the represented image. Alice Walker describes just this phenomenon in "The Civil Rights Movement: What Good Was It?" an essay which is directly relevant to the intersection between the media and the Civil Rights Movement. There Walker explains her mother's fascination with the soap operas that she watched as a maid:

> She placed herself in every scene she saw, with her braided hair turned blond, her two hundred pounds compressed into a sleek size-seven dress, her rough dark skin smooth and *white*. Her husband became "dark and handsome," talented, witty, urbane, charming. And when she turned to look at my father sitting near her in his sweat shirt with his smelly feet raised on the bed to "air," there was always a tragic look of surprise on her face. Then she would sigh and go out to the kitchen looking lost and unsure of herself. (123)

*African American Review*, 31 (3) Fall 1997: pp. 463–79. © 1997 Deborah E. Barker

The soap operas are a form of escape, but they also help to perpetuate the image of a glamorous white world. As Walker explains her mother's situation, "Nothing could satisfy her on days when she did not work but a continuation of her 'stories,'" and she "subordinated her soul to theirs and became a faithful and timid supporter of the 'Beautiful White People'" (122-23).

To say that we are all profoundly marked by the media in our most immediate understanding of racial and sexual identity is by now almost a commonplace, but the exact nature of this marking is much more difficult to assess. In *Meridian* Alice Walker enacts a literary analysis of the *interaction* between the media and the public as dramatized through the character of Meridian Hill, who, as a young black woman participating in the Civil Rights Movement, represents an intersection between race and gender as it was being culturally redefined during the political upheaval of the sixties and seventies.[1] Meridian not only confronts the image of "Beautiful White People" promoted by an objectifying white-dominated mass media, but, more importantly, she sorts through the often uncomfortable interaction between mass media images and self-generated representations of racial and gender identity in African-American art and culture, including the legacy of black motherhood.[2] Through this confrontation, Meridian learns how to "see" herself.

While much critical attention has been focused on the interaction between music and language in African-American culture, the visual arts, as Michelle Wallace asserts, have been under-represented and under-analyzed. This is an especially egregious oversight, because the visual element of race is inexorably linked to racial identity: "How one is seen (as black), and, therefore, what one sees (in a white world), is always already crucial to one's existence as an Afro-American. The very markers that reveal you to the rest of the world, your dark skin and your kinky / curly hair, are visual" (Wallace 207). This corporeal recognition of race, Wallace maintains, allows white Americans to "overlook" African Americans, while assuming that blacks cannot "see" that they are being treated as invisible. The result produces a mutually dependent cultural invisibility and blindness based on the visual markers of race. In *Meridian*, movies, magazines, television, and the visual arts play a vital role in this process because they reinforce and reproduce on a mass scale certain cultural images of ourselves that are virtually impossible to ignore.

As Walker shrewdly demonstrates, the force of any given cultural representation is, in part, related to the power of the medium in which it is displayed, and therefore it is also subject to the economic and ideological underpinning of that medium. Noam Chomsky explains that

> the major media—particularly, the elite media that set the agenda that others generally follow—are corporations "selling"

privileged audiences to other businesses. It would hardly come as a surprise if the picture of the world they present were to reflect the perspectives and interests of the sellers, the buyers, and the product. Concentration of ownership of the media is high and increasing. (8)

Walker, however, does not depict the media as a monolithic structure that simply shapes a passive audience. She brings to the novel what an analysis of the media alone cannot: Individual reactions to the media images in turn become events which shape the images of the media, and this is most powerfully demonstrated in a fictional format, especially one set during the Civil Rights Movement, a time when images of African Americans were undergoing incredible change.

To illustrate the rich and complex history of representations of African-American women, I will highlight various forms of this representation that help to contextualize Walker's analysis of the impact of the media on our perceptions of race and gender. These examples will cover a wide terrain both historically and generically, but I have chosen them because they reveal the pervasive logic behind the cultural construction of racial and gender identity in America. It is important to keep in mind, however, in examining *Meridian*'s opposition to the cultural depictions of African-American women that, although black women have been historically marginalized or "erased" in the mass media, they do not stand outside the culture; they do play and always have played an integral role in shaping culture. Regardless of the prevalent segregation of our society, ultimately it is impossible to segregate mass culture; its influence is too pervasive and, at the same time, too subtle. In the novel there is no single effect of the media just as there is no single reaction to the media.[3] The characters—male and female, black and white, old and young—use media images as a touchstone for their understanding and analysis of the world around them. They variously reject, emulate, parody, valorize, destroy, interpret, romanticize, and/or revolutionize the images they encounter. The mass media, therefore, provide an intersection between the cultural representations of the past and the present, between black and white culture, and between high art and popular culture.

## Movies: A White Dream World

In *Meridian* it is the Hollywood movies that serve as the site of unobtainable desire. The movies are not only white-dominated, but are largely controlled by a few major studios that have the financial backing to produce and distribute large-budget, major-release films. Hollywood represents a white dream world which is based on the viewers' identification with the valorization of white culture over that of people of color: "Movies: Rory Calhoun, Ava Gardner, Bette Davis, Slim Pickens. Blondes against brunettes and cowboys against Indians, good men against bad, darker men" *(Meridian* 75). Not only do the movies transmit an implicit racist message, but they also create a seductive and unattainable dream of glamour, a glamour that is particularly attractive to young schoolgirls. For Meridian the movies provide the dream world she moves through as a girl to alleviate the boredom and limitations of her own life. Her identification with the movie images is so powerful that in her memory they actually replace the events of her own life:

> . . . she could herself recall nothing of those years, beyond the Saturday afternoons and evenings in the picture show. For it was the picture show that more than anything else filled those bantering, galloping years. . . . This fantasy world made the other world of school—with its monotony and tedium—bearable. (75)

The movies are satisfying only if the viewer can completely identify with that world, but any actual comparison between the images of everyday life and the movie images creates the "tragic look of surprise" and a sense of discontentment. As Meridian sits alone all day looking out the window after the break-up of her marriage, she understands the young girls that go by on their way home from school and their lack of awareness of the world around them:

> They simply did not know they were living their own lives— between twelve and fifteen—but assumed they lived someone else's. They tried to live the lives of their movie idols; and those lives were fantasy. Not even the white people they watched and tried to become—the actors—lived them. So they moved, did the young girls outside her window, in the dream of happy endings: of women who had everything, of men who ran the world. So had she. (75)

For Meridian, a seventeen-year-old high school dropout, divorcee, and unenthusiastic mother, the discrepancies between her own life and that of the movie idols, or even the other young girls, are too extreme; the realities of her life are unavoidable.

## Magazines: The Ideology of Enforced Motherhood

As a young wife and mother Meridian turns away from the movies and turns to magazines that target young black women. She reads *Sepia, Tan, True Confessions, Real Romance,* and *Jet,* but these do not provide an attractive alternative to the dream world of the movies. Meridian's assessment is that, "according to these magazines, Woman was a mindless body, a sex creature, something to hang false hair and nails on. Still, they helped her know for sure her marriage was breaking up" (71) and that she is not ready for motherhood. Instead of instilling an ideology of femininity based on marriage and motherhood, the magazines serve as a yardstick by which Meridian measures her own alienation. The magazines cannot provide an escape for Meridian because it is her own story that is repeatedly presented in the articles, yet she resists their version of the "happy ending." The articles illustrate the reification of the "legacy of black motherhood" from which Meridian feels excluded because of her decision to give up her child. Motherhood is defined in such strict parameters in the magazines that they espouse an ideology of enforced motherhood, an ideology that stresses lady-like behavior and depicts a sacrificial motherhood which is incongruous with individual ambition or political participation.

To understand Meridian's reaction to images of motherhood it is necessary to bring to light those forms of the media (black teen magazines) which have not been given the same critical attention as more widely circulating magazines such as *Look* or *Life,* but which have had, perhaps, an even greater influence on their target audience, young African-American women. A content analysis of the stories and advertisements from *Tan* (December 1959 and January to April 1960, roughly the time period when Meridian is reading the magazine) can help to elucidate both the connection and conflict between Meridian's own stories and the narratives she reads in the magazines. *Tan* in particular is appropriate because, as a confessional romance magazine directed at a young black female audience, it shares the qualities of all the abovementioned magazines, and it provides the greatest concentration of representations of young black women aimed precisely at this group.

On one level these magazines are an antidote to the glamorous myth of Hollywood romance because they explore the everyday details of married life.[4] The romantic allure of sex is undercut in articles such as "What Makes a Girl Bad," "Married at Seventeen," and "I Can't Have Your Baby," which depict women, like Meridian, who find themselves pregnant before they are ready to assume that responsibility. Meridian's decision to give her child up for adoption violates the norms of the black community as they are presented in *Tan.* "I Was a Victim of the Beat Generation" and "No Fathers for Their Babies," which combine personal confessions with a kind of sociological analysis, warn of the double or triple standard applied to black women regarding premarital sex and illegitimate children. As the article describe it, in the white community a pregnancy is generally kept quiet; the young woman goes away for a time and gives her baby up for adoption, resuming her former life as if nothing had happened. In the black community adoption is not so acceptable an option, and a pregnant teen is more likely to assume the responsibilities of motherhood.

Although the magazines warn against being "fast," the unmarried mothers in the stories are not condemned; they generally return to their families and, by the end of the story, marriage is suggested as a future reward. The real condemnation and most severe consequences are accorded not to women with illegitimate children but to women like Meridian who reject their own mothers and/or reject becoming mothers themselves. In "Married at Seventeen" and "I Can't Have Your Baby," the two articles most directly applicable to Meridian's story, both women are married to respectable black men with good jobs; the problem is that these women, like Meridian, have rejected their mothers' advice and in doing so have cut themselves off from the "legacy of black motherhood." Their desire for individual autonomy is presented as the source of their problems, problems that ultimately endanger their unborn children.

Any discussion of the legacy of black motherhood must, of course, include the problematic position of the slave mother and the complex representations associated with black motherhood. As Meridian is well aware, a slave mother would not have had the choice to keep her own child, while Meridian is choosing to give hers away (91). According to Claudia Tate, nineteenth-century African-American women writers reconstructed the norms of true womanhood "to inscribe moral indignation at the sexual and maternal abuses associated with slavery" and "to designate black female subjectivity as a most potent force in the advancement of the race" (107). In other words, a narrative of a former slave who marries and raises her own children constituted a sign of personal and social liberation, of civic enfranchisement and social responsibility. Tate persuasively argues that it is inappropriate to read nineteenth-century African-American women's fiction against "modernist allegories of desire" which "characterize marriage and freedom as antithetical." However, in following this reconstruction of womanhood and refuting the antebellum representation of black women as sexualized breeders, the twentieth-century romance magazines that Meridian reads (while still retaining some aspects of the "discourse of racial liberation" by encouraging fidelity and respect for the family and community) have taken on a more conservative and limiting view of female subjectivity. While Tate can argue that in the postbellum period black female subjectivity as depicted in women's sentimental novels was a "most potent force in the advancement of the race" (107), in 1960 the magazine narratives encouraged a maternal devotion that precluded political involvement.

In "Married at Seventeen," Shirley's decision to quit school and to get married against her mother's wishes leads not only to her estrangement from her parents but ultimately to her attempted suicide, which results in the loss of her unborn baby. The story's "happy ending" is Shirley's reunion with her parents in her hospital room and the doctor's assurance that she will have other children. The story ends with Shirley's confession and her prayer that she will be worthy of her "wonderful children" and her "husband's love." Her confession, however, is not just an acknowledgment of wrongdoing, or bad judgment, but a confirmation that there is only one set of standards and one role that is acceptable:

> My parents *had* been right. Marriage was a mistake for me. A mistake because I was not an adult, not a mature enough person to face the problems of life. I had wrapped my future in rosy dreams of romance and the first time the bubble broke, I did not know where to turn. Or when I did know—that my parents would have helped—I made a martyr of myself by refusing their aid. It takes a real person to stoop with dignity. My heart was heavy with the bitter price I had to pay, the loss of my baby. It wasn't just the attempted suicide and lack of oxygen but the run down condition I had let myself get into from improper diet and lack of exercise.
> "I guess I'm not fit to be a mother." (53)

Ironically, although Shirley's confession is that she is not ready for marriage or motherhood, the solution to her problem is to have more children. As long as she can be recuperated into the ideology of enforced motherhood, she can be forgiven for the attempted suicide that caused the death of her baby, but it is seemingly unthinkable that she might have had the child and given it away. Meridian has clearly internalized this message. As the novel indicates, Meridian "might not have given [her son] away to the people who wanted him. She might have murdered him instead. Then killed herself. They would all have understood this in time" (90). Unlike adoption or abortion, suicide, while considered tragic, can be forgiven because, rather than violating enforced motherhood, it reinforces the concept by making death a woman's only alternative to motherhood, and it has the added consequence of getting rid of women who are "monsters," the way in which Meridian's mother characterizes any woman who would give away her child.

Meridian feels that she has lost her mother's love and that she is cut off from the legacy of black motherhood. As in Walker's "In Search of Our Mothers' Gardens," Meridian too has a legacy of artistic/creative ancestors who created out of the materials and circumstances available to them. Most prominent is her great-grandmother, who decorated barns and who earned the money to buy her own freedom and that of her children and her husband. Meridian's great-grandmother represents the positive image of the strong African-American mother / artist (pro)creator who through her own work and sweat was able to free and protect her children from slavery, but who was also a creative artist whose work survived after her.

Mrs. Hill, however, no longer embodies the positive elements of motherhood or the artist; she is another example of the negative ramifications of enforced motherhood. While Meridian sees her mother as "Black Motherhood personified" and as "worthy of [her] maternal history," the narrator states that Mrs. Hill "was not a woman who should have had children. She was capable of thought and growth and action only if unfettered by the needs of dependents, or the demands, requirements, of a husband" (49). She raised her children though she never wanted them, and she refused her own creativity as a form of protest for the role she had to adopt as a mother. Mrs. Hill's garden is not a living garden but a cluster of "fake" flowers made of paper and wire, and her walls are covered with photographs of other people's children—not her own. For Mrs. Hill to accept Meridian would challenge her own definitions of the proper role of women and would challenge the necessity of her own sacrifice of motherhood and question even the desirability of having raised six children "though I never wanted any." Rather than bringing mothers and daughters together, the legacy, when viewed as a requirement rather than a right, keeps them apart and condemns any woman who cannot live up to its standards while also limiting all women to only one role in life.

Becoming a real woman, according to the magazines, seems to involve a masochistic selflessness which cannot brook anger or resentment. "I Can't Have Your Baby" presents the most direct attack on the duties of a daughter and the value of motherhood. Lora, who as a girl was responsible for her brothers and sisters, admits that she resented and at times even hated her mother, whose "only purpose in life was to bear babies with disgusting regularity" (27). Like Meridian, Lora's desire for independence leads to a rift between her and her mother. She leaves home, gets a job, and eventually marries her boss. When she finds out that she is pregnant, her first thought is to have an abortion. Although ultimately she decides to have the baby, she pretends that it isn't really happening to her. Like Shirley, she does not take proper care of herself and ends up in the hospital needing a transfusion from her youngest brother, the very brother whose birth she had resented because she had to stay home to help raise him. For Lora the happy ending comes with the birth of her daughter. The "awful pain of birth seemed to have purged my heart of the hatred and resentment I felt toward my family," and she was at last "well on the way to becoming a real woman, just as Mom said" (62). Pain therefore has a cathartic effect which rids women of individual desires and turns them into "real" women.

The twentieth-century magazines do, of course, offer some very sound advice: It is helpful to have familial support during pregnancy, and it is important to take care of yourself mentally and physically. But the proper role of the mother as portrayed in the articles goes beyond such good advice. The article "Devil Child" best exemplifies the stringent requirements of the "good-enough" mother. Elfreda, who tells her own story, commits none of the transgressions of the other women (she is not pregnant before she marries, nor does she take improper care of herself during pregnancy), yet her transgression produces the most tragic outcome: She murders her son to prevent him from raping her.

Elfreda, who marries a hard-working, honest young black man, still enjoys going out with her friends after the birth of her first child, Leonard. Elfreda has an understanding and sympathetic mother and a loving grandmother (named Grandma *Hill)* who agree to look after her son on the evenings she goes out with her friends. Five years later, when her second child is born, Elfreda is older and ready to settle down. The extra attention her daughter receives makes her son jealous, and, despite his parents' increased attention over the years, the damage cannot be repaired. Leonard goes from bad to worse, hurting his sister and attacking her friend. It is this assault, which his mother breaks up, that causes Leonard to turn on her and leads to his death. The lesson here as explained directly in the narrative is that Leonard's death is ultimately attributable to his mother's desire to have fun when she was young. Despite the fact that "he got lots of attention from his relatives," he did not get enough from his parents. The implied lesson is that any deviation from total devotion to one's children can lead to the most dire consequences, and ultimately it is the mother's fault.

## The Art of Advertising

Ironically (and despite the fact that their titles invoke the visual recognition of color—*Tan, Sepia, Jet)*, these magazines downplay the Hollywood version of romantic love by dramatizing the realities of "giving in" to passion, even as they depict acceptable forms of sexuality (those associated with marriage) by invoking the visual tropes of whiteness: long hair and light skin. The article "How to Keep Your Husband Happy," for example, advises women to "look feminine" and concludes that "most men associate femininity with longish softly waved hair" (66). The ads in particular associate romance and marriageability with light skin and long hair. An ad for Nadinola Bleaching Cream shows a woman smiling brightly while the man behind her holds up her left hand to reveal her engagement ring; the copy reads "Give romance a chance! Don't let a dull, dark complexion deprive you of popularity." An ad for Raveen shows only the heads of a woman and a man, who is smiling intently at her. The woman's head is turned so that her face is seen only in a limited profile while her long hair dominates the picture and is three times the size of her face. The caption reads, "Men love women with lovely, lustrous, thrilling hair appearance!" For Meridian this association of marriage and acceptable sexuality with the visual symbols of whiteness is particularly unappealing. As a girl she had accepted her mother's view that white women were "frivolous, helpless creatures, lazy and without ingenuity" (108) whose only notable asset might be "a length of hair, if it swung long and particularly fine. But that was all. And hair was dead matter that continued—only if oiled—to shine" (109).

Walker parodies the "dead matter" of long hair as a trope of white female sexuality in her depiction of Marilene O'Shay, the "mummy woman" whose husband drags her "preserved" body across the country in a circus wagon that is inscribed in red letters: "Obedient Daughter, Devoted Wife, Adoring Mother, Gone Wrong." In the opening chapter of the novel Meridian challenges the power of the myth of the white woman as a means of marginalizing blacks by exposing the mummy woman as fake. The artificially created/preserved corpse of Mrs. O'Shay brilliantly embodies the contradictory representations of race and gender in American culture by alluding to the historical representations of these categories and how they have been used to shape and define each other.[5]

In the pamphlet which he distributes to those who pay to see his wife, Mr. O'Shay assures his audience that his wife is indeed white and that the darkening of her skin (which his attempts to whitewash have not concealed) has been caused by exposure to salt and "only reflects her sinfulness" and not her race. The mummy woman exemplifies Hazel Carby's assertion that the nineteenth-century ideology of the cult of true womanhood with its attendant features of purity, delicacy, and sexlessness not only excluded black female sexuality but was dependent on it to define acceptable white female behavior. "Black womanhood was polarized against white womanhood in the structure of the metaphoric system of female sexuality, particularly through the association of black women with overt sexuality and taboo sexual practices" (32). White women, however, retained the status of "true womanhood" only so long as they conformed to the sexual limits associated with that status. White women, like Marilene O'Shay, who are sexually transgressive are represented as being visually recognizable because they take on the attributes of racial difference. As Mary Ann Doane describes the relationship between nineteenth-century representations of race and sexuality, "The hyperbolic sexualization of blackness is presented within a visual framework; it is a function of 'seeing' as an epistemological guarantee" (214). Marilene's representation as the dark-skinned mummy woman therefore reinforces the "epistemological guarantee" of purity or the lack of it; the salt has preserved her both as a sign of past sinfulness and as a reminder that death is the ultimate form of control over female sexuality.[6]

Carby's and Doane's analyses of nineteenth-century sexual and racial politics are particularly appropriate for understanding the significance of the mummy woman because of its own nineteenth-century antecedents. Mr. O'Shay's touring side show and his promotion of the mummy woman embody the sensationalistic use of sexuality and race that marks the concurrent development of art and advertising in an emerging mass culture, particularly as manifest in the nineteenth-century freak show and the traveling art show. In the early 1840s (before the completion of the transcontinental railway or the mass availability of photography, television, or the movies), one of the most effective ways to reach the masses was literally to take your show on the road. Two such touring shows, which on the face of it seem to have nothing in common, have particular relevance to the presentation of the mummy woman: P. T. Barnum's notorious "Fejee Mermaid" (1843) and Hiram Powers' *The Greek Slave* (1844). Powers' *Slave* is an example of ideal sculpture, the epitome of American high culture, while Barnum's freak show is associated with the worst aspects of popular culture—fraud and sensationalism. However, like the mummy woman, both *The Greek Slave* and the "Fejee Mermaid" were carefully promoted through the use of visual images interpreted by supporting texts that were predicated upon the polarization of black and white female sexuality.

In 1843 Barnum sent his uncle, Alanson Taylor, on a Southern tour to exhibit the "Fejee Mermaid," one of Barnum's most notorious frauds. Although the "mermaid" ultimately was declared to be simply the body of a fish sewn onto the head of a monkey, Barnum used a publicity strategy of combining drawings of an exotic mermaid accompanied by pamphlets which supported the mermaid's authenticity.[7] The image of the mermaid has long been associated with irresistible female sexuality. Barnum was able to heighten the erotic association of the mermaid by coupling it with the Fiji Islands, a location which was often the site of the exotic adventures chronicled in the popular sea narratives of the nineteenth century, but the "Fejee Mermaid" also played on the image of the sensual black woman. Although the Fijian mermaid is, of course, not African, many white Americans' propensity to associate all dark-skinned people is evidenced by the fact that Barnum was able, in his later exhibition of Fijian cannibals, to include an African-American woman from Virginia. In Charleston the controversy over the mermaid's authenticity as a new species was set amid the backdrop of the growing scientific debate over "polygenesis," a theory promoted by Dr. Josiah C. Nott, who used his hypothesis that African Americans were a separate and inferior species to support his proslavery position (Fredrickson 78–80). Reverend John Bachman, a critic of Nott, declared the mermaid a hoax and began the scientific debate that was played out in the newspapers. Despite the free publicity, the public controversy ultimately backfired and the mermaid, like the mummy woman, was declared a hoax, and the tour was canceled (Harris 62–67).

Despite the mermaid's ultimate demise in the South, Barnum made record profits in New York, and he certainly proved the power of manipulating racial and sexual representations for promotional purposes. The lesson was not lost on the art world. Four years after the American tour of the "Fejee Mermaid," Hiram Powers, an American sculptor, began a traveling exhibition of his most famous work, *The Greek Slave*. In promoting his tour of *The Greek Slave* Powers' problem was the opposite of Barnum's.[8] Powers needed to downplay the erotic connotation of his nude statue and disassociate it from the American slave trade. The touring show of *The Greek Slave*, like that of the mummy woman, was accompanied by a pamphlet. However, in the case of *The Greek Slave* the pamphlet stressed her modesty and purity and included testimony from ministers who attested to the morality of the work. *The Greek Slave* employs the visual markers of whiteness and Christianity to present a woman under attack by the barbarian Turks, thus reversing the racial politics of slavery and presenting a victimized white (marble) woman:

> Visual details carefully informed the audience that the subject was a pious, faithful woman: a locket and a cross hanging on her abandoned clothing suggest a lost love and a sustaining Christian faith. Stripped naked, displayed for sale in the marketplace, her hands chained, the Greek slave, unlike Eve, was absolved from responsibility for her own downfall. (Kasson 49)

Supporters of *The Greek Slave* claimed that she was "clothed all over with sentiment; sheltered, protected by it from every profane eye" (Kasson 58). The accompanying narrative was apparently quite effective; viewers wept and wrote poetic tributes to the victimized Greek slave, and the tour was also a financial success.

The rationale behind the purity of *The Greek Slave* is that she "civilizes" the baser instincts of her viewers, thereby controlling how they "see" her. The black woman is also assumed to be in control of how she is seen. The corollary to white female purity, as Carby explains, was the belief that black women by definition were not pure and therefore could not possibly be victims of male desire, but were instead the instigators (27). The black slave woman is therefore "seen" as responsible for inciting male desire, on the one hand, and for not eliciting pity, on the other. The difference between the mummy woman and *The Greek Slave* revolves around the issue of sexual desire and sexual autonomy. *The Greek Slave* retains her "epistemological guarantee" of purity by demonstrating her lack of desire in the face of sexual transgression. Marilene O'Shay, who goes "outside the home to seek her pleasuring," revokes her status as a white woman, as a symbol of restrained and contained sexuality, and takes on the visual markers of racial difference.

In the context of the mummy woman and its nineteenth-century antecedents, the artistic productions of Truman Held, Meridian's former lover and fellow Civil Rights Worker, are equally suspect. Truman has turned the stereotype of the strong, fecund black woman into a marketable aesthetic object, and potentially the money he makes through the sale of his work will provide him with the means for not dealing with black women in his future—by marrying another white woman. As Truman works "night and day on the century's definitive African-American masterpieces," he still has not come to terms with his own ambivalent feelings about black women. "'Black women let themselves go,' he said, even as he painted them as magnificent giants, breeding forth the warriors of the new universe. 'They are so *fat*,' he would say, even as he sculpted a 'Big Bessie Smith' in solid marble, caressing her monstrous and lovely flanks with an admiring hand" (168). Truman can appreciate black women only as art. Lynne, Truman's white ex-wife (who has her own problems with viewing black women as art[9]), assumes that Truman's art will have an impact on his own life, that having fought through his art to the reality of his own mother, aunts, sister, lovers, to their beauty, their greatness, [he] would naturally seek them again in the flesh" (169) and that she is magnanimously giving him back to Meridian. Yet when she comes to his apartment she meets his new "tiny blonde" girlfriend who explains, "'We've been livin' together for two months. Truman says soon as he sells some more of his paintings we're goin' to be married'" (171).

Truman's art becomes his substitute for dealing with the black women in his past. He can paint and sculpt Meridian over and over, but he cannot fully accept her as a lover and a friend. Truman's art does not challenge his own stereotypes about black women, nor does it prompt him to "seek them again in the flesh." It is precisely their flesh that Truman finds threatening. His objection to large women is clearly not on aesthetic grounds because in his art he can admiringly caress the large flanks of Bessie Smith. It is the flesh itself, the reality of actual black women, that he cannot come to terms with. Seeking black women "in the flesh" also carries a sexual connotation and is directly connected to Truman's avoidance. While he can control the flesh/sexual representation of black women in his art, he fears that real black women do not control their flesh; they "let themselves go." Truman has incorporated the cultural representation of black women as sexually wanton to such a degree that he now fears them in the flesh. Ultimately Truman's definitive American masterpiece is, like Mr. O'Shay's mummy woman, the only way he can control and limit female sexuality. When Truman sees the circus wagon of Marilene O'Shay with its description of her preservation and her dutiful nature as daughter, wife, and mother, he immediately declares, "'That's got to be a rip-off'" (19). Yet these are the same attributes that he has required of his own wife and which prevent him from accepting Meridian as she is (110). Rather than challenging media images of African-American women, Truman is depicted as someone who too quickly embraces and imitates media images, incorporating them into his own artistic creations of black women.

A sign of Truman's complicity with the media is that, while Meridian uses women's magazines as a measure of her alienation and her unwillingness to comply with the gender codes, Truman uses popular magazines as a blueprint for his ever-changing persona. When Truman ponders the issues of his own life he repeatedly turns to the mass media for his cue. Ironically, Truman explains to Meridian that he dates Lynne and the other white exchange students because they read the *New York Times*. The exchange students, therefore, symbolically link Truman to the white, Eastern media. And it is again the mass media that influences Truman's decision whether or not to stay married to Lynne, since it is no longer fashionable to have a white wife:

> He had read in a magazine just the day before that Lamumba Katurim had gotten rid of his. She was his wife, true, but apparently she was even in that disguise perceived as evil, a castoff. And people admired Lamumba for his perception. It proved his love of his own people, they said. But he was not sure. Perhaps it proved only that Lamumba was fickle. That he'd married this bitch in the first place for shallow reasons. (135)

Although Truman is able to question the motives and sincerity of the celebrities he reads about, he still does not fully question his own motives and his need to be politically and publicly correct.

As the new revolutionary artist of the '70s, Truman explains that the revolution of the '60s was just a fad. "'The leaders were killed, the restless young were bought off with anti-poverty jobs, and the clothing styles of the poor were copied by Seventh Avenue. And you *know* how many middle-class white girls from Brooklyn started wearing kinky hair'" (189). Truman's critique is, of course, equally applicable to his own dress and lifestyle. Like a cultural chameleon, each time Truman is described he has adopted a new, updated image.[10]

### Television: Black Exposure

That Meridian would turn to the Civil Rights Movement after rejecting the magazine version of black womanhood is not surprising. It is a lesson that she would have learned from the magazines themselves. Although

*Tan* and *True Confessions* dealt very little with politics, *Jet*, which aimed at a wider audience, dealt more extensively with current affairs and with the Civil Rights Movement in particular. And it was only in connection with the Movement that women were accorded status independent of their role as "sex creatures." *Jet*, which was blatant in its depiction of black women as sexual objects, regularly featured photographs of women in bathing suits in 1960. Even when women were being lauded for intellectual or social distinctions in the magazine, the text was accompanied by a "cheesecake" photo. For example a Chicago housewife who is promoting National Library Week is pictured in heels and a swimsuit reading a book; the caption accompanying the picture reads "Stacked High." A University of Chicago coed who is majoring in international relations is also depicted in a bathing suit, and the caption includes her measurements as well as her major. A "pinup" calendar, again depicting women in bathing suits, was another regular feature of the magazine. In fact, there are very few pictures of women which do not emphasize their bust line or show them wearing bathing suits. The one very noticeable exception to the rule is the cover of the April 21, 1960, issue, which shows an unsmiling young woman who does not even look into the camera and whose bust-line is not visible in the photograph. She is standing behind bars and the caption reads, "Sit-in Student Freedom Fighters." The Movement, therefore, afforded contemporary African-American women an alternative form of representation in the mass media as serious participants in a political cause. At the same time that Meridian's involvement in the Civil Rights Movement has cut her off from her mother and the version of sacrificial motherhood put forth by the black women's magazine, it also marks her self-conscious participation in history.

Walker demonstrates that the same media which propagate oppressive fantasies can also be a source of opposition. In Walker's own life it was the presence of a black face on television which provided her with an alternative and ruptured the influence of the television images and white "stories":

> The influence that my mother's soap operas might have had on me became impossible. The life of Dr. King, seeming bigger and more miraculous than the man himself, because of all he had done and suffered, offered a pattern of strength and sincerity I felt I could trust. . . . I saw in him the hero for whom I had waited so long. ("Civil Rights" 124)

Meridian's listless television watching is interrupted when she sees her own neighborhood on the TV news. Through this event she is thrust into history and becomes "aware of the past and present of the larger world" (73). It is only through a televised press conference that she learns that a house nearby is a headquarters for a voter registration drive, and again it is through the TV news that she learns that the house has been bombed.

Meridian is stunned, not only that such things could happen in her own neighborhood, but that the Civil Rights workers were already aware of the danger and had hired a guard. Meridian's reaction to this scene points to her own lack of knowledge of the larger world, but it also emphasizes the lack of representation of blacks on television. As Meridian indicates, blacks are not usually on the news "unless of course they had shot their mothers or raped their bosses' grandparent—and a black person or persons giving a news conference was unheard of" (72). By calling a press conference, the Civil Rights workers use the media as a form of resistance to represent their own goals, rather than being depicted as reflections of the white community's fears. (Access is still limited, however; it is the white newscaster who controls the handkerchief-covered microphone as if to filter the words of blacks or to protect himself from contamination.) Still, the power of television works two ways: The black youths have made themselves heard, but they have also made themselves and their whereabouts public knowledge, and have subsequently been the victims of a bombing. Like Louvinie, the slave who was silenced because of the terrifying power of her stories, which literally scared her young, white master to death, the black youths have also been silenced by death for challenging racial segregation.

*Meridian* also scrutinizes the less dramatic effects of black access to the media. Again, there is no single reaction to resistance. As Foucault explains, "Focuses of resistance are spread over time and space at varying densities, at times mobilizing groups or individuals in a definitive way, inflaming certain points of the body, certain moments in life, certain types of behavior" (96). Walker demonstrates the ripple effect of the media coverage. The TV depiction of the brutality used against marching Civil Rights workers indirectly influences Meridian's ability to go to college. As her high school principal states, ". . . a generous (and wealthy) white family in Connecticut— who wished to help some of the poor, courageous blacks they saw marching and getting their heads whipped nightly on TV—had decided, as a gesture of their liberality and concern, to send a smart black girl to Saxon College in Atlanta, a school this family had endowed for three generations" (86). Although at face value this would seem to be a positive effect of TV coverage, the narrator's ironic tone serves as an implicit critique. The word *wealthy,* in parentheses, mediates the generosity of the white family by indicating that this was no financial sacrifice for them. And the sincerity of their action is undermined by its being described as "a gesture of their liberality and concern"; its real import is to enhance their own "positive" image as liberals. Television brings the violence of the marches into their Connecticut home, but the family's reaction of sending a smart black girl to a school that is segregated by race and sex does very little to combat racism and sexism, as is indicted by the fact that the family for three generations has been giving money to Saxon, a school which enforces middle-class standards of lady-like decorum and does not condone involvement in the Civil Rights Movement.

## Photography: Through a Different Lens

If, as suggested earlier, movies provide some of the most limiting and limited forms of media representations, photography is one of the most widely accessible and varied forms, and it serves as an important symbol of self-representation in *Meridian*. The family photo album became an important means of documenting the major events and activities of the family, and with the advent of affordable cameras photography became a popularly accessible art form. (For Lynne and Meridian one of the signs of their alienation from their families is the fact that Lynne has no photos of her parents and Meridian's mother has photos of other people's children, not her own.) The history of photography is one associated not only with recording the lives of the wealthy and famous but also one of capturing everyday people and places. Photography, more than any other visual medium, has been used to record the lives of the poor and the disenfranchised.[11]

Walker, of course, does not condone all aspects of photography. She is well aware of its objectifying potential and the history of the visual depiction of black women as the exotic Other. As Mary Ann Doane explains, "Within a photographic discourse which brought the dark continent home to Europeans, the exotic and the erotic were welded together, situating the African woman as the signifier of an excessive, incommensurable sexuality" (213). Walker demonstrates this with the example of the white exchange student at Saxon who takes "photographs of the girls straightening their hair and also of them coming out of the shower" as if they were natives in the *National Geographic*. The exchange student is informed by the Saxon students that "'this here ain't New Guinea'" (103). The camera, however, in its most positive aspect facilitates a link between the object and the subject. Truman, through his art, is able to create Meridian as a profitable and silent object that cannot question or challenge his motives or his art. However, when he uses the camera to take a picture of Lynne surrounded by black children, who take turns combing her hair, he finds he cannot take the picture. The camera forces him to see (though not fully acknowledge) the contradictions in his life. He cannot aestheticize his ambivalent relationship with Lynne. "What stops him he will not, for the moment, have to acknowledge: It is a sinking, hopeless feeling about opposites, and what they do to each other" (129).

For Meridian the camera serves as a symbol of her ability to see her world through a different lens. While at college Meridian begins to develop her own representation of the world through her photographs (she "decorate[s] the ceiling, walls, backs of doors and the adjoining toilet with large photographs of trees and rocks and tall hills and floating clouds, which she claim[s] she *knew*" [38]). Her photographs of nature, while soothing, cannot insulate her from the harsh external realities that she encounters in her involvement in the Civil Rights Movement, nor from the repressive rules of Saxon's code of lady-like behavior. At the end of the novel, however, the metaphor of the camera and two key photographs (a picture of a slain Civil Rights worker and the rejuvenated Sojourner tree) help her to recontextualize the stifling aspects of religion, as represented by her mother, and the unrelenting aspects of revolutionary politics, as represented by her friend Anne-Marion. Meridian's insight occurs during a visit to a reformed church:

> She was aware of the intense heat that closed around the church and the people moving slowly, almost grandly up the steps, as *if* into an ageless photograph. And she, standing across the street, was not part of it. Rather, she sensed herself an outsider, as a single eye behind a camera that was aimed from a corner of her youth, attached now only because she watched. If she were not there watching, the scene would be exactly the same, the "picture" itself never noticing that the camera was missing. (193-94)

In using the metaphor of the camera, Meridian does not disturb or appropriate the past (the ageless photograph); it is independent of her gaze and has its own importance and autonomy, but simultaneously the camera gives her a perspective from which to view the scene. This is an important passage because it holds the key to Meridian's struggle to define herself as a woman and an activist within the black community. In the past she has resisted both the conservative elements of the church and the radical and potentially violent aspects of the black power movement. Meridian's return to the reformed church allows her to embrace those things in her past that have separated her from her friends and family, but she does it on her own terms and not on theirs.

The church which Meridian attends is changed from the inside out. The building itself is different; the preacher is not only understandable but he is blatantly political, attacking Nixon, forbidding young men to participate in the Vietnam War, and mentioning God only "as a reference." The music and the icons of the church have been transformed from passive signs of conformity to signs of active resistance (198). But the most radicalizing element of this new-old church is the inclusion of a photograph of a young man killed for his revolutionary beliefs. The impact of hearing his father's story and the congregation's reaction brings Meridian to the realization that "she *would* kill, before she allowed anyone to murder his son again" (200). It was her refusal to kill in the name of the revolution which marked her break with the radical movement and her friend Anne-Marion. The photograph allows Meridian to reconcile her ambivalent feelings both toward the church and to the revolutionary groups of her past. By combining the radical and the righteous Meridian can accept what formerly was unacceptable: "Only in a church surrounded by the righteous guardians of the people's memories could she even approach the concept of retaliatory murder. Only among the pious could this idea both comfort and uplift" (200).

The final photograph of the novel, that of the new branch on the Sojourner tree (which Meridian hangs next to her own poems and Anne-Marion's letters), serves as a visual sign of the reintegration of Meridian's cultural, political, and artistic interests. The fact that Anne-Marion has sent her the picture confirms Meridian's reconciliation with the ideas of the revolutionary groups of her past. And the new sprout signals her return to health and her return to writing poetry. (Walker has described her own early poems as "new leaves sprouting from an old tree" [*Gardens* 249].) The Sojourner, which was destroyed in the Saxon student riot, links Meridian to her African heritage, to music, sexuality, and resistance. The Saxon slaves believed the tree had magical powers, could talk and make music, and "possessed the power to obscure vision. Once in its branches, a hiding slave could not be seen" (44). The Saxon students, including Meridian, believing the tale, used the tree to shelter their lovemaking.

The "obscured vision" fostered by the Sojourner's leaves seems benevolent in comparison to Wallace's concept of cultural invisibility, yet it is necessitated by the oppression of slavery in the past and the repression of female sexuality in the present. Such invisibility can be enabling, but it is not a solution. The solution for Meridian is not simply to reject the cultural images of African-American women, nor to sacrifice herself to them as a revolutionary martyr. She finds a way to see them in a new critical context which no longer obscures her vision. In the final chapter of the book, Truman has taken Meridian's place, implying that he is now going to see the world from her perspective and to see her within a new critical context which no longer obscures his vision.

## NOTES

1. Barbara Christian, in her thorough reading of *Meridian*, discusses the importance of the circular structure of the novel in connecting Meridian's personal history with her cultural milieu and with the development of the Civil Rights Movement (*Women* 204-34).

2. As Barbara Christian observes of Walker's writing in general, "Walker's peculiar sound, the specific mode through which her deepening of self-knowledge

and self-love comes, seems to have much to do with her contrariness, her willingness at all turns to challenge the fashionable belief of the day, to reexamine it in the light of her own experiences and of dearly won principles that she has previously challenged and absorbed" (*Feminist* 82-83).

3. As Foucault explains, "Resistance is never in a position of exteriority in relation to power. . . . These points of resistance are present everywhere in the power network. Hence there is no single locus of great Refusal, no soul of revolt, source of all rebellions, or pure law of revolution. Instead there is a plurality of resistances, each of them a special case: resistances that are possible, necessary, improbable; others that are spontaneous, savage, solitary, concerted, rampant, or violent; still others that are quick to compromise, interested, or sacrificial; by definition, they can only exist in the strategic field of power relations" (96).

4. The article "Is Love Really Necessary," for example, undercuts the glamour of romance by stressing the difference between the romance of dating and the reality of marriage. The author agrees that love in marriage is preferable, but lists six areas of compatibility that are equally important: sexual relations, money matters, social and entertainment activities, relations with in-laws, religion, and mutual friends.

5. Critics have expressed various, but interrelated, interpretations of the importance of the mummy woman. According to Barbara Christian the opening scene "satirizes the lavish trademarks of the South—the white woman protected, indeed mummified, by the sanctimonious rhetoric of her society, but losing even these questionable privileges when she exercises any sexual freedom" (*Women* 207-08). For Deborah McDowell "the mummy woman is a metaphor for the preservation of dead, no longer viable traditions and institutions" (264). Picking up on McDowell's statement, Alan Nadel asserts that the scene "makes clear the connection between Meridian's body and the body politic." Her paralysis links her to the mummy woman at the same time that her activism "suggests an alternative to the untenable roles of womanhood produced by white and male culture and replicated in the mummy-woman's alleged history" (60). Karen Stein, Martha McGowan (31), and Peter Erickson (89), view Meridian's encounter with the mummy woman as an ironic depiction of the decline of the Civil Rights Movement. According to Stein, "Walker suggests that a primary reason for the Movement's failure was its lack of a sustained sociopolitical critique" (131).

6. The pattern of death and violence (intentional, accidental, or even self-induced) as a means to silence and/or punish women who have abrogated their traditional duties as daughters, wives, or mothers (especially mothers) is repeated throughout the novel in the stories of Wild Child (who observes no social conventions and whose only language is obscenities and farts), Louvinie (who was silenced because of the force and power of her speech), Fast Mary (who killed her illegitimate child and then herself), and Lynne (who is dead in the eyes of her family because of her interracial marriage). The silencing of these women is also directly connected to the death of a child, often their own. Each of these women represents the devastating consequences of going outside prescribed limits and serves as a warning to Meridian, whose own struggles correspond to those of the silenced women: Wild Child, the violation of lady-like behavior imposed at Saxon; Louvinie, the ability to speak out in the Civil Rights Movement; Fast Mary, the decision to have an abortion; and Lynne, estrangement from the family, especially from the mother. Hence, Meridian, as a twentieth-century black woman, is not excluded from the cult of true womanhood, but instead suffers from the severity of its behavioral codes. The

artificial preservation of the mummy woman and the fundamental question of her authenticity characterize the basic inadequacy of the cult of true womanhood as a realistic or desirable model of conduct for a twentieth-century woman.

7. However, even Barnum had his limits. He was persuaded to cancel the eighteen-foot-long banner of a mermaid which he planned to fly outside his New York museum (Werner 56-63).

8. Powers' earlier nude, *Eve Tempted*, was considered too indiscreet by an American buyer who canceled his order. Other art tours that featured nudes had also received unfavorable press in America (Kasson 48-49).

9. Lynne reifies the life of poor, Southern blacks through a romantic, artistic perspective that undermines the principles of her participation in the Civil Rights Movement and her attempt to change the South: "To Lynne, the black people of the South were Art. This she begged forgiveness for and tried to hide, but it was no use . . . 'I will pay for this,' she often warned herself. And yet, she would stand perfectly still and the sight of a fat black woman singing to herself in a tattered yellow dress, her voice rich and full of yearning, was always—God forgive her, black folks forgive her—the same weepy miracle that Art always had for her" (130). Lynne "pays for" her objectified view of blacks by living out the negative ramifications of the stereotype that she has romanticized. Living in poverty on the Lower East Side, Lynne dramatically represents that there is nothing romantic or artistic about her plight. The real dangers of poverty, inadequate housing, and poor living conditions are graphically brought home to Lynne by the brutal death of her daughter Camara (174). Lynne exemplifies Walker's criticism that white women have not included black women under the heading of "women" because that would mean having to deal with the implication of poverty for black women as mothers (*Gardens* 373).

10. Truman is first the "preppie," French-speaking, jeans-and-polo-shirt-clad, clean-cut young man of the early Civil Rights Movement. His affinities are with Western culture (especially anything French) and the middle class. Meridian notes that he has the face of an Ethiopian warrior that you see in magazines, and when we next see him he has picked up on the increased emphasis on African culture: He wears a "flowing Ethiopian robe of extravagantly embroidered white, his brown eyes aglow with excitement" (100). As the New York artist, Truman smokes little cigars and has his hair in two dozen small braids. When he returns to the South to find Meridian, he has adopted yet another persona—the "revolutionary artist." Meridian notes ironically that he looks like Che Guevara, "not by accident I'm sure," in his "tan cotton jacket of the type worn by Chairman Mao" (24).

11. While Hollywood responded to the Depression with big-budget musicals, documentary photographers traveled the South and Southwest recording the devastating effects of the drought and Depression. Richard Wright's *Twelve Million Black Voices*, which recorded the movement of blacks from the rural South to the urban North, relied on the Farm Service Administration's archives for its photos.

## WORKS CITED

Carby, Hazel V. *Reconstructing Womanhood: The Emergence of the Afro-American Woman Novelist.* New York: Oxford University Press, 1987.

Chomsky, Noam. *Necessary Illusions: Thought Control in Democratic Societies.* Boston: South End Press, 1989.

Christian, Barbara. *Black Feminist Criticism: Perspectives on Black Women Writers*. New York: Pergamon Press, 1985.

———. *Black Women Novelists: The Development of a Tradition, 1892-1976*. Westport: Greenwood, 1980.

"Devil Child." *Tan* 10 (Apr. 1960): 32+.

Doane, Mary Ann. *Femmes Fatales: Feminism, Film Theory, Psychoanalysis*. New York: Routledge, 1991.

Erickson, Peter. "'Cast Out Alone / To Heal / And Re-create / Ourselves': Family-Based Identity in the Work of Alice Walker." *CLA Journal* 23 (1979): 71–94.

Foucault, Michel. *The Histoiy of Sexuality: An Introduction*. Vol. 1. Trans. Robert Hurley. New York: Vintage, 1980.

Fredrickson, George M. *The Black Image in the White Mind: The Debate on Afro-American Character and Destiny, 1817–1914*. Middletown: Wesleyan UP, 1971.

Harris, Neil. *Humbug*. Boston: Little, 1973.

"I Can't Have Your Baby." *Tan* 10 (May 1960): 26+.

"I Was a Victim of the Beat Generation." *Tan* 10 (Feb. 1960): 10–12.

"Is Love Really Necessary?" *Tan* 10 (Jan. 1960): 16+.

Kasson, Joy. *Marble Queens and Captives: Women in Nineteenth-Century American Sculpture*. New Haven: Yale University Press, 1990.

"Married at Seventeen." *Tan* 10 (Apr. 1960): 15+.

McDowell, Deborah. "The Self in Bloom." *CLA Journal* 24 (1981): 262–75.

McGowan, Martha J. "Atonement and Release in Alice Walker's *Meridian*." *Critique: Studies in Modern Fiction* 23.1 (1981): 25–36.

Nadel, Alan. "Reading the Body: Alice Walker's *Meridian* and the Archeology of Self." *Modern Fiction Studies* 34 (1988): 55–68.

"No Father For Their Babies." *Tan* 10 (Dec. 1959): 10+.

Perkins, Ann. "What Makes a Girl Bad?" *Tan* 10 (Mar. 1960): 38+.

Stein, Karen. "Alice Walker's Critique of Revolution." *Black American Literature Forum* 20 (1986): 129–142.

Tate, Claudia. "Allegories of Black Female Desire; or, Reading Nineteenth-Century Sentimental Narrative of Black Female Authority." *Changing Our Own Words: Essays on Criticism, Theory, and Writing by Black Women*. Ed. Cheryl A. Wall. New Brunswick: Rutgers University Press, 1989. 98–126.

Walker, Alice. *In Search of Our Mothers' Gardens*. San Diego: Harcourt, 1983.

———. *Meridian*. New York: Simon, 1976.

Wallace, Michele. "Modernism, Postmodernism, and the Problem of the Visual in Afro-American Culture." *Aesthetics in Feminist Perspective*. Ed. Hilde Hein and Carolyn Korsmeyer. Bloomington: Indiana University Press, 1993. 205–17.

Werner, M. R. *Barnum*. New York: Grosset & Dunlap, 1923.

Wright, Richard. *Twelve Million Black Voices*. New York: Viking, 1941.

MARCIA NOE AND MICHAEL JAYNES

# Teaching Alice Walker's "Everyday Use" Employing Race, Class, and Gender, with an Annotated Bibliography

"Because I'm black and I'm a woman and because I was brought up poor and because I'm a Southerner . . . the way I see the world is quite different from the way many people see it" —Alice Walker

"The whole point of reading literature, it seems to me, is to learn to have sympathies, imaginative relationships with people who are different from one's self." —Irving Howe

We write as a teacher and a student who have found that race, class, and gender can function heuristically to complicate and enrich students' readings of Alice Walker's, "Everyday Use" and to encourage students to take a more reflective approach to this story. We have found that reading and discussing the story from these perspectives can help students question the easy conclusions they might be tempted to draw from the story and understand the complexities that lie beneath its surface. This approach can also help students transcend their personal circumstances and gain a better understanding of people who are culturally different from themselves.

For Marcia "Everyday Use" is a story, popular with students, that can appear deceptively simple and one-dimensional to the casual reader, perhaps because it is focalized through the first-person narrator, Mama. As Susan Farrell suggests, this narrative strategy can have the effect of persuading

*Eureka Studies in Teaching Short Fiction*, 5:1; Fall 2004: pp. 126–136. ©2004 Marcia Noe.

155

students that Mama's statements are completely accurate and her values are co-extensive with those of the implied author; this dependence on an unreliable narrator can lead to an oversimplified and distorted reading of the story. Students who engage with the story only superficially tend to identify Maggie, the stay-at-home country daughter, as the "good daughter" and Dee, her sophisticated city sister, as the "bad daughter," taking their cues from Mama's descriptions of them. When students are asked to discuss the story first from the perspective of gender, then race, and finally class, they are able to move away from identifying with Mama to engage critically with the story and interrogate the narrator and her values. A related problem concerns the story's denouement, in which Mama gives her heirloom quilts to Maggie, even though Dee has asked for them. Students tend to draw a simplistic moral lesson from the fact that humble, self-effacing Maggie wins out over her better educated elder sister rather than to examine the story's movement and components carefully and critically to arrive at a more nuanced reading, which can be facilitated if the story is approached from the perspectives of race, class, and gender and the ways in which they are imbricated.

For Michael, looking at the story through the lenses of gender, race and class helped him transcend the self-involved sphere of his personal existence to experience the reality of the Other. Discussing the ways that race, class, and gender are important in "Everyday Use" helped Michael to see himself in a way that he had never before: as an educated, middle-class, Christian, heterosexual white male who is privileged in many ways. In his opinion, this story is most valuable to a reader such as himself, who had never fully examined his place and role in a patriarchal society until he read the story from these perspectives. Doing so helped him to move closer to the possibility of seeing the story from the point of view of a poor black southern woman. By seeing how Maggie, Dee, and Mama deal with issues of their past, their femininity, their class, and what it means or doesn't mean to be black, he gained a small amount of understanding of his race, class, and gender's role in the oppression of people like these characters.

Focusing on gender can help students see how different the story is from the typical story or play by a male author. "Everyday Use" is gynocentric; it is not a story about fathers and sons, as is often the case in Western literature, but about mothers and daughters. Stories about fathers and sons usually involve rivalries, competitions and the passing down of goods. Often the object of contention is an inheritance of land or money. In canonical plays, such as *Cat on a Hot Tin Roof* and *Desire Under the Elms*, there is typically much lying, cheating, and bickering to get the inheritance; often it is the oldest son who comes out on top. There are similar elements in "Everyday Use," but instead of the usual father-to-son inheritance plot as seen in the plays of Miller, Williams, and O'Neill, it is cultural heritage, rather than land or money, that is at stake in the story, represented by the quilts and butter churn that Dee wants to appropriate. And while the eldest son often inherits wealth in patriarchal works, in "Everyday Use" Mama gives her legacy of quilts to Maggie, the uglier, scarred, less flamboyant, less confident, more traditional, less-educated younger sister rather than to her elder sister, Dee. The story thus is an inversion of the canonical story of masculine inheritance and thereby offers an alternate value system as well as an alternate plot.

Patricia Kane, in "The Prodigal Daughter in Alice Walker's 'Everyday Use,'" emphasizes that Dee—the prodigal, wandering daughter of the story— does not receive the inheritance, unlike the prodigal son of the Biblical version of the tale: "The reversals and variations from the Biblical prodigal son story suggest that when women make the choices, the tale expresses different values" (7). "Everyday Use" establishes a more community-focused value system, as seen in Mama's giving the quilts to Maggie, that is thus placed in sharp opposition to the more patriarchal values of a play like *Cat on a Hot Tin Roof* or *Desire Under the Elms*. While land is worked, cared for, and overseen by individuals and handed down from one individual to another, usually from a father to an eldest son, quilts are communal, woven into existence with the hands and skill of women, testaments to the importance of women's space and values. In "Patches: Quilts and Community in Alice Walker's 'Everyday Use,'" Houston Baker and Charlotte Pierce-Baker point out that while Dee is the one who is most intent on possessing the quilts, it is Maggie who actually is skilled in quilting, capable of making her own quilts, and thus, in Mama's eyes, the daughter who is best able to understand, care for, and cherish the quilts, and by extension, the family's history and culture.

While employing gender as an analytical category to discuss "Everyday Use," Alice Walker's essay, "In Search of Our Mother's Gardens," can further elucidate this story. In this essay Walker asks what it must have meant for "[a] black woman to be an artist in our grandmothers' time? In our great-grandmother's time? It is a question with an answer cruel enough to stop the blood" (233). Walker writes of nameless great-grandmothers who lived lives of oppression while longing to model "heroic figures of rebellion, in stone or clay"(233). This statement led Michael to consider the popular image of artists. Picasso, Michelangelo, Pollack came immediately to mind: all males. He then realized that he had no conception of what it must mean for a woman, whether black or a member of any other race, to be an artist today. He realized that while it is difficult enough for a contemporary woman artist to be taken seriously in a male-dominated culture, it would have been nearly unimaginable for women of our great-grandmothers' time to be considered serious artists. In this context, "In Search of Our Mother's Gardens" illuminates the first paragraph of "Everyday Use," in which Mama and Maggie have readied the front yard in anticipation of Dee's visit, sweeping "the hard clay . . . clean as a floor" and lining "the fine sand around the edges . . . with tiny, irregular grooves . . ." (2012). We can thus see Mama not only as poor, unsophisticated, and uneducated, but also as a twentieth-century incarnation of those would-be artist grandmothers and great-grandmothers that Walker writes about in her essay. Lacking the education and background to create through elite media such as sculpture or painting, Mama expresses her heritage and creativity through ordering her front yard and furnishing her home with artifacts crafted by her ancestors.

Another way in which the lens of gender can help students see more complexity in the characters is the way that this perspective foregrounds their androgynous dimensions. Mama is female, yet quite masculine in appearance and in her self-proclaimed ability to "kill and clean a hog as mercilessly as a man . . . eat pork liver cooked over the open fire minutes after it comes steaming from the hog . . . and [knock] a bull calf straight in the brain between the eyes with a sledge hammer and [have] the meat hung up to chill before nightfall" (2013). Dee is more feminine in dress and appearance, yet she is very assertive. She seems to command Hakim-A-Barber, the story's only male character, according to her will. It could even be argued that the homely Maggie, lacking the traditional feminine attributes of beauty, grace, and style, is somewhat androgynous as well. None of the female characters is completely, traditionally "feminine." They all contain worlds of female experience. By reading the story from the perspective of gender, we are better able to understand and appreciate the complexity of the female personality and the female values and world view that the story endorses. Conversely, the story can help male students understand what it means to be a man in a patriarchal society, enabling them, the traditional holders of power and privilege, to be able to step back and examine their own status as well as to see how minorities view them. As a result of reading "Everyday Use" with an emphasis on gender, male students can begin to become more understanding, tolerant, and better men.

Race is a second lens through which a productive reading of "Everyday Use" can proceed. Toward this end, Barbara Smith's seminal essay, "Toward a Black Feminist Criticism," can be usefully placed in dialogue with the story. Smith says that "[w]hen white women look at Black women's works they are of course ill-equipped to deal with the subtleties of racial politics" (170). If this is the case, then white males are doubly removed from Walker's racial politics; therefore, it is doubly important that they read and attempt to understand "Everyday Use." For example, Michael was surprised by the question that Mama—a confident, intelligent woman—asks: "Who can even imagine me looking a strange white man in the eye?" (2013). It would never have occurred to Michael that a black woman could feel this way; to him, white men are simply men like any others. However, the story has shown him that his assumption may not be true, and this revelation makes the story important to study—especially for white men.

Race plays a critical role 'in the forming of Mama's character; she received a meager education because the colored school she went to closed down while she was in the second grade. Mama's sense of herself as black is also reflected in her statement, regarding the Johnny Carson daydream, that she couldn't imagine looking a white man in the eye or talking back to one. But while it may appear that Mama is self-conscious about being black while Dee is proud of her black heritage, looking at the story through the lens of race promotes a more nuanced reading; it is Dee's African heritage but not her African American heritage that she wants to claim. She adopts an African name and African dress but is plainly not thrilled about the simple cabin in which Maggie and Mama live. She admires the churn top and dasher, the benches, the quilts of her ancestors; they are in the distant past, not in the present, like Mama and Maggie, who threaten to embarrass Dee with their simple country ways. The objects of contention in the story, the Lone Star and Walk Around the Mountain quilts, are significant not only because they are family heirlooms but because of their role in African American history, a history of which Dee demonstrates no awareness: since the time of slavery, African American women have used quilts to tell stories and send messages; moreover, quilts are widely believed to have been used as signals in the Underground Railroad (Tobin and Dobard 26–33, 80–81, 118–119; Baker and Pierce-Baker 309; Perry).

At the beginning of the story, Mama imagines that she is too black for Dee, saying, in her self-description at the end of the Johnny Carson daydream, "But of course all this does not show on television. I am the way my daughter would want me to be: a hundred pounds lighter, my skin like an uncooked barley pancake" (2013). Dee brings race directly to the forefront of the story when she explains why she changed her name: "I couldn't bear it any longer, being named after the people who oppress me" (2015). Mama points out that Dee is named after her aunt, and the name has a long history in their family. Ironically, Dee takes on an African name, Wangeroo Leewanika Kemanjo, and in doing so, she elides her African American heritage at the same time that she embraces her African heritage. And, as Helga Hoel points out, the "African" name she adopts is of questionable authenticity (37-38). Further, we can see this pattern continuing with her request for the quilts. Dee wants the quilts, not for "everyday use," as their African American makers intended, but for objects of art to link her back to her African roots. Dee is more attractive, more curvaceous, and more stylish than her sister Maggie. She has the benefit of the trendy African mystique while Maggie is scarred from the fire that consumed the family's first house, a loss that Dee did not mourn. Maggie's scars suggest the scars of three hundred years of African American slavery.

Dee has the university education while Maggie and Mama have the much different education of the fields, the crafts, the country folkways of their African American heritage. Even the two-dimensional Hakim emphasizes how far removed is Dee from her African American heritage; Hakim and his hair, his long goatee, his unpronounceable name, and philosophical doctrines are an index of how African Dee has become. Since Maggie, in the end, gets the quilts that Dee has asked for, the value system of the story is seen to be quite different from that of Dee, whose objections to Maggie's using the quilts are tantamount to a rejection of her African American heritage of manual labor and simple lifestyle.

Reading the story from the perspective of class can help the student to focus on and better understand the turning point of the story and denouement: when Dee asks for the family heirloom quilts and is refused them by Mama. Although Mama and Dee are alike in personality, confidence, assertiveness, and intelligence, Mama and Maggie have something more important in common; they are both working-class characters, while Dee has moved into the middle class. She carries herself, dresses, speaks, and conducts herself according to middle-class norms. Before she became educated and realized that her humble roots could be used to enhance her status, she was ashamed of her working-class origins. Mama tells us, "She wrote me once that no matter where we 'choose' to live, she will manage to come see us. But she will never bring her friends" (2014). We also learn that the "priceless" quilts that Dee now wants were the same ones that Mama tried to give her when she went away to college; at that time Dee didn't want them: "[She told me they were old-fashioned, out of style" (2017). Dee's new interest in her roots stems from her new awareness that aspects of her history can be used as accessories of style and as elements of interior decoration to elevate her in other people's eyes and to solidify her middle-class status; she can appear more intelligent, more compassionate, more thoughtful, more in touch with her heritage. She has brought Hakim to visit her family in order to use Mama and Maggie and the house she hates and the quilts she didn't want earlier to show him her humble roots. For her the dasher, the churn top, the quilts, and Hakim himself are fashion accessories, status symbols that Dee uses to show Mama and Maggie that she has a greater understanding and appreciation of her heritage than they do. She even tells Mama, "You just don't understand . . . your heritage" (2018). The irony is that the African American past Dee is denying links Mama and Maggie to the African heritage she desires so intently in a way that she could never experience, at least without a considerable change in mindset. Maggie will marry John Thomas, the local boy, and carry on the African American traditions and lifestyle that Mama taught her. Maggie will continue to quilt and churn butter and raise children and live proudly and simply; Dee, in objecting to Maggie's getting the quilts because "[s]he'd probably be backward enough to put them to everyday use" (2017) is rejecting her working-class black roots and substituting, in her plan to hang the quilts rather than use them, a more middle-class ethos, ironically getting further and further from the roots she thinks she is attempting to reclaim.

The irony of Dee's plan can be further emphasized by honing in on the quilts themselves and the way that their intended uses differentiates between classes. Mama and Maggie see them as items of everyday use. They both know how to make them and know that they are made to keep people warm. However, Dee sees them as works of art to hang on walls. Poor people make quilts; rich people buy them. To the poor, quilts are made to keep people warm and dashers are made to churn butter; to the rich these items become fashionable art objects with which to decorate dwellings. Dee says that she wants the quilts, but not the ones that have been stitched by a machine around the edges. Mama says, "That'll make them last better." Again, the emphasis is on use. Dee says, "That's not the point. . . . These are all pieces of dresses Grandma used to wear. She did all this stitching by hand. Imagine!" (2017). This statement is also ironic. Mama doesn't have to imagine; she knows. She quilts by hand also. Again we see the irony in Dee's words: she is out of line by proclaiming these facts as if Mama didn't know them first hand. Dee didn't want these quilts until they became fashionable, a fact that Walker emphasizes.

When students are divided into small groups and asked to use first gender, then race, and finally class as analytical categories in their consideration of "Everyday Use," with each group sharing their insights with the class as a whole on the first topic before moving on to discuss the next, they experience both enlightenment and frustration. While the close focus on each discrete topic can generate many insights, such as those discussed by Michael above, this method also demonstrates to students how difficult it is to discuss how race functions in the story, for example, without also discussing class or gender. For example, is Mama consigned to a life of poverty because she is black, because she is a female, or because she is working class? All three factors would seem to be causative here and not easily separated. At this point the formula *race + gender = class* can be brought up for discussion. It is equally difficult to separate gender and race in considering how the central symbol of the story, the quilts, functions in "Everyday Use." This exercise is valuable because it demonstrates how powerful the categories of gender, race, and class can be when used as heuristics; it is also useful in showing students how these terms are imbricated.

A review of the scholarship on "Everyday Use" reveals that almost no one has discussed how the story should be taught. As a starting point, we recommend, for an undergraduate class, the third chapter of Robert MacMahon's *Thinking About Literature*, "Alice Walker's 'Everyday Use': A Summary and Analysis of Characters and Motives." There are a number of other secondary sources that we have found most useful when examining the story from the perspectives of race, class, and gender; they are listed in the annotated bibliography that appears at the end of this essay. Also available is a two-part series of films from Films for the Humanities & Sciences (www. films.com; 800-257-5126): *Alice Walker: "Everyday Use"* and *Alice Walker: A Stitch in Time*. The former is a 26-minute dramatization of the story and the latter is a 22-minute interview with Alice Walker that focuses on specific issues of gender, race, and class that the story raises.

We believe that "Everyday Use" is an ideal story with which to demonstrate both the power and the pitfalls of using gender, race, and class as analytical categories with which to approach a work of fiction in the undergraduate literature classroom. In reading "Everyday Use," Michael experienced a story about black, working-class women and thereby became more open to the history, values, and concerns of people who are completely different from him in terms of gender, race, and class. Thus, the story is valuable not only as a well-crafted work of fiction but as a means of eroding the cultural egocentrism that many students bring to college. If these students are exposed to "Everyday Use" and its complexities, a shift in cultural consciousness may occur. As Gary Saul Morson says,

> To engage with a work, one projects oneself into the alien world of another culture and another time, into the mind of any author who judged and saw things differently from the way we usually do, and into the thoughts and feelings of characters quite unlike ourselves.

Walker's story can stand on its own as a work of art, but it can also function as a catalyst to put us on the road to a multicultural, enlightened society. This change can begin with a close examination of Walker's "heroic figures of rebellion" in "Everyday Use."

## WORKS CITED

Baker, Houston, and Charlotte Pierce-Baker. "Patches, Quilts and Community in Alice Walker's 'Everyday Use.'" *Alice Walker: Critical Perspectives Past and Present*. Ed. Henry Louis Gates, Jr., and K A. Appiah. New York: Amistad Press, Inc. 1993. 309–316.

Farrell, Susan. "Fight vs. Flight: A Re-evaluation of Dee in Alice Walker's 'Everyday Use.'" Electronic Collection A83585372: RN A83585372. 1998 Newberry College.

Hoel, Helga. "Personal Names and Heritage: Alice Walker's 'Everyday Use,'" *American Studies in Scandinavia* 31.1 (1999): 34–42.

Kane, Patricia. "The Prodigal Daughter in Alice Walker's 'Everyday Use.'" *Notes on Contemporary Literature* 15.2 (1985): 7.

MacMahon, Robert. "Alice Walker's 'Everyday Use': A Summary and Analysis of Characters and Motives." *Thinking About Literature.* Portsmouth, New Hampshire: Heinemann, 2002.

Morson, Gary Saul. "Teaching as Impersonation." *Literary Imagination* 4.2 (Spring 2002). 145–151.

Perry, Regenia. *Harriet Powers's Bible Quilts.* Rizzoli Art Series. Series Editor Norma Broude, n.p.; n.d.

Smith, Barbara. "Toward a Black Feminist Criticism." *The New Feminist Criticism: Essays on Women, Literature, and Theory.* Ed. Elaine Showalter. New York: Pantheon Books, 1985. 168–85.

Tobin, Jacqueline L., and Raymond G. Dobard. *Hidden in Plain View: The Secret Story of Quilts and the Underground Railroad.* New York: Doubleday, 1999.

Walker, Alice. "Everyday Use." *Anthology of American Literature,* Vol. 2, Eighth Edition. Ed. George McMichael and others. Upper Saddle River, New Jersey: Pearson Prentice Hall, 2004. 2002–2018.

———. "In Search of Our Mothers' Gardens." *In Search of Our Mothers' Gardens: Womanist Prose by Alice Walker.* 1974. New York: Harcourt, Brace Jovanovich, 1983. 231–243.

Below appear some secondary sources that will be helpful to the instructor who wishes to use race, gender, and class as analytical categories in teaching "Everyday Use":

Baker, Houston, A. Jr., and Charlotte Pierce-Baker. "Patches: Quilts and Community in Alice Walker's 'Everyday Use'." *Alice Walker: Critical Perspectives Past and Present.* Ed. Henry Louis Gates, Jr., and K. A. Appiah. New York: Amistad Press, Inc. 1993. 309–316.

Quilting patches could be defined as the faded glory of the already gone, and they are compared to women as they are a liminal element between wholes. Weaving, shaping, sculpting and quilting provide responses to chaos; they are survival strategies in the face of dispersal. Traditional African cultures were scattered by the Europeans, and the female European tradition of quilting became a black women's folk art. Those outside the sorority of quilting often fail to understand the dignity and grace of quilt makers taking haphazardly scattered patches and combining them into articles of everyday use. A discussion of the short story "Everyday Use" with particular emphasis on the black woman's art of quilting and what the quilts represent follows. Maggie is described as the "arisen goddess" of the story. She goes from inglorious to goddess due to her long ancestral memory and knowledge of quilt-making. Links between "Everyday Use" and *The Color Purple* are discussed.

Bauer, Margaret D., "Alice Walker: Another Southern Writer Criticizing Codes Not Put to 'Everyday Use'." *Studies in Short Fiction* 29 (1992): 143–151.

Parallels are drawn between the stories in Alice Walker's *In Love and Trouble* and works by authors such as Katherine Anne Porter, Flannery

O'Connor, William Faulkner, and Eudora Welty. Walker writes about the South as a place and a group of people she loves but is troubled by also.

Christian, Barbara, T., "Alice Walker: The Black Woman Artist as Wayward." *"Everyday Use" Alice Walker.* Ed. Barbara T. Christian. New Brunswick: Rutgers University Press, 1994: 123–148.
Walker's large body of writing contains recurrent motifs, including the black woman as creator and the black woman's level of wholeness reflecting the health of the community. Walker's works tend to be centered on black women, especially *In Love and Trouble, Can't Keep a Good Woman Down,* "In Search of Our Mothers' Gardens," *Meridian, and The Color Purple,* This tendency is also reflected in her personal effort to rescue the works of Zora Neale Hurston from oblivion. Rather than being elaborate in her writing, she is organically spare, and she uses a concentrated distillation of language. Several works are discussed in the context of black protagonists, other black authors, cultural nationalism, and the psychological impact of oppression.

Walker is drawn to the process of gat-making as a model for her own craft. Out of everyday, random, unconnected pieces come clarity, imagination and beauty. Walker not only embraces quilts as "high" art; she also admires their functional beauty as well. "In Search of Our Mothers' Gardens" and "Everyday Use" are discussed in relation to women's art and quilt-making. *Meridian* and other stories are discussed along with a more lengthy treatment of Celie and other characters in *The Color Purple.*

Farrell, Susan. "Fight vs. Flight: A Re-evaluation of Dee in Alice Walker's 'Everyday Use'." Electronic Collection: A83585372 RN: A83585372. 1998 Newberry College.
Most people agree that Walker's story is about a mother's awakening to one daughter's superficiality and to the other's deep-seated understanding of heritage. A reading such as this condemns the older, more "worldly" sister. This popular view is far too simple, and Dee should be commended for several things. Because the story is told through the first-person narration of Mama, and all first-person narrators tend to be unreliable, the reader needs to reflect critically upon Mama's narration. For example, Mama may be projecting her fears onto Maggie about Dee's arrival. We are told through Mama, and since we never get inside Maggie's head, it is impossible to know what Maggie is thinking. We find out, during the Johnny Carson fantasy, that Mama is ashamed of her appearance and will be nervous until Dee leaves. Mama says Dee would wish her to be more slender and lighter in color, but we cannot know if this is truly Dee's wish or not.

Mama remembers Dee as being self-centered and demanding, but she also remembers her as determined fighter who has style. Mama can't imagine looking a white man in the eye, and Dee acts as if she has never heard the world tell her "no." Dee is educated, and perhaps the "simple pleasures" Mama and Maggie enjoy are not enough for complex, modern African-Americans. Dee will move on, and Maggie will remain. She will remain the same as she and many of her ancestors have been for centuries. She will remain unchallenging, uneducated, and unconvinced that the world owes her more. Dee's power and fire and active seeking of a better lot in life should be admired, not deplored.

Dee's new name is not a throwing off of her heritage but a reclaiming of her past. It is an active step to rising above what has been allowed her by the dominant class and ideology. Walker's novel *Meridian* is also mentioned in the same light in a short discussion.

Kane, Patricia. "The Prodigal Daughter in Alice Walker's 'Everyday Use.'" *Notes on Contemporary Literature.* 15.2 (1985): 7.

Walker's story is a variation on the prodigal son story with which we are all familiar. It is humorous and it pleases us by having the fatted calf received by the stay-at-home, not the wanderer. The difference in the ending suggests that when the story is told by and about women, the tale takes on different values. This is a useful look at a variation of the archetypal prodigal child vs. the familiar daughter and the inversion of values it suggests.

Keating, Gail. "Alice Walker: In Praise of Maternal Heritage." *The Literary Griot.* 6.1 (1994): 26–37.

This is a look at maternal heritage that utilizes Alice Walker's essay, "In Search of Our Mothers' Gardens," as a framework from within which to discuss *The Color Purple* and "Everyday Use." Walker acknowledges the huge contributions of women and traces the influence of women through her own matrilineage. Nina Auerbach's book *Communities of Women* is also cited as demonstrating how males are out to conquer the world while women have no such aspirations. Virginia Woolf's *A Room of One's Own* is also examined. Walker says we must broaden our conception of Art. Women use all sorts of creative media in artistic expression, even though they are often not recognized as such. The same idea is ingrained in Walker's "Everyday Use." Both Mama and Dee recognize the value of the quilts in question because they both realize, in different fashions, that they are art. They are made with pieces of their history and heritage and they have been assembled with love. Dee doesn't understand that Mama and Maggie have found a natural outlet for their creativity.

Willa Cather's fiction examines some of the same values. Cather was much concerned with the female tradition and its roots. Walker's hugely successful novel *The Color Purple* is also examined in the same light as the other works. Quilt-Making (and therefore matrilineal heritage) is found in *The*

*Color Purple* as well. Celie, the main character in this novel, also understands and values the simplicity in her life, and this makes her wise. Celie's freedom is provided through her ability to sew. Maternal heritage is examined in each of the works with special attention to the two by Walker.

McMahon, Robert. *Thinking About Literature*. Portsmouth: Heinemann, 2002.

This book provides practical advice about how to teach a variety of topics and stories. Chapter three, "Alice Walker's 'Everyday Use': A Summary and Analysis of Characters and Motives," is of special interest. A summary of the story is given which ties the story to the prodigal son story, and then some pedagogical advice is given. The chapter provides some "getting acquainted" reading exercises and some thought-prompting questions to get students' minds on the subject and theme of the story. Then, different situations are outlined, including "Dee vs. Maggie," "Mama's Moral Character," "Why Does Mama Take the Quilts from Dee and Give Them to Maggie?" More class-related exercises are given with suggested readings of the story designed to motivate students to think about the story in less obvious ways.

Tuten, Nancy. "Alice Walker's 'Everyday Use'." *Explicator*. 51.2 (1993):25–28.

Tuten focuses on the way in which both Dee and Mama use language to their advantage. Dee uses language to condescend to and subjugate her sister and mother. The first-person narrator/mother seems helpless, at the beginning of the story, but this changes as the story progresses. Mama gains control through her language. Mama and Maggie are definitely joined as a team when Dee shuns her family identity. Taking a new name is an exercise in language. Dee trades the language of her oppressors for the language of her past. Mama gains power when she does this. This shift in power is subtly illustrated in a late-story shift in tense from present and future to past. In the end, Mama shows power by not mentioning Dee at all in the final paragraph of the story while she mentions Maggie twice by name. The characters' power is achieved by language, and it is Mama who retains the most power by the end of the story.

Walker, Alice. "In Search of Our Mothers' Gardens." 1974. *In Search of Our Mothers' Gardens: Womanist Prose by Alice Walker*. New York: Harcourt Brace Jovanovich, 1983: 231–243.

Walker asks from where does she, the writer, come and what is her tradition? She explores these questions by relating a female heritage that makes her different from other writers. She traces the images of black women in literature and discusses in depth the creative legacy of ordinary, unknown black women in the South. She uses her own matrilineage as an example. Black women of yesteryear had no traditional creative outlet for their genius, so they made their own in everyday activities such as quilting because these were the only outlets the dominant society left them. Gardening, quilting and cooking are similar such arts, so subtle, natural, and culturally ingrained that the artist may have been unaware of her creation. Time has transformed such creation—considered mundane in the past—into high art, as the anonymous quilt in the Smithsonian testifies. A discussion of that quilt's impact on the author ties in her more recent work, with its themes of black women's creativity, and her own transformation.

LAURIE MCMILLAN

# *Telling a Critical Story: Alice Walker's* In Search of Our Mothers' Gardens

Since the 1970s, the personal voice has been brought to bear more and more often on literary criticism, leading Nancy Miller to describe the 1990s as a time of "confessional culture" that manifested itself in academia with "personal criticism and other autobiographical acts" (*But Enough* xiv, 1–2).[1] Though we have now entered a new century, the trend does not appear to be waning, yet autobiographical criticism is still often greeted with hesitation. While many scholars using personal writing in their criticism claim with Ruth Behar that such work is well-suited to addressing "serious social issues" (B2), critics point out that the personal voice does not actually effect change. Daphne Patai, for example, announces that "personal disclosures" and "self-reflexivity [do] not change reality. [Such approaches do] not redistribute income, gain political rights for the powerless, create housing for the homeless, or improve health" (A52). Despite the clear lack of *direct* political intervention wrought by personal criticism, however, I am not willing to dismiss it as completely irrelevant to questions of social justice. Alice Walker's *In Search of Our Mothers' Gardens* (1983) is one text that shows how self-conscious autobiography can be a useful tool to wield in a politically-motivated critical practice. Three of Walker's essays in particular—"Beyond the Peacock," "Looking for Zora," and "In Search of Our Mothers' Gardens"—demonstrate how personal criticism can use performative ele-

*Journal of Modern Literature* 29:1 (2004): pp. 107–123. © 2004 Indiana University Press.

ments to increase its effectiveness. Walker's particular style of performance involves the use of story narratives that emphasize the highly constructed and textually mediated qualities of her self-representation. Readers are thus encouraged to interpret Walker's writing on multiple levels—not only as personal testimony but also as literary criticism and allegory—effectively bringing the personal voice into criticism without falling into traps of essentialism. As it renegotiates readings of the past, then, *In Search of Our Mothers' Gardens* demonstrates the way literary criticism can use performative autobiography to influence cultural practices and potentially change material lives.

## The Debate Over Personal Criticism

### i. The pros

Although the reasons why critics choose to write autobiographically vary enormously, three factors are central to the use of personal criticism in Alice Walker and other writers who are committed to literary criticism as a vehicle for social change. First, autobiography allows scholars writing from traditionally marginalized positions to simultaneously assert the legitimacy of their viewpoints and challenge perspectives that have been presented as disinterested and universal. Pamela Klass Mittlefehldt thus claims the personal voice as a way "to assume the validity and authority of one's voice, the significance of one's experience, and the implicit value of one's insight and perspective" (197). Such a gesture is political in itself on occasions when it challenges ideas about who is allowed to speak. At the same time, autobiographical criticism has the power to change dominant discourses by raising awareness of views outside of the mainstream. Many black feminist critics especially prize the disruptive power of scholarship: Barbara Smith proposes a "highly innovative" literary criticism that the black feminist critic "would think and write out of her own identity" (137), while scholars such as Deborah McDowell and Valerie Smith believe that attention to the experiences of black women may potentially radicalize discourses of race and gender. When followed to its logical outcome, the wariness of false universals and the valuing of multiple viewpoints lead to a vision of literary criticism that perpetually attends to issues of difference. Mae Henderson thus calls for "a multiplicity of 'interested readings' which resists the totalizing character of much theory and criticism" (162). Such a vision may be at least partially realized through autobiographical criticism as it focuses on the local and the particular.

Autobiographical criticism may do political work not only by acting as an antidote to universalizing tendencies but also by affirming the value of personal writing, a genre long devalued in its associations with both women and African Americans. The slogan connecting the personal and the political in the Women's Liberation Movement implicitly points to a long tradition of women's writing that includes diaries, memoirs, and letters. Autobiography has also figured strongly in African American traditions, often in variations of the slave narrative.[2] However, such personal writing has begun to receive widespread critical attention only in the last twenty-five years, and it still is often read as a sign of the times instead of being considered on the basis of its own literary merit.[3] Embracing autobiography in literary criticism, then, is one way of claiming personal writing as a valuable genre. Jane Tompkins further suggests that traditional scholarly writing tends to maintain "the public-private dichotomy, which is to say, the public-private *hierarchy*" that "is a founding condition of female oppression" (1104). She calls for more personal modes of writing because "to adhere to the conventions is to uphold a male standard of rationality that militates against women's being recognized as culturally legitimate sources of knowledge" (1105). Other scholars have similarly turned to autobiographical criticism as part of an effort to reclaim and revalue a heritage of life-writing while introducing alternative methods into a critical realm long dominated by white males.

The use of autobiography in criticism may finally be important as it inspires change not only in the academy but also outside it, as readers are drawn into a culture of activism. Personal criticism has the potential to inspire political action in its readers in two ways: through the author's engagement in the subject matter and through connections forged between literary criticism and material conditions. Many scholars who have experimented with autobiographical criticism have brought new enthusiasm to their work, leading Marianne Torgovnick to suggest that a personal investment is important because it can infuse writing with an "eloquence" that engages both the author and the reader (qtd. in Williams 421). Frances Murphy Zauhar concurs, observing that when "the model of the detached analytical" critic has been replaced with the critic "engaged in and even transformed by [. . .] literature" (107), the reader is more likely to become personally invested in the project as well (115). As personal criticism appeals to both the "heart and intellect," readers are more likely to continue the political work initiated by the text (Behar B2). Furthermore, the personal voice often renders criticism more widely accessible than would traditional academic prose. As Ruth Behar argues, one of the most compelling reasons to use a personal voice is the "desire to abandon the alienating 'metalanguage' that closes, rather than opens, the doors of academe to all those who wish to enter" (B2). Autobiographical criticism, then, often sparks enthusiastic responses in a wide range of readers who are drawn into the text by the scholar's visible personal investment.

Personal criticism may also move readers towards activism by bringing literary criticism out of a purely textual realm and into contact with the socio-material. Jane Tompkins thus turns to personal writing because academic language is too far "from the issues that make feminism matter. That make *her* matter" (1104); she hopes that using an openly subjective discourse will allow her to better connect scholarship to her lived experiences. The autobiographical anecdote (a distinct kind of personal writing) enacts a similar gesture toward material conditions.[4] Catherine Gallagher and Stephen Greenblatt suggest that the anecdote acts as "an interruption that lets one sense that there is something—the 'real'—outside of the historical narrative" (50), while Joel Fineman explains that the anecdote is always literary but "is nevertheless directly pointed towards or rooted in the real" (qtd. in Gallop 3).[5] Of course, literary criticism tends to be connected in many ways to the cultural milieu whether or not it includes personal anecdotes, but autobiographical writing makes such connections explicit. Readers are then more likely to recognize what is at stake in the particular critical project, and they may feel compelled to join the dramatized struggle in which the author is engaged. Bringing autobiography to criticism can potentially inspire social change, then, as it challenges dominant views, values personal writing, and inspires activism through its investment in the criticism as a response to lived conditions.

## ii. The cons

While many scholars have used the personal voice to invigorate their critical work and address injustices, the reactions of other scholars have not been wholly positive. Although some resistance to personal criticism may stem from defensiveness or unwillingness to reconsider received paradigms, four potential problems may keep personal criticism from being politically effective. First, because personal writing by nature has an inward focus, it can end up being self-absorbed and limited in scope rather than ultimately moving towards social change. If a narrative is meaningful only to the person who wrote it or to a select group of listeners, its political power becomes moot. Linda Kauffman thus wonders, "Are 'we' feminist scholars solipsistically talking only to ourselves?" (1156), and Nancy Miller explains, "At its worst, the autobiographical act in criticism can seem to belong to a scene of rhizomatic, networked, privileged selves" (*Getting Personal* 25). Daphne Patai puts it even more forcefully: "I doubt that I am the only one who is weary of the nouveau solipsism [in academic writing]—all this individual and collective breast-beating, grandstanding, and plain old egocentricity" (A52). Any personal writing that does not consider who the audience is and what it hopes to accomplish is likely to fall into such a pattern.

Second, because the personal is often considered less valid than traditional styles of academic writing, those who use such an approach risk being silenced and/or reinforcing gendered dichotomies. Many academics will immediately take scholarship less seriously when it incorporates a personal voice, leading Nancy Miller to comment, "[W]e're not sure we want ourselves going to the bathroom in public—especially as women and feminists—our credibility is low enough as it is" (*Getting Personal* 8). Using the personal voice may also be problematic in feminist work since the implied values of "sincerity and authenticity [. . .] inevitably lock us back into the very dichotomies (male intellect versus female intuition; head versus body, etc.) that so many feminists have spent so much time trying to dismantle" (Kauffman 1162). Such risks are serious matters because criticism intended to effect social change may end up contributing to the binary thinking that is one of the major roots of unjust practices.

Third, autobiographical criticism can inhibit dialogue by relying on the authority of experience. Here, an "authentic" voice uses subjectivity as a way of silencing alternate opinions, perpetuating rather than disrupting the claim to authority traditionally associated with the objective voice. David Simpson calls this maneuver "invok[ing] 'liberal authenticity'" and says it "can be reduced to a statement like 'I felt it, therefore it is true'" (qtd. in Heller A9). Linda Kauffman further explains, "By insisting on the authority of my personal experience, I effectively muzzle dissent and muffle your investigation into my motives" (1156). In some cases, the association between personal experience and scholarship can dictate, either implicitly or explicitly, who is "allowed" to discuss women's literature or minority literature.[6] If literary criticism hopes to address injustices, a personal voice that silences other voices is ineffective because it reinforces a model of relation based on domination.

Finally, personal criticism often rests in an identity politics as one member of a group speaks representatively, ignoring differences within that group. That is, many times when scholars write from a personal perspective, they point to their position based on gender, race, or another cultural marker, and they seem to be "speaking *as*" a member of a particular group or "speaking *for*" a particular group (Miller, *Getting Personal* 20). David Simpson labels this a "native identity politics," and he translates it as, "I felt it. I am white. Therefore, this is what white people feel'" (qtd. in Heller A9). Such positioning becomes ineffective on the one hand because it can reduce cultural groups to biological functions, as if all women are the same or all African American women are the same. In addition, however, even when cultural influences are acknowledged, an identity politics can develop in which differences among people within a single group are ignored. Furthermore, when people speak representatively of an entire group, they also tend to assert that group's difference from (an)other group(s), reinforcing problematic oppositions and stabilizing categories that tend to be fluid and hybrid in actuality. Each of these four drawbacks to personal criticism could lead to a critical practice that inadvertently perpetuates rather than changes oppressive practices.

### iii. Self-conscious negotiations and Alice Walker

Using the personal voice in literary criticism may potentially be either revolutionary *or* conservative. As scholars have used autobiography and encountered both its inspirations and its frustrations, however, they have worked through my list of "pros" and "cons" in a number of fruitful ways. The most successful negotiations tend to bring poststructural theory into autobiographical practice, so that the critics simultaneously construct and deconstruct a personal story as they write with highly self-conscious and self-reflexive styles.[7] Such literary criticism is *performative* rather than naturalized. "Naturalized" personal criticism would use an autobiographical voice that presents itself as transparent, as if reading about a person is to fully know and understand that person and his or her experiences. "Performative" personal criticism, on the other hand, highlights the way an identity is taken up and used in a certain way, drawing attention to autobiography's mediation through language and cultural context. As a performative approach keeps people from being reduced to their representations, notions of identity remain fluid and changeable; an essentialist identity politics can then be resisted rather than enacted through the autobiographical criticism.

Although Walker's *In Search* essays were written before the heyday of poststructural theory, they anticipate the theoretical turn to performative writing to a great degree. Walker uses the story narrative to combine her highly particularized experience with literary allusion and symbolism, helping her to bring "real life" onto the page while paradoxically highlighting the fictionalized presentation of that "life." Walker is thus able to achieve the positive effects of personal criticism while largely avoiding its pitfalls. Like much personal criticism aiming to effect socio-political change, Walker's volume challenges dominant ideas of the time by asserting the value of marginalized voices (those of African American women in particular in this case); it explicitly values autobiographical writing; and it calls readers "beyond contemplation to action" through Walker's own investment in the text and through attention to unjust social conditions (Mittlefehldt 206).[8] If Walker presented herself in naturalized terms, however, much of her political work would be sabotaged with the implication that race and gender are stable categories that define the individual. Instead, Walker presents herself as a somewhat fictionalized character, inhabiting certain roles in each narrative. This turn to performance not only moves beyond self-absorption as it attends to audience reception, but it also implies a fluid and changing notion of subjectivity that avoids gendered dichotomies, resists claims to authenticity, and problematizes an identity politics. In other words, while Walker's autobiography accomplishes political goals, its performative story elements keep it from operating within foundationalist assumptions that could ultimately reinforce the status quo.

## Alice Walker tells a critical story

Although Alice Walker's *In Search of Our Mothers' Gardens* works as an integrated whole in many ways, three essays in particular—"Beyond the Peacock" (1975), "Looking for Zora" (1975), and "In Search of Our Mothers' Gardens" (1974)—exemplify a personal criticism performed through story narratives.[9] The three essays share a sense of quest and tend to comment upon one another as themes and symbols are woven together among and between them, yet each moves in a distinct direction. The importance of personal story narratives is suggested not only through the quest themes but also as Walker "signifies" on the writers Flannery O'Connor, Zora Neale Hurston, and Virginia Woolf. "Signifying," as Henry Louis Gates explains it, is a critical approach with African American roots that enacts repetition with difference. The repetition pays tribute to the precursor writer, while the difference is a way of revising the precursor's story or practice, often exposing its limitations.[10] Walker's particular choices of precursor writers highlight the importance of story that guides her personal critical voice. The fictional elements of Walker's personal stories are finally suggested in the use of three motifs in the essays—houses, mother(s), and gardens—that bring the literal and symbolic together. As the motifs are introduced in detailed and concrete ways, they perform several functions: they particularize Walker's background; they bring Walker's critical work in touch with material existence; *and* they operate as symbols with significance beyond Walker's personal experience. The work that the essays aim to do, the writers that they draw upon, and the symbols that they use come together to create a model of a radical and performative personal criticism.

Although "Beyond the Peacock," "Looking for Zora," and "In Search of Our Mothers' Gardens" are guided by different purposes, they share a sense of quest that is suggested in their titles. The phrases "beyond," "looking," and "in search" all point to dissatisfaction with what is currently visible and a commitment to bring into sight that which has remained hidden. This sense of quest manifests itself in the essays with an emphasis on process— Walker writes about journeys, both literal and figurative, which the essays simultaneously recount and enact. That is, the essays present an ongoing process of discovery and recovery rather than a final destination of completed work. The focus on quest positions the essays within a long story tradition, and it also adds a mythic dimension to Walker's writing. Quests, after all, are grand and important rather than ordinary or everyday. In Walker, however, the ordinary and grand are brought together: she tells simple stories of ordinary lives, but these stories are written as a matter of communal survival. Walker is very aware of the history of oppression of African Americans, and she recognizes the importance of building a heritage to help African Americans thrive. Ruth Behar might have been characterizing Walker's essays when writing that "the best autobiographical scholarly writing sets off on a personal quest and ultimately produces a redrawn map of social terrain" (Behar B2). Walker's quest to help claim, recover, and build upon stories is a means to her own survival as a writer, but it is also a way to support the African American community.

Despite the common quest theme, the essays move in quite distinct directions. "Beyond the Peacock" both problematizes and affirms an integrationist approach to literature through the specific example of Flannery O'Connor. Here, Walker recounts a visit she and her mother made to one of their former homes and the former home of O'Connor, just down the road. In the course of the visit, Walker muses on O'Connor's significance and on her own troubled response to a privileged white Southern writer. "Looking for Zora" turns to the building of a black women's literary heritage as it enacts and encourages recovery work that can provide markers of the past for future generations. Walker tells of her journey to Florida, where she tracked down Hurston's burial spot so as to mark the site with a headstone. "In Search of Our Mothers' Gardens" continues to affirm an African American women's literary heritage. In order to explore the roots of black women's literature, Walker considers the plight of black women and the creative work of both Phillis Wheatley and her own mother under incredibly adverse conditions. While Wheatley may be the more conventional literary foremother, Walker values her own mother's use of gardening as an alternative expression of black women's creative ability. Together, the essays turn again and again to the invisibility of a black women's literary heritage and begin to build—or rebuild—a tradition of storytelling and creative expression that can help support the African American community.

Walker's commitment to story as a way of moving her personal voice into a cultural conversation becomes apparent as she signifies upon Flannery O'Connor, Zora Neale Hurston, and Virginia Woolf. In "Beyond the Peacock," Walker adopts O'Connor's mission in writing but modifies her use of fiction. As Walker understands it, O'Connor writes about characters "in times of extreme crisis and loss" in order to help readers recognize their "responsibility for other human beings" (56).[11] Walker similarly seems intent on inspiring "both personal and cultural levels [of transformation]" (Mittlefehldt 206). However, O'Connor tends to offer negative examples while Walker portrays positive, even utopic, models. This difference becomes apparent as Walker retells O'Connor's "Everything That Rises Must Converge" to her own mother. While O'Connor's story focuses on a mother and son who have trouble getting along because of their different perspectives, Walker and her mother tend to respect one another's viewpoints. For example, Walker changes her description of O'Connor's character from "old" to "middle-aged" due to her mother's objections (49). Walker's narrative also varies from O'Connor's because it uses a first person autobiographical voice rather than a third person fictional perspective, allowing Walker to highlight the way her background affects her reading of O'Connor. Still, Walker comments on O'Connor's Catholicism in order to bring fiction and biography together, and she embeds the retelling of O'Connor's stories in her own narrative. Despite the differences, then, the connections between the two writers throughout this essay draw attention to the stylized aspects of Walker's personal narrative.

Zora Neale Hurston stands in contrast to O'Connor, for Walker fully embraces Hurston as a role model in "Looking for Zora" and, in the process, makes storytelling more central.[12] Dianne Sadoff argues that the "structure and material [of "Looking for Zora"] imitates and so recalls [Hurston's] *Mules and Men*" (12), in part because both Hurston and Walker return to the South with an "ideal" vision that is revealed as false through their use of "self-irony" (14). More importantly, both Hurston and Walker are interested in claiming and preserving their African American heritage. Their journeys and interviews allow them to come to story in community with others, while their publications are a means of both saving and sharing what they have found. Additionally, although both Hurston and Walker present their quests autobiographically, they both use the term "lies," which subtly recasts expectations of autobiography. In *Mules and Men,* the people Hurston interviews commonly call their folktales and legends "lies." When Walker references these "black folk tales that were 'made and used on the spot,' to take a line from Zora" (98), she echoes her own lines from a few pages earlier, where she had described her claim to be Hurston's niece as a "profoundly *useful* lie" (95, Walker's emphasis). In each case, stories ("lies") are treasured for their usefulness rather than their factual veracity. Walker thus demonstrates her willingness to take on a role (such as that of Hurston's niece) in order to accomplish a mission, and she also suggests that even "lies" can contain some measure of truth: Hurston "*is* [her] aunt," even though the familial bond is a figurative rather than a literal one (102). As she uses the term "lies" and Hurston's approaches, then, Walker implies that her personal writing may be partly folktale—a narrative to be shared on a storefront where its significance is based on what it might symbolize—what it might accomplish—rather than on how closely it follows actual events.

Walker finally signifies on Virginia Woolf, particularly her *A Room of One's Own,* in "In Search of Our Mothers' Gardens." Both writers combine attention to socio-material conditions with performance and symbolism. However, the African American oppression Walker writes of tends to be more horrific than the injustices suffered by the middle-class white women of Woolf's text, and Walker becomes more personally involved in her text than does Woolf. In her well-known volume, Woolf argues that women have been categorically denied the conditions necessary to produce literature—a fixed income and a private space in which to work. Walker similarly considers the material circumstances that have affected the literary production of African American women, but to do so, she inserts relevant details into passages quoted from Woolf's work:

> "For it needs little skill and psychology to be sure that a highly gifted girl who had tried to use her gift for poetry would have been so thwarted and hindered by contrary instincts [add 'chains, guns, the lash, the ownership of one's body by someone else, submission to an alien religion'], that she must have lost her health and sanity to a certainty."
>                   (Woolf qtd. in Walker 235; bracketed phrases are Walker's)

Walker thus uses Woolf's ideas but re-contextualizes them so that they speak to the experiences of Phillis Wheatley, as well as to the situation of the many black women who were unable to produce creative writing despite a potential talent. At the same time, the change Walker is working towards becomes more pressing because the oppression she catalogues makes Woolf's concerns pale in comparison.

Walker also signifies on Woolf's use of a persona in *A Room of One's Own.* Although Woolf uses "I" throughout her text, she separates herself from this "I" near the start of the volume: "'I' is only a convenient term for somebody who has no real being. Lies will flow from my lips, but there may perhaps be some truth mixed up with them" (Woolf 4).[13] The use of a persona allows Woolf to use symbolism throughout her text to make points on multiple levels. For example, she writes that "a man's figure rose to intercept" her just as her thoughts were running wild, and he compelled her to walk on the path (6), an image related to the discussions of boundaries, transgressions, and gendered positions that Woolf continues throughout her text. Such an approach calls for readers to actively interpret rather than passively receive ideas, so that "it is for [the reader] to seek out [. . .] truth and to decide whether any part of it is worth keeping" (Woolf 4-5). Alice Walker does not adopt a persona as Woolf does, but neither does she "reject her predecessor's self-neutralizing aesthetic and voice-dropping narrative practice" (Allan 132). Instead, Walker combines the performance of Woolf with an insistence on her own material and interested existence in relation to her text. Walker emphasizes the text as performance by introducing the importance of story and using metaphorical language. "In Search" thus begins with a metaphorical poem, and Walker insists on her own identity as a storyteller: "[T]hrough years of listening to my mother's stories of her life, I have absorbed not only the stories themselves, but something of the manner in which she spoke, something of the urgency that involves the knowledge that her stories—like her life—must be recorded" (240). Here, "stories" and "lives" become intermingled, and stories themselves become ubiquitous—they are unconsciously "absorbed." Walker's extensive use of literary symbolism continues to foreground performative aspects of her narrative. Still, Walker clings to her own material situation in a way that Woolf does not, explaining that she looks in her own backyard—her personal past—in order to answer larger questions about black women's literary heritage. Walker's combination of allegory and direct involvement in her text encourages readers to engage in textual interpretation in order to understand and act on issues that affect actual human beings.

While Walker's playful recuperations of O'Connor, Hurston, and Woolf constantly highlight the importance of storytelling in her personal criticism, the use of figurative language reinforces the performative elements of her autobiographical writing. Nancy Miller suggests that symbolic language is particularly suited to writing that calls for social change:

> [M]etaphors are to be taken very seriously [. . .] as an economical way both to theorize outside of systems dependent on a unitary signature [. . .] and to imagine in the material of language what hasn't yet come [. . .] into social being. [. . .] Perhaps what seems most "feminist" to me about the uses of both metaphor and narrative criticism is the self-consciousness these modes of analysis tend to display about their own processes of theorization.
>
> (*Miller Getting Personal* xii)

Walker's essays use three important motifs to render their work both con-cretely specific *and* symbolically representative: houses, mothers, and flow-ers or gardens. As the personal becomes presented as story complete with metaphorical language, readers are encouraged to interpret the narrative both literally and figuratively rather than reduce it to either one person's experience (and thus not terribly important in a wide-ranging sense) or to a "mere" story (and thus not terribly pressing because it is not "real" or "true"). Each of the three motifs functions among the essays in particular ways to forward Walker's project and her call for others to engage in issues of social justice and literary heritage. While each is always literal on one level, houses also symbolize literary roots and traditions that take various forms, the mother points to literary precursors, and flowers or gardens represent an idealized field of African American women's literary heritage. The images together work within a single though diverse project of literary recuperation and growth.

The houses, as concrete manifestations of injustices, graphically communicate the disparity between the preservation of white and black cultural heritages.[14] In "Beyond the Peacock," Walker's former house is in the middle of a muddy pasture, surrounded by fences and "no trespassing" signs (43–44). When Walker and her mother eventually reach it, they see that two of the four rooms have rotted away; the two that remain are used to store hay. The whole scene represents the roots and the history of African Americans and their literatures—difficult to access and left to disintegrate, with some irrevocable losses already apparent. Such a theme is reinforced in "Looking for Zora," for Walker has a difficult time finding Hurston's grave because the area is covered with waist-high weeds and a map to mark the location has to be hand-drawn from memories and oral communication. As a final "home" for Hurston, such a grave graphically indicates the neglect that black writers have suffered, which Walker explicitly notes by including a quote from Robert Hemenway describing Hurston's "resting place" as "generally symbolic of the black writer's fate in America" (93). Walker also visits the last neighborhood in which Hurston had resided which, like Walker's former home, is difficult to access: Walker and her companion need to ask several people for directions, and the street is unpaved and "full of mud puddles" (113). This dire physical setting seems appropriate when the young people who live there "had no idea Zora ever lived, let alone that she lived across the street" from them (115). While all of these experiences can be (and should be) read symbolically as signs of an undervalued black heritage, Walker introduces affect into her narrative in order to bring the symbolic in touch with the material actuality of what she describes. She thus explains in restrained tones that "normal responses of grief, horror, and so on do not make sense because they bear no relation to the depth of emotion one feels" (115). As such passages combine attention to the specific scene of devastation with a sense of its overwhelming communal implications, readers are called to join Walker in responding to the problem.

O'Connor's house in "Looking Beyond" stands in startling contrast to Walker's former home and Hurston's former neighborhood and gravesite. O'Connor's last residence is close to the road and is attended to by a caretaker, with a small, shabby house set behind it where slaves had probably once lived. Walker writes, "Her house becomes—in an instant—the symbol of my own disinheritance, and for that instant I hate her guts" (57). In such a way, Walker again simultaneously invokes raw emotion and explicitly draws attention to the way material signs of disparity operate as symbols, representing oppressions that might be less tangible. Symbols, then, are not illusive or without effect. On the contrary, Walker relates the psychic burden of acknowledging injustices: "For a long time I will feel Faulkner's house,

O'Connor's house, crushing me" (58). In other words, Walker feels oppressed by the white literary heritage that has been preserved and honored at the expense of her own black roots, and the concrete structures provide a visual manifestation of a weighty cultural problem.

The house symbolism is rather discouraging, but it is answered with a more positive focus on mothers and the maternal.[15] It is Walker's mother who ignores the "no trespassing" signs when they revisit their former home, and the presence of Walker's blood mother keeps O'Connor from intruding into the maternal position that threatens Walker with the dispossession of her specifically black roots. Walker's "mother" is thus a literal woman at the same time that she serves as a figurative path to the preservation of a black woman's heritage. In "Looking for Zora," Walker claims that Hurston is her aunt in order to access information about her, but Hurston becomes Walker's "metaphorical mother as well" (Sadoff 8). "In Search" most significantly places importance on the mother as a source of inheritance, support, inspiration, life, nourishment, and instruction—in short, the mother empowers the daughter, whether she takes the form of a literary precursor, a peer, or a literal maternal figure.

The mother is always intertwined with the final motif of importance in the three essays: flowers or gardens. "In Search" begins with an epigraph that pictures the relationship between the mother and daughter as that of a plant. The poem, "Motheroot," suggests that the mother acts like a nourishing root that eventually helps the flower (daughter) blossom, though the root herself remains invisible. More often, however, the mother is not part of a plant herself but instead is the gardener, able to plant gardens (literary works) that grow and multiply, building and sustaining communities with their beauty and life. Thus, in "Beyond the Peacock," Walker's mother is not impressed with the pretentious peacock that blocks O'Connor's driveway. The peacock, associated with O'Connor, damages gardens, just as the white literary tradition has damaged that of blacks.[16] In "Looking for Zora," Walker discovers that Hurston enjoyed gardening just as her own mother did (114), and even among the weeds at Hurston's gravesite Walker notices that some "are quite pretty, with tiny yellow flowers" (104). The importance of gardening is most noticeable in "In Search" when Walker discovers her own creative roots:

Whatever she [Walker's mother] planted grew as if by magic, and her fame as a grower of flowers spread over three counties. [. . .] And I remember people coming to my mother's yard to be given cuttings from her flowers; I hear again the praise showered on her because whatever rocky soil she landed on, she turned into a garden. [. . .] [T]o this day people drive by our house in Georgia [. . .] and ask to stand or walk among my mother's art. (241)

The "rocky soil" indicates the oppressive conditions under which African Americans have produced art, the "cuttings" suggest that art can inspire other art to "grow" or flourish, and the recognition of the gardens (or art) becomes a source of communal pride that draws people together. In "Beyond the Peacock," a similar testament to the creative ability of African American woman counters the rotting house of Walker's childhood: the daffodils planted by Walker's mother "have multiplied and are now blooming from one side of the yard to the other" (44). Such an image keeps despair at bay by encouraging the valuing of nontraditional sources of creativity, and it simultaneously suggests literary writings will flourish and multiply as the daffodils have done.

As Walker makes language and style work for her on multiple levels, *In Search of Our Mothers' Gardens* brings personal writing, storytelling, and literary criticism together to form meaningful narratives that can both draw attention to problematic conditions and provide hopeful alternatives. Walker's literary criticism is thus connected directly to the way people live at the same time that it brings orderliness to the messiness of lives; indeed, recasting lived experiences into a tightly-knit narrative is a key way to begin transforming a history of abuse and neglect into a vision of renewed life. By drawing on the work of other authors and using literary devices, Walker keeps her writing from becoming simplistic or reductive. Instead, its mediated qualities are consistently highlighted even as its bearing on material lives is made clear. While not all personal criticism needs to take on Walker's approach of storytelling, Walker does provide a strong example of autobiographical writing that uses performance to move its readers to political activism. Readers are called to engage in and actively interpret Walker's text in order that they more fully engage in and actively interpret their own worlds.

## Notes

1. Jane Tompkins's "Me and My Shadow," first published in *New Literary History* in 1987, is one of the earliest texts to receive attention for its use of personal criticism. The autobiographical trend in scholarship visibly gained momentum during the nineties, evidenced by a number of articles published in *The Chronicle of Higher Education* (see, for example, Scott Heller, Liz McMillen, Ruth Behar, and Daphne Patai) as well as by anthologies such as *The Intimate Critique: Autobiographical Literary Criticism* (1993; edited by Diane P. Freedman, Olivia Frey, and Frances Murphy Zauhar), *The Politics of the Essay* (1993; edited by Ruth-Ellen Boetcher Joeres and Elizabeth Mittman), and *Confessions of the Critics* (1996; edited by H. Aram Veeser). See these texts and Jeffrey Williams for analyses of why personal criticism and other forms of experimental scholarship have become widely used since the nineties.

2. Houston Baker writes, "The generative conditions of African life in the New World that privilege spiritual negotiation also make autobiography the

premiere genre of Afro-American discourse" ("There Is No More" 136). Richard Yarborough further explains that, before the twentieth century, black writers were primarily interested in "establishing the credibility of their literary voices and thus their view of reality," and autobiography made a more fitting weapon than fiction did "in the battle to gain a hearing for the true version of the Afro-American experience" (111).

3. William Andrews explains, "[C]ritics [. . .] have treated Afro-American autobiography [. . .] as a commentary on something extrinsic rather than as statements of something intrinsic to themselves" (79). He calls for Afro-American autobiography to be considered as its own genre, "important to study for its own sake" (80).

4. Much of Alice Walker's personal writing in "Beyond the Peacock," "Looking for Zora," and "In Search of Our Mothers' Gardens" can be considered anecdotal. While any autobiographical anecdote would fall under the heading "personal writing," not all personal writing is anecdotal. The anecdote is generally a brief story based on an actual event that is used to illustrate a point.

5. Gallagher and Greenblatt are referring specifically to the use of the anecdote in new historicist criticism, but their observation can be applied to the kind of personal anecdote Walker uses without distorting their argument.

6. Black feminist critics, especially, have recognized the problems that arise when black women's fiction is viewed as continuous with the lives of black women. At the same time, scholars recognize the dangers of ignoring the social position of the critic, for scholars of color do need to dominate the study of minority literature rather than become silenced, once again, by the voices of white critics. See Deborah McDowell, Houston Baker, and Tania Modleski for more elaborate discussions of the twin dangers of marginalization and exclusivity.

7. Rachel Blau DuPlessis, for example, uses the repetition of the stilted phrase "Now did I" in order to include the interruption of kitchen routines in her scholarship without naturalizing her experiences: "Now did I go downstairs, now did I cut up a pear, eight strawberries, now did I add some cottage cheese," and so on (4). Linda Kauffman tells a story of her childhood but follows it with multiple interpretations *and* critiques of those interpretations. Nancy Miller refuses the division of theory and the personal, partially by bringing "occasional" writing into her scholarship (that is, essays that were written for particular occasions, some of which called for less formal tones than Miller may have generally used when writing a book) (*Getting Personal* xi, 15). Jane Gallop uses the "anecdote" as a point of departure, bringing theory and personal writing together in a manner somewhat akin to Miller's approach. A great many other variations of performative personal criticism could be recounted, but Jane Tompkins's "Me and My Shadow" is notably absent from my list. Her self-presentation tends to be "naturalized" rather than "performative." She writes, "This is what I want you to see. A person sitting in stockinged feet looking out of her window" (1108) and "That is why, you see, this doesn't sound too good. It isn't a practiced performance, it hasn't got a surface. I'm asking you to bear with me while I try, hoping that this, what I write, will express something you yourself have felt or will help you find a part of yourself that you would like to express" (1107). Tompkins seems intent on having readers "see" her and "connect" with her, while the writers I label performative are more interested in showing readers portraits with very visible frames, making the mediated quality of representation quite clear without sacrificing contact with lived experiences.

8. For more on the political power of Walker's essays, see Pamela Klass Mittlefehldt.

9. I spend more time developing the importance of narrative, the critical framework of womanism, and a sense of Walker's entire volume of essays in my dissertation, *Practice, Practice, Practice: Innovative Feminist Literary Criticism,* a work in progress from which this essay is taken. For ideas about the value of narrative, see Susan Stanford Friedman's *Mappings,* Jay Clayton's *The Pleasures of Babel,* and Toni Morrison's "Memory, Creation, and Writing." For comments on *In Search of Our Mothers' Gardens,* see Tuzyline Jita Allan, Pamela Klass Mittlefehldt, and Dianne Sadoff.

10. Gates emphasizes signifying as an approach that disrupts racism: "The ironic reversal of a received racist image of the black as simianlike, the Signifying Monkey—he who dwells at the margins of discourse, ever punning, ever troping, ever embodying the ambiguities of language—is our trope for repetition and revision, indeed, is our trope of chiasmus itself, repeating and simultaneously reversing in one deft, discursive act" ("Blackness of Blackness" 286). I am not arguing that Walker signifies on O'Connor, Hurston, and Woolf because the precursor writers are racist, but instead because revising these writers' approaches allows Walker to bring conventions of fiction and performance into her writing without losing her own personal investment in the text. 11. Parenthetical citations refer to Walker's *In Search* unless otherwise noted.

12. Walker's writing has often been linked to that of Hurston, especially in terms of storytelling as a theme. See, for example, Molly Hite's *The Other Side of the Story* and Henry Louis Gates's *The Signifying Monkey.*

13. Woolf's use of the term "lies" is consistent with that of both Hurston and Walker.

14. See Henry Louis Gates for an analysis of house symbolism in *The Color Purple* and in Hurston's *Their Eyes Were Watching God* (*The Signifying Monkey* 253).

15. See Sadoff for an analysis of matrilineage in Walker.

16. Walker finds the peacock that blocks the driveway "inspiring," but her mother answers that "they'll eat up every bloom you have, if you don't watch out" (59)—an exchange that effectively expresses Walker's mixed feelings about O'Connor as a literary precursor.

## Works Cited

Allan, Tuzyline Jita. "A Voice of One's Own: Implications of Impersonality in the Essays of Virginia Woolf and Alice Walker." Joeres and Mittman: 131–147.

Andrews, William L., "Toward a Poetics of Afro-American Autobiography." Baker and Redmond: 78–91.

Baker, Houston A., Jr., "There Is No More Beautiful Way: Theory and the Poetics of Afro-American Women's Writing." Baker and Redmond: 135–155.

Baker, Houston A., Jr., and Patricia Redmond, eds. *Afro-American Literary Study in the 1990s.* Chicago: University of Chicago P, 1989.

Behar, Ruth. "Dare We Say 'I'? Bringing the Personal into Scholarship." *Chronicle of Higher Education,* 29 June 1994: B1+.

Clayton, Jay. *The Pleasures of Babel: Contemporary American Literature and Theory.* Oxford: Oxford University Press, 1993.

DuPlessis, Rachel Blau. *The Pink Guitar: Writing as Feminist Practice.* New York: Routledge, 1990.

Freedman, Diane P., Olivia Frey, and Frances Murphy Zauhar. *The Intimate Critique: Autobiographical Literary Criticism.* Durham, NC: Duke University Press, 1993.

Friedman, Susan Stanford. *Mappings: Feminism and the Cultural Geographies of Encounter.* Princeton, NJ: Princeton University Press, 1998.

Gallagher, Catherine, and Stephen Greenblatt. *Practicing New Historicism.* Chicago, IL: University of Chicago Press, 2000.

Gallop, Jane. *Anecdotal Theory.* Durham, NC: Duke University Press, 2002.

Gates, Henry Louis, Jr. "The blackness of blackness: a critique of the sign and the Signifying Monkey." *Black Literature and Literary Theory.* Ed. Henry Louis Gates, Jr. New York: Routledge, 1984. 285–321.

———. *The Signifying Monkey: A Theory of Afro-American Literary Criticism.* New York: Oxford University Press, 1988.

Heller, Scott. "Experience and Expertise Meet in New Brand of Scholarship." *Chronicle of Higher Education,* 6 May 1992: A7+.

Henderson, Mae G. "Speaking in Tongues: Dialogics, Dialectics, and the Black Woman Writer's Literary Tradition." 1989. Napier 348–68.

Hite, Molly. *The Other Side of the Story: Structures and Strategies of Contemporary Feminist Narrative.* Ithaca: Cornell University Press, 1989.

Joeres, Ruth-Ellen Boetcher, and Mittman, Elizabeth, eds. *The Politics of the Essay: Feminist Perspectives.* Bloomington: Indiana University Press, 1993.

Kauffman, Linda S. "The Long Goodbye: Against Personal Testimony, or An Infant Grifter Grows Up." 1992. Warhol and Herndl 1155–1171.

McDowell, Deborah. *"The Changing Same": Black Women's Literature, Criticism, and Theory.* Bloomington: Indiana University Press, 1995.

McMillen, Liz. "Don't Leave Out the Juicy Things: Campus Writing Groups Provide Advice, Support to Authors." *Chronicle of Higher Education,* 9 Feb. 1994: A18+.

Miller, Nancy K. *But Enough About Me: Why We Read Other People's Lives.* New York: Columbia University Press, 2002.

———. *Getting Personal: Feminist Occasions and Other Autobiographical Acts.* New York: Routledge, 1991.

Mittlefehldt, Pamela Klass. "'A Weaponry of Choice': Black American Women Writers and the Essay." Joeres and Mittman: 196–208.

Modleski, Tania. *Feminism Without Women: Culture and Criticism in a "Postfeminist" Age.* New York: Routledge, 1991.

Morrison, Toni. "Memory, Creation, and Writing." *Thought* 59 (1984): 385–390.

Napier, Winston, ed. *African American Literary Theory: A Reader.* New York: New York University Press, 2000.

Patai, Daphne. "Point of View: Sick and Tired of Scholars' Nouveau Solipsism." *Chronicle of Higher Education,* 23 Feb. 1994: A52.

Sadoff, Dianne F. "Black Matrilineage: The Case of Alice Walker and Zora Neale Hurston." *Signs* 11 (1985): 4–26.

Smith, Barbara. "Toward a Black Feminist Criticism." 1977. Napier 132–146.

Smith, Valerie. "Black Feminist Theory and the Representation of the 'Other.'" 1989. Napier 369–384.

Tompkins, Jane. "Me and My Shadow." 1987. Warhol and Herndl: 1103–1116.

Veeser, H. Aram. *Confessions of the Critics.* New York: Routledge, 1996.

Walker, Alice. *In Search of Our Mothers' Gardens: Womanist Prose*. San Diego: Harcourt Brace, 1983.

Warhol, Robyn R., and Diane Price Herndl, eds. *Feminisms: An Anthology of Literary Theory and Criticism*. Rev. ed. New Brunswick, NJ: Rutgers University Press, 1997.

Williams, Jeffrey. "The New Belletrism." *Style* 33 (1999): 413–442.

Woolf, Virginia. *A Room of One's Own*. San Diego: Harcourt Brace, 1929.

Yarborough, Richard. "The First-Person in Afro-American Fiction." Baker and Redmond 105–121.

Zauhar, Frances Murphy. "Creative Voices: Women Reading and Women's Writing." Freedman, Frey, and Zauhar 103–116.

DEBORAH ANNE HOOKER

# Reanimating the Trope of the Talking Book in Alice Walker's "Strong Horse Tea"

In a 1970 essay, "The Black Writer and the Southern Experience," Alice Walker qualifies her refusal to "romanticize the Southern black country life" of her upbringing, recalling that while she "hated it, generally . . . no one could wish for a more advantageous heritage than that bequeathed to the black writer in the South: a compassion for the earth, a trust in humanity beyond our knowledge of evil, and an abiding love of justice" (21). Essays published in the 1980s, such as "Am I Blue" and "Everything is a Human Being," and her more recent response to the events of September 11, 2001, *Sent by Earth*, coalesce that southern, rural-bred "compassion for the earth" into a recognizable ecocritical world view. In "The Universe Responds," for example, Walker unabashedly stakes the richness of human creativity to the health of the natural world: "we are connected to [animals] at least as intimately as we are connected to trees," she says. "Without plant life human beings could not breathe. . . . Without free animal life . . . we will lose the spiritual equivalent of oxygen. Magic, intuition, sheer astonishment at the forms the Universe devises in which to express life—itself—will no longer be able to breath in us" (191-92).

In this regard, Walker explicitly diverges from the anti-pastoral strain in the African-American literary tradition that, since the time of Frederick Douglass, has "expressed a profound antipathy toward the ecological niches

*The Southern Literary Journal*, 37.2 (2005): pp. 81–102. Copyright © 2005 by the Southern Literary Journal and the University of North Carolina at Chapel Hill Department of English. All rights reserved.

usually focused on in ecocriticism: pastoral space and wilderness" (Bennett 208). Reacting to the early black experience of the rural South, in a landscape distorted by slavery's crimes and the decades of violence and racism following its abolition, the tradition, Michael Bennett argues, has tended to view "the relative safety of the urban environment" as a more promising landscape of economic opportunity and social justice denied in more conservative and isolated, rural enclaves (198).

Walker's 1967 short story, "Strong Horse Tea," appears, in many ways, to echo this anti-pastoral tradition.[1] Her brutally poor protagonist, Rannie Mae Toomer, literally lives in a pasture surrounded by the "fat whitefolks' cows and an old gray horse and a mule" (462).[2] And there is no hint of pastoral romance in the image of the "fat winter fly" roosting on the forehead of her child, Snooks, who will ultimately die of "double pneumonia and whooping cough" (459). However, Walker refuses to privilege a contrasting and more urban, albeit southern, domain: the narrative tension of the short story is, in fact, created by Rannie's waiting for "a real doctor" from town to arrive with his presumably superior arsenal of cures; having refused the help of the community witchwoman, Aunt Sarah, and the "swamp magic" she proffers, Rannie realizes too late that a more urban world, the traditional anti-pastoralist preference, has ignored her plight and abandoned her to the meager resources of her home community (459).

To complicate matters further, however, the story concludes on an apparently anti-pastoral note, with Rannie "slipping and sliding in the mud" of the pasture, soaked to the bone from a tremendous thunderstorm, collecting the only thing, according to Sarah, that stands a chance of reviving Snooks: mare's urine, the strong horse tea of the title (466).[3] That final scene also depicts a come-uppance of sorts for Rannie: as she catches the tea in her flimsy plastic shoe, she discovers "a leak, a tiny crack, at her shoe's front"; with no other recourse, she "stuck her mouth there over the crack, and ... freezing in her shabby wet coat, ran home to give the good and warm strong tea to her baby Snooks" (466). Since Snooks dies while she is in the pasture, Rannie obviously takes the medicine. But in the context of the many polarities that critics have identified—between town/country, folk medicine/white medicine, black roots and heritage/white technological progress—the particular allegiance for which she is being chastened is not so clear.[4] Rannie's isolation from her home community before Aunt Sarah appears argues against its idealization, and Sarah herself acknowledges that Rannie's preference for the white doctor, though naïve, is almost inevitable.

The story is ambivalent, I would argue, precisely because traces of Walker's emerging ecoconsciousness are embedded in the traditional anti-pastoral elements alluded to above. In an important sense, her story takes us back to what is arguably the inception of that tradition through a reconsideration of what Henry Louis Gates has identified as the "ur-trope" of African-American literature—the trope of the talking book, or as he later qualifies it, the "trope of the untalking book" (131, 165). Predating and prefiguring Douglass's anti-pastoral texts, the trope appears first in James Gronniosaw's 1770 *Narrative of the Most Remarkable Particulars in the Life of James Albert Ukawsaw Gronniosaw, An African Prince, As Related by Himself*, and is subsequently repeated and revised in a number of narratives published between 1770 and 1815, by Olaudah Equiano, John Jea, John Marrant, and Ottobah Cugoano. (The writings of Gronniosaw, Equiano, and Cugoano are of most interest to me here.) This trope typically depicts untutored auditors from predominantly oral cultures encountering the print technology of their white masters for the first time, a confrontation that incites the desire to speak with the book as they perceive their masters to be doing. As Gates makes clear, this trope figures the incitement to literacy, an acquisition that would confirm the human status of the black non-European according to criteria set by white Enlightenment thought (127-132).

In Walker's revision, a similarly untutored Rannie repeatedly encounters the advertising circulars delivered to her daily by a white mailman, and it is in the scenes with the circulars that Walker signifies most directly on the trope of the talking book and the texts in which they appear; her retroping, moreover, allows us to see how the dynamics of desire at work in "Strong Horse Tea" parallel and retroactively illuminate some of the unexamined consequences of identifying with the worlds and the values signified by the mystifying texts in the earlier narratives. These consequences suggest that anti-pastoralism arises not only from a history of brutality enacted on black bodies against a rural backdrop but is, in philosopher David Abram's words, an "unnoticed and unfortunate" tendency inherent in literacy itself (273). The ambivalence of Walker's story arises from the tension between the historical status of the trope as a figure for literacy, the sign refuting the animal status ascribed to the African, and a modern awareness of the peril of estrangement from the "more-than-human world"[5] that technologies of literacy can orchestrate.

That Walker's text grapples with the tension between the spoken and written word that the talking book trope thematizes can be discerned from the many parallels her text erects with those earlier narratives. The most obvious parallel is the appearance of printed texts to illiterate auditors whose amazement reveals both a simple lack of literacy and a profound unfamiliarity with the dominant forces shaping and controlling their worlds. In three of the earlier narratives on which "Strong Horse Tea" signifies, we see black (or, in Cugoano's case, Native American) auditors mystified by the appearance of a printed object—in many cases, a holy book—which excludes them from the conversation the text apparently "carries on" with its white interlocutors. In the 1770 edition of his narrative, for example, the enslaved African prince

Gronniosaw observes his master as he "read prayers . . . to the ship's crew every Sabbath day" (11). I was "never so surprised in my life as when I saw the book talk to my master, for I thought it did, as I observed him to look upon it, and move his lips. I wished it would do so with me" (11). In secret Gronniosaw took the book, "opened it, and put my ear down close upon it, in great hopes that it would say something to me; but I was . . . greatly disappointed, when I found that it would not speak." Its silence, he assumes, is a hostile response to his blackness (11).

The more well-known slave narrative, *The Interesting Narrative of the Life of Olaudah Equiano, Or Gustavus Vassa, the African, Written by Himself*, first published in 1789, follows a similar trajectory: Equiano, too, sees his master and a friend, Richard Baker, "employed in reading" and, like Gronniosaw, feels "a great curiosity to talk to the books, as I thought they did" (48). Like his precursor, Equiano has "often taken up a book, and have talked to it, and then put my ears to it, when alone, in hopes it would answer me" (48). The book's silence provokes a similar insecurity: Equiano has "been very much concerned when I found it remained silent" (48).

Unlike Equiano and Gronniosaw, Cugoano's revision of the trope does not occur in his autobiography but in his *Thoughts and Sentiments on the Evil and Wicked Traffic of the Slavery and Commerce of the Human Species*, first published in Great Britain in 1878 as a response to major eighteenth-century justifications for slavery. With its uneasy endorsement of expanded trade between Europe and Africa as a means of lifting black culture to the level of white, his text, in many respects, is the one with which Walker's is in most intimate dialogue.[6] In Cugoano's *Thoughts and Sentiments*, the trope surfaces in an exemplum within his overall argument, in his account of the Spanish conquest of the Incan people. Demonstrating the perverse use of scripture to justify imperialism, he dramatizes Pizarro's meeting with the Incan King, Atahualpa, in which a Spanish Father, Vincente Valverde, uses a breviary, "pretending to explain some of the general doctrines of Christianity" in addition to informing the Incan King that Pope Alexander had "invested their master as the sole Monarch of all the New World" (63). When Atahualpa asks where the Father had learned "things so extraordinary . . . the fanatic Monk" held out the breviary: "in this book" (63). Like Equiano and Gronniosaw, Atahualpa puts his ear to the pages of the book, with the same silent reaction from the book, but not from the nascent reader: "This, says he, is silent; it tells me nothing; and [he] threw it with disdain to the ground" (64) a noble, if futile, act of defiance, and one of Atahualpa's last, as he is soon murdered by Pizarro's forces.

Echoing Cugoano's exemplum, Walker situates the illiterate Rannie within a recognizably modern permutation of that old imperializing ethos. And, as in the earlier versions of the trope, Walker's revision emphasizes her protagonist's amazement at texts that exclude her from the symbolic exchanges it apparently engages in with others. When the advertising circulars come to the desperately poor Rannie, she had to ask the mailman

> what certain circulars meant that showed pretty pictures of things she needed. Did the circulars mean that somebody was coming around later and give her hats and suitcases and shoes and sweaters and rubbing alcohol and a heater for the house and a fur bonnet for her baby? Or why did he always give her the pictures if she couldn't have what was in them? Or what did the words say . . . especially the big word written in red: "S_ A_ L_ E"? (460-461)

The mailman explains that "the only way she could get the goods pictured on the circulars was to buy them in town and that town stores did their advertising by sending out pictures of their goods" (461). Rannie would then "exclaim in a dull, amazed way that *she* never had any money. . . . *She* couldn't ever buy any of the things in the pictures—so why did the stores keep sending them to her?" (461) Like the Spanish clergyman, the mailman delivers, along with the circulars, a message proclaiming the inevitability of this particular form of economic hegemony: he explains to Rannie "that *everybody* got the circulars whether they had any money to buy with or not. That this was one of the laws of advertising, and he couldn't do anything about it" (461).

Obviously, like her precursors, Rannie cannot read, as her question about "the big word written in red—S_A_L_E" demonstrates, a question, like the silent book of her predecessors, emphasizing the exchanges that exclude her. Unlike those earlier auditors, however, she does not put her ear to the pages, expecting a literal voice to emerge from the flat surface of the text, nor, like Equiano and Gronniosaw, does she see someone mouthing words over the text. The seeming peculiarities of these earlier representations can be explained by recalling that those scenes exemplify the relative novelty of print technology in the eighteenth century, when orality was still a dominant medium for European and non-European alike, and orally-influenced behaviors and perceptions were still evolving into the more modern behaviors we associate with reading. For instance, the moving lips of the masters above the text depict the residual effects of orality on reading, when interacting with a text retained some of the behaviors associated with face-to-face encounters. In such transitional stages, as Walter Ong reminds us, "the written words had to be mouthed aloud, into their full being, restored to and made to live in the oral cavities in which [it was believed] they came into existence" (259). What Gronniosaw and Equiano *are* correctly "reading," then, is the behavior of white readers in this transitional period and interpreting that behavior in light of the oral dominance of their lives.

But beyond that gesture and its interpretation by these illiterate auditors, their prior immersion in oral culture also causes them to "anthropomorphize" the book, a judgment connoting naiveté only when delivered from this side of the literate/oral divide. Their perception of the text as alive grows out of oral culture's attribution of animation to all that can possibly "speak." In such cultures, the word "is of its very nature a sound, tied to the movement of life itself in the flow of time" (Ong 20). Because it possesses aural qualities, not just visual ones, it is not reducible to a sign on the page of a book (Ong 20-21). David Abram argues further that in non-literate cultures, which have not yet "fully transferred their sensory participation to the written word . . . [people] still dwell within a landscape that is alive, aware, and expressive . . . 'language' remains as much a property of the animate landscape as of the humans who dwell and speak within that terrain" (139). In oral cultures, then, words are tied to speech, and speech is allied to sound, which can issue from the mouths of men, animals, or other naturally-occurring elements. In the environment of the strange new world that stolen people like Gronniosaw and Equiano were confronting, speech could very well emerge from exotic objects that may thus be animate, possessing unfamiliar mouths of their own.

Because Rannie's encounter with her mystifying texts occurs after some three hundred years of print technology's dominance, Walker does not represent her as expecting the pages to literally speak, nor, despite his role as conveyor of the medium, does Walker depict the mailman "in conversation" with the print. Yet Rannie's behavior demonstrates that the texts do speak to her, with effects reminiscent of those produced by the silent talking books in the earlier tropes.

Despite failing to grasp why she repeatedly receives the pictures of all the objects she "couldn't ever buy," Rannie paradoxically invests her trust in the world from which these texts emerge. Consequently, when Aunt Sarah appears at her doorstep, having been summoned by the mailman in lieu of the white doctor, Rannie derogates her skills as "swamp magic" and "witch's remedies." Your "old home remedies I took as a child," she tells Sarah, "come just short of killing me" (459). Rannie holds out for the real medicine from town, "some of them shots that makes people well. Cures 'em of all they ails, cleans 'em out and makes 'em strong, all at the same time" (460). Since the story presents no other forms of outside intervention, we must assume that Rannie's misplaced trust in the white world is somehow constructed by the ubiquitous circulars that appear again and again, like harbingers of future bounty, within her impoverished world. Her belief that the doctor will eventually appear is predicated on the perpetual appearance of the mailman and the circulars, bearing all those images of hats and suitcases that she mistakenly assumes will be "coming around later," too, an assumption with tragic consequences for her child Snooks.

In this context, Rannie appears to succumb to what critics of twentieth-century advertising have identified as one of its most potent mechanisms: ads function not merely to inform potential buyers of the availability of a particular product, but in fact construct "consumers as an integral part of the social meaning of goods" (Ewen and Ewen 21). Like the circulars that bombard Rannie, the modern marketplace is flooded "with suggestions that individuals should buy products in order to encounter something in the realm of social or psychological experience that previously had been unavailable to them" (Ewen and Ewen 21).[7] The circulars confront Rannie with what she lacks—the heater, the bonnet, the shoes and sweaters, and the money to procure them—certifying, in their wake, the inferiority of her local world. In the earlier encounters with the talking book, literacy simultaneously confronts the auditors with their inferiority and functions as the currency whereby Equiano and Gronniosaw can acquire the value they lack. In this regard, the holy books function like the advertising texts of "Strong Horse Tea," in that both discourses align the auditors' desires with the value systems the texts promote and, even more importantly, with the value systems their technologies embody. To borrow Marshall McLuhan's famous dictum: the medium *is* the message.

Gates' extensive study of the trope of the talking book testifies to the holy books' creation of the desire for "something in the realm of social or psychological experience . . . previously . . . unavailable to" its black auditors: "What seems clear upon reading the texts created by [these first] black writers in English . . . is that the production of literature was taken to be the central arena in which persons of African descent could, or could not, establish and redefine their status within the human community" (129). Demonstrating a mastery of arts and sciences through writing—the hallmarks of reason and thus the eighteenth-century criteria for human status—could refute the African's placement on the Great Chain of Being as "the lowest of the human races or as first cousin to the ape" (Gates 167). Like Rannie's reification of the white doctor, Equiano comes to regard these who produce the texts he encounters "as men superior to us" (56). After acquiring some English, he admits that he "relished [the] society and manners" of his English masters, and desiring "to resemble them; to imbibe their spirit, and imitate their manners, [he] took every opportunity to gain instruction" in reading and writing (56). Like Equiano, "Cugoano uses book learning and Christian religion to distinguish Britons positively from Africans" (Wheeler 27).

Thus, for these former slaves, literacy, often first embodied in religious discourse, signifies the unavoidable and practical acquiescence to the Enlightenment standard prescribing human status and value. The ubiquity

of the circulars in Rannie's world retroactively signifies on the inescapability
of such a discourse in the eighteenth century, which was carried on the ships
that trafficked in the human commerce of slavery and, ironically, set the
terms by which human status would be ascertained. These terms and, more
importantly, the symbolic systems like alphabetic literacy by which they were
conveyed institute the first disconnect from an animate landscape, and in
them we can trace the emergence of the anti-pastoral tradition.

The anti-pastoral tendency inherent in an Enlightenment discourse that
correlates literacy with human status has its inception in even earlier writings
that attempted to solve the problem of "classifying the people of color" that
"sea-faring Renaissance Europe" had encountered in its myriad voyages of
discovery (Davis and Gates xxiv). In *The New Organon* in 1620, for example,
Sir Francis Bacon attempts to de-emphasize skin color as an index of cultural
value, but in so doing he clearly negates the reciprocity between a people and
the natural elements amid which they exist: the differences between "the most
civilized province of Europe" and "the wildest and most barbarous districts
of New India," he asserts, arise "not from the soil, not from climate, not from
race, but from the arts" (qtd in Davis and Gates xxiv).[8] This critical disconnect
from the land that Bacon asserts is figured in the earlier tropes of the talking
book through a particular motif that Walker also retropes in her story: the
rejection of "home," which is more than a rejection of geographic locale. It
involves a disinvestment in the concrete, sensual, earthy values the home
culture embraces: Rannie rejects Aunt Sarah's remedies with their intimate
connection to the landscape and animals—"the arrowroot or sassyfrass and
cloves, or sugar tit soaked in cat's blood" (460)—in favor of "some of them
shots" that come pre-packaged, obscuring any immediate perception of the
materials out of which they were concocted or their connection to a larger
environment.

The rejection of home in Gronniosaw's narrative is embedded in a
disagreement over religious faith, which nevertheless shares with Rannie's
rejection a triumph of the abstract over the concrete.[9] Like Rannie, Gronniosaw
is beguiled by advertisements—in his case, the verbal promises of "a merchant
from the Gold Coast," who promised that he "should see houses with wings
to them walk upon the water" and "also see the white folks" (7). Despite the
fact that he is tricked by the merchant and enslaved, Gronniosaw's narrative
paints this deception as a blessing in disguise because it introduces him to
the Christian faith. The slavery separating him from his family is, in fact,
prefigured in an earlier spiritual alienation from them. Delivering him to
Christianity, slavery is the vehicle that allows him to validate an intuition
of monotheism he claims to have had held "from [his] infancy," that there
existed "some great Man of Power which resided above the sun, moon, and
stars," the objects of his family's worship (5). He refutes his "dear" mother's

pagan insistence that the "sun, moon, and stars" had, indeed, "made all our country" (7), a stance estranging him from his family, who accede to his wishes to depart with the Gold Coast merchant.

Rannie's attribution of greater powers to a white doctor she has never seen as opposed to the old home remedies of Sarah echoes Gronniosaw's intuition about the "Man of Power"—the Christian God who, by definition, doesn't materialize. But more significantly, both rejections of home represent investments in abstraction, pointing to what scholars of literacy identify as one of the most profound transformations worked by the acquisition of alphabetic literacy. As Gronniosaw's rejection of his [End Page 89] mother's pantheistic explanation suggests, this act of abstraction diminishes the value of the felt connection between the human and the natural world.[10]

The way in which literacy enables abstraction, according to David Abram, is by instituting a "new order of participation" with one's surroundings:

> To read is to enter in a profound participation, or chaism, with the inked marks upon the page. In learning to read, we . . . break the spontaneous participation of our eyes and our ears in the surrounding terrain (where they had ceaselessly converged in the synaesthetic encounter with animals, plants, and stream) in order to recouple those senses upon the flat surface of the page. (131)

With the pictographic and ideographic ciphers that predated the phonetic system, Abram explains, reading certainly "involved a displacement of our sensory participation from the depths of the animate environment to the flat surface of our walls, of clay tablets, of the sheet of papyrus." However, the pre-alphabetic character still embodied the "animate phenomenon of which it was the static image" and "provoked from us the sound of its name." With the evolution of a strictly phonetic system, however, one that was instigated by the Semitic aleph-beth and modified by the Greeks and Phonecians, these "written characters no longer refer us to any sensible phenomenon out in the world . . . but solely to a gesture . . . made by the human mouth" (Abram 100). Words severed from the environment lose their connection to place, which is "superceded by a new abstract notion of 'space' as a homogenous and placeless void" (Abram 184). And as many students of the oral/literate divide have observed, this paring away of sensual external referents, in effect, enables the reflective intellect; it makes possible the conceptual leap of abstraction, the derivation of "an entirely placeless notion of eternity—a strictly intelligible, nonmaterial realm of pure Ideas resting outside of the sensible world" (Abram 197).[11]

One of these studies, Jean-Joseph Goux's *Symbolic Economies After Marx and Freud*, correlates alphabetic literacy's displacement of affect from the sensuousness of the surrounding world with the triumph of monotheism over polytheism or the pagan animism that Gronniosaw's mother, for example, espouses. The inception of monotheism, given with the Mosaic laws, corresponds to the advent of the Semitic aleph-beth around 1500 B.C. Like the alphabetic letters, monotheism involves a paring away of investment in external referents and transfers that investment to "to the letter, to writing, to alphabetic signifiers" (Goux 145). This paring away of external referents is echoed in the Mosaic prohibition against making images of God, which also "implies a shift of emphasis from sensorial perception to the abstract idea" (Goux 136). Studies of myth also point to this prohibition against idolatry as the historical passage from rituals that involved the worship of female deities, mother goddesses, and all the connections to the sensual and to the earth such worship implied.[12]

Thus monotheism, Gronniosaw's "intuition," which severs him from his pagan homeland religion, is a form of iconoclasm congruent with the paring away of sensual referents in the alphabet, and, in fact, the two are interdependent. In learning to read, Gronniosaw, Equiano, and Cugoano not only acquire the status of human being as defined by Enlightenment thought, they also move from the wider, more sensual worldview of orality into the more ascetic straits of monotheistic Christianity, something they embrace at the philosophical level, which is itself, according to Ong, Abram, and Goux, a noetic state arising from alphabetic culture. To escape commodity status/ animal status, they master the denatured logic of the word via one of its more prominent discourses—Christianity. In so doing, they abandon certain prior kinds of relationships with the world, self, and others, a move that, obviously, offers other compensations. As Ong affirms, "With writing, the earlier noetic state undergoes a kind of cleavage, separating the knower from the external universe and then from himself. This separation makes possible both 'art' (techne) in the ancient Greek sense of the detached abstract analysis of human procedures and science, or detached abstract analysis of the cosmos" (18).[13]

Rannie certainly does not become literate in the course of the story, and in that regard deviates from the course of her precursors who do go on to write their way into human history. However, her son's death, which is precipitated, in part, by her misplaced faith in the developed, literate world, one that advertises itself to her daily through the circulars, suggests certain liabilities inherent in the conceptual leap of abstraction: Rannie identifies with an abstraction instead of with the concrete resources of her community and suffers for it.

In fact, the images in the advertising circulars function like a parody of the ideal forms of Platonism, concepts that could not have assumed the form of "concept" without the transformations wrought by alphabetic writing that Ong, Goux, and Abram describe. Realistically, because Rannie has no money, the perfect forms of hat, heater, sweater, and suitcase exist only in a "nonmaterial" plane. Because she has nothing to exchange for them, they will remain out of her reach, fundamentally outside of her sensible world. She will never touch them, smell them, taste them, feel their heat, their warmth, or their comfort. And yet, like the ideal forms of Platonism or the invisible god of monotheism, the world from which they emerge comes to act as the standard for all meaning and value. Rannie places her belief in the invisible white doctor—an abstraction—who has also come to exist, in her mind, in a higher, albeit distant realm of perfection and authority than Aunt Sarah. With her sassyfrass tea, cat's blood, and strong horse tea, Sarah and her "nigger magic" are, to Rannie, imperfect replications of that ideal form.

The way in which Walker constructs Sarah's response to Rannie's perception deepens the story's ambivalence: that response not only certifies the efficacy of her connection to the landscape of orality, with its intimate investments in the natural world, but also reveals her recognition of the almost inescapable and perverse identification by those who are culturally oppressed with that culture's dominant interests and modes of exchange. In her most compassionate commentary, she initially chides Rannie for her belief in the "white mailman, white doctor," but then admits to feeling "sadly glad that the young always grow up hoping. It *did* take a long time to finally realize that you could only depend on those who would come" (463).[14] Walker's emphatic "did" suggests Sarah's familiarity with this phenomenon: perhaps she, too, had grown up hoping, and it had taken her a long time to lose that hope and adopt a certain fatalism with regard to the beneficence of the outside world. What she sees in Rannie, she has seen before; her paradoxical "sadly glad" signifies both her compassionate understanding of inexperience and youth denigrating tradition in favor of the new and the potential losses and gains inherent in choosing one world view to the exclusion of the other.

But Sarah's summation of the cure for that ambivalence—"You could only depend upon those who would come"—is more than a fatalistic affirmation of the pragmatism of using who or what is at hand (463); it is a statement conveying the logic of the word in an oral culture, which is a logic of presence. And because Sarah represents Rannie's only hope, the story affirms this logic.[15] As Ong writes, "Real words are always sounds, always events, which exist only while they are going out of existence.... In oral or oral-aural communication both speaker and hearer must be alive" and present to one another. "The case is quite different with writing. Once I have put a message into writing, it makes no difference so far as the text goes whether I am dead or alive" (233).[16] Like the word passed between two interlocutors in an oral situation, Sarah and her help are present to Rannie. And as she continually reminds Rannie about the white doctor from town, an abstract derivative of the printed circulars, "He ain't" (463).

Sarah and her swamp magic are poised against the influence of the advertising circulars and the white doctor from town in a way that affirms the power inherent in an oral culture's perception of a landscape that is, according to Abram, "alive, aware, and expressive" (139). In this opposition, Walker complicates the anti-pastoral representation of literacy as liberation when the texts in her story are directly linked with impotence and death. The circulars take on their most ominous signification when they are metonymically associated with Snook's death. When Walker introduces us to the child, "his hard wasted skull" partially concealed "under a pile of faded quilts," she calls attention to the sound of his breath with a particular simile: his fretful breathing "caused a faint rustling in the sheets near his mouth like the wind pushing damp papers in a shallow ditch" (459). This sound haunts Rannie's final meeting with the mailman. Standing in the pouring rain, she desperately begs him to fetch the white doctor from town. Uneasy in the face of her "hungry desperation," he "stuffed a wad of circulars advertising hair dryers and cold creams into her hands" instead (461). In her anguish, Rannie drops the circulars, "trampling [them] under her feet" as she crossed back under the fence into the pasture where she lived" (462). As the only printed texts introduced in the story, the circulars are the "damp papers" pushed by the wind, resurrecting the sound of Snook's labored breath, and implicating the circulars in the circumstances of his death.

In another instance, the circulars are figured in such a way to demonstrate their impotence in the face of other natural forces. While Rannie prevents Aunt Sarah from ministering to Snooks as she waits for the doctor, "a cold wind . . . shoot[s] all around her from the cracks in the window framing; faded circulars blew inward from the wall" (463). Unable to buy the items represented, Rannie has converted the circulars to a particular kind of use value, futilely plastering them on her walls of her house against the onslaught of the cold Georgia weather.

On the one hand, both figurations involving the circulars can be read as an indictment of all that Rannie has been denied by the forces of a dominant and racist culture, which routinely relinquishes the welfare of its neediest members to the invisible hand of the market. Snooks' death results, in part, from Rannie's implicit exclusion from the avenues that might have alleviated her poverty—education, jobs, and all the fundamental opportunities literacy enables. The texts plastered on the walls would thus metaphorize the only "insulation" available to her against her present deprivation. In this kind of reading, literacy would assume the same potentially redemptive status as in the anti-pastoral narratives of Frederick Douglass and, as Gates asserts, of "virtually all the slave narratives published between 1789 and 1865" (148).

But there are alternative ways to read this contest between wind and the text, which Walker emphasizes by situating the entire narrative within a disturbance of the air, in a thunderstorm that reaches its crescendo when Rannie fetches the tea. Walker implies the wisdom of reconnecting with what Abram identifies as one of the casualties of the advent of both Christianity and alphabetic literacy: the "ancient association" of language "with the invisible breath" of the wind (254). "In the oral, animistic world of pre-Christian and peasant Europe," Abram says, "all things—animals, forests, rivers, and caves—had the power of expressive speech, and the primary medium of this collective discourse was the air. In the absence of writing, human utterance, whether embodied in songs, stories, or spontaneous sounds, was inseparable from the exhaled breath" (253-54).

Walker contrasts both the impotence and death-dealing connotations of the circulars to the oral ministrations of Aunt Sarah, which are beneficent precisely because they are "of a piece" with the "invisible breath" of the wind. When Rannie finally relents and allows Sarah to examine Snooks, the old woman "hum[s] a thin pagan tune that pushed against the sound of the wind and rain with its own melancholy power" (464). Imitating the sound and breath of the wind, she knows, is important for her sympathetic medicine; accordingly, she "blew against his chest," giving Snooks the only relief he will know (464). His breathing eases, momentarily responding to her "pagan tune," her breath, and her touch, suggesting the vitality and power of her connection to the greater-than-human world. Unlike Rannie, Sarah has not severed her connection to the elements but, as is characteristic in an oral culture, responds to them in kind, recognizing the wind as an animate force, conveying important information, speaking to her in a meaningful way.

The etymology of the word describing Sarah's tune—pagan—obviously refers to landscapes beyond the city or town, those rejected by the anti-pastoral tradition and those historically most resistant to the initial spread of Christian dogma. Walker's depiction of the vitality of Sarah's pagan medicine as opposed to the impotence and death associated with the written texts retroactively figures one of the sacrifices involved for those who created those earlier texts of the trope of the talking book, where Enlightenment thought, reason, and literacy demanded a thorough divorce from any association with the "lower" animals in the Great Chain of Being, and, by extension, to any investment in the power they or other elements in an animate environment might represent.

As the holy book's appeal to Gronniosaw, Cugoano, and Equiano affirms, Christianity was one of "the greatest factors in the advancement of alphabetic literacy in both the medieval and modern eras," particularly because it brought with it "the technology upon which that faith depended" (Abram 254). Conversion often involved "training the senses to participate with the written word," and as such, it was one means by which pagan associations with the enveloping environment could be broken. Gronniosaw's rejection of his mother's paganism aptly exemplifies such an effect: "As the written text began to speak . . . the voices of the forest, and of the river, begin to fade" (Abram 254).

Walker further complicates our typically positive acceptance of literacy's superiority by retroping one of the most familiar anti-pastoral motifs: the black body that bears the impress of the animal. Most famously, Douglass affixes the image of the "brute" to the moment "the dark night of slavery closed in upon [him]," when the slave breaker Covey had momentarily eroded Douglass's desire to read (95). In other instances, Douglass "uses the same animalistic imagery to describe the slaveowner as that which had been applied to him as a slave" (Bennett 205), a frequent motif in many abolitionist texts at least as far back as the 1830s, used to figure slavery's degrading effects on master and chattel alike.

The animal images linked to Rannie's body are clearly connected to this tradition, suggesting how vestiges of slavery continue to shape the harsh conditions in which Rannie and those like her exist. She lives in abject poverty, in a house within a pasture, "surrounded by dozens of fat whitefolks' cows" (462), a locale placing her literally and categorically in the same field with animals. Other negative animal imagery resurrects the precise ideology of black subhumanity that the prior texts of the trope of the talking book were created to refute: Rannie's neglect of herself and her anguish over Snooks mark her face in "a long row of whitish snail tracks" (459). When the mailman encounters her waiting to send him for the doctor, he is repelled by Rannie's "wet goat" smell, a characteristic combining the connotations of dark, pre-Christian sensuality and modern squalor (461).

But with Sarah, the animal markings work to different effect. In Walker's first description of the conjure woman, Sarah wears "magic leaves around her neck sewed up in a possum skin next to a dried lizard's foot" (459), her eyes "aged a moist hesitant blue that gave her a quick dull stare like a hawk" (460). Sarah's hawk-like stare and her subsequent wisdom suggest her access to a broader, more transcendent perspective than that available to Rannie; while her perspective and her powers may be god-like in the context of her locale, the hawk imagery also implies that neither is so lofty and abstract, like those of the invisible Christian god, so as to divorce her entirely from the landscape she surveys. Sarah wears animal parts like totems, out of respect for the power they contain and "in order to draw to herself the power of those plants and animals with which she treats illness" (Estes 215), a recognition of her felt connection to the larger world upon which her ability to heal depends.

The story's climactic scene seems to offer Rannie a very painful experience of this felt connection to the animal world; in it her body is literally marked *by* an animal, and she is drawn into a kind of exchange that illuminates all that she has rejected in her preference for what the print circulars represent. When Sarah sends her into the pasture to collect the "strong horse tea," Rannie, in her anxiety, forgets a container in which to catch the urine. She ends up "slipping and sliding in the mud, rac[ing] after the big mare, holding out, as if for alms, her plastic shoe" (466). As the term "alms" suggests, Rannie goes looking for a handout, a gift from the animal world. This act involves her in a kind of exchange that delivers markedly different effects than the commodity exchanges called for by the advertising media, exchanges isomorphic to alphabetic literacy in a crucial way.

Commodity exchange is, like the acquisition of literacy, a minimalist drama, staged with all excess environmental distractions pared away. Unlike barter or gift-giving, for example, commodity exchange forestalls the emotional engagement of the parties involved. "A market exchange has an equilibrium . . . you pay to balance the scale . . . the whole point is . . . to make sure the exchange itself doesn't" affectively involve one person with another (Hyde 10). The equivalent exchange of goods for money is like the reduction of each signifying mark in the alphabet to a single sound, suppressing all excess emotional or "sentimental" investments that might inhere in the objects being sold. In so doing, each symbolic register of exchange reveals a remarkable kind of efficiency, reminding us of the historical coincidence of alphabetic writing and the appearance of monetary economies.[17]

On the positive side, this type of exchange prevents, for example, entangling relationships with every person with whom one exchanges money for goods or services, situations that would be emotionally exhausting as well as inefficient. However, the mailman's polite disengagement from Rannie's anguish negatively epitomizes the pervasive effects of this kind of exchange, a form clearly underwriting the circulars he delivers. Conversely, in the giving of alms, in the giving of any gift, Lewis Hyde reminds us, "there is momentum, and the weight shifts from body to body," creating the phenomenon of reciprocity, and in a broader context, constructing sociality itself (9). The pastoral scene at the end of Walker's story is a literalization of that particular abstraction: the body of the mare literally empties a part of itself, admittedly a distasteful part of itself, into Rannie's shoe. The sociality figured in this act is thus that between animal and human.

The gift is an erotic form of exchange; it institutes a bond, whether the bond is desired or not. And in this story, the gift comes from an animal, and it is inscribed as a cure. Admittedly, it does Snooks no good, but it is a cure inasmuch as it involves Rannie in a drama that signifies her indebtedness to the more than human world that she has rejected by rejecting Aunt Sarah and her "swamp magic." But this gift comes with a parting volley, another literalization of the shift of weight from body to body involved in the gift transaction that Hyde describes above: "In parting, the old mare snorted and threw up one big leg, knocking [Rannie] back into the mud" (466). Her body is once again marked by an animal in this final scene.

In the context of the larger opposition set up by the narrative, Rannie's body ironically bears the deepest and most painful imprint of animality precisely because she buys into the value system represented by the advertising circulars, instituting a delay that leads her finally into the encounter with the pastured mare. Walker thus revises the progression seen in the earlier texts of the talking book trope, where identification with print culture and the values its technology embodies refute the connection to "lower" forms of life. In Walker's retroping, the negative connotations of animality can be seen as a construct of alphabetic literacy, which, as Abrams' explanations lucidly show, tends to diminish the felt connections, common to oral culture, between humanity and the other inhabitants of its natural environment. The animate world is silenced, cast aside, regarded as inferior, in alphabetic culture; those not possessing literacy, like Equaino, Groniossaw and Cugoano, are similarly regarded and regard themselves as inferior until they, understandably, choose to learn to read and write. If alphabetic literacy has historically tended to distance us from a living environment, then "Strong Horse Tea" complicates the notion of literacy as it has often been constructed in those texts it retropes, as an unqualified and uncomplicated signifier of cultural superiority. As Walker later asserts, in a more explicit statement of her ecocritical perspective, in the essay, "Am I Blue": what "animals try to tell us" is this: 'Everything you do to us will happen to you; we are your teachers, as you are ours. We are one lesson" (7). Rannie's marking and the reminder of reciprocity it signifies are early indicators of such a view.

The mare's kick, David Estes reminds us, also takes place in an environment "charged" by the lightning bolt, that archetypal image of epiphany (225). That kick, the imprint of the animal world on the human, insists that, like Rannie, we forget that external reference and ground of all grand human abstractions at our peril. Yet despite the "unnoticed and unfortunate side-effects" of alphabetic literacy that I have explored here, Walker's own writing clearly shows us that words can be used to point the way back to our senses, to involve us in richer and more profound relationships with the more-than-human world. This recognition, as many other ecocritical writers have pointed out, carries profound implications for all systems of exchange and thus for all current and future terrestrial dramas.

## Notes

1. The 1967 edition of Walker's *In Love & Trouble: Stories of Black Women*, in which "Strong Horse Tea" first appeared, was unavailable at the time of this writing. I am using the version reprinted in the 1986 expanded edition of *Modern Stories of the*

*South.* Notably, the story appearing in this anthology differs in many ways from that appearing in the 1973 edition of *In Love & Trouble*, the earliest edition containing the story that I was able to locate. While it is impossible to document each alteration here, significant variations from the 1973 version will be noted as I cite corresponding passages in the 1986 version.

2. In the 1973 version of the story, the phrase reads "fat whitefolks' cows and an old gray horse and a mule or two." An additional sentence following this phrase in the 1973 version emphasizes Rannie's poverty: "Animals lived there in the pasture all around her house, and she and Snooks lived in it" (93).

3. David C. Estes acknowledges a lack of documentation for the efficacy of mare's urine as a cure for Snooks' diseases in two standard folklore references: Harry Middleton Hyatt's *Hoodoo—Conjuration—Witchcraft—Rootwork* (Hannibal, MO: Western Publishing Co, 1970) and Newbell Niles Puckett's *Folk Beliefs of the Southern Negro* (Chapel Hill: University of North Carolina Press, 1926); however, Estes does catalogue a number of African American folk beliefs about the use of human and animal urine to cure certain physical ailments as well as to alter the nature of one's luck (221-222). For other folk medicine sources for the story, see also Mark Royden Winchell's "Fetching the Doctor: Shamanistic House Calls in Alice Walker's 'Strong Horse Tea'" (*Mississippi Folklore Register* 15.2 [1981]: 97–101).

4. For example, in a 1993 essay, "Our People, Our People," in *Alice Walker and Zora Neale Hurston: The Common Bond.* (Ed. Lillie P. Howard [Westport, CT: Greenwood P, 1993] 31–42), Trudier Harris contexualizes "Strong Horse Tea" within the framework of Walker's inconsistent depiction of African American folk culture over a twenty-year period. The story, Harris argues, opposes Walker's depiction of folk culture to "feminist politics." Rannie Mae Toomer is drawn so as "to show the futility of her position as a lone female, with a child, in the middle of nowhere. Walker imposes feminist politics upon folk culture and makes it one of the villains . . . a monster used to degrade Rannie" (35).

Earlier, in "Folklore in the Fiction of Alice Walker: A Perpetuation of Historical and Literary Traditions" (*Black American Literature Forum*, 11 [1977]: 3–8), Harris reads the story as symbolically depicting the "consequences of moving on to better things—the technology of the white world, here or the white world in general—at the expense of something more valuable—one's heritage and roots" (7). Similarly, Keith E. Byerman's brief commentary on "Strong Horse Tea" in *Fingering the Jagged Grain: Tradition and Form in Recent Black Fiction* (Athens: U of Georgia P, 1985) identifies the tension "between folk wisdom and conventional systems of order" wherein "a strong folk female figure must deal with the unbelief of a woman who has, either consciously or unconsciously, adopted an antifolk system of values. The validity of that system must be called into question and then the folk alternative given primacy" (139).

Estes' argument frames the story within the tradition of African American folk medicine, techniques employed by slaves to assert some modicum of control over and undermine the master's propertied claim to their bodies. For him, the story confronts a belief in modern medicine with subversive folk medical traditions, practices by which "the power and self-esteem" of these folkways are preserved (214).

5. The term, the "more-than-human world," is David Abram's.

6. As the presence of the advertising circulars indicates, the story is obviously concerned with the issue of capitalistic production, specifically the inequalities and allure of wealth and status that such a system produces. Cugoano confronts similar

issues in his *Thoughts and Sentiments on the Evil and Wicked Traffic of the Slavery and Commerce of the Human Species.* Noting the contradictions that inevitably mark his polemic, given the extant discourses on racialism (17), Roxann Wheeler points out that Cugoano's Christian sentiments make him fully aware of the "corrupting influence of attractive foreign commodities" on native populations while he nevertheless proposes "social commerce (of non-human commodities) tempered by Christian convictions" as "the only route to civil, commercial society in Africa" (27).

7. In the context of eighteenth-century commercialism, Wheeler identifies [End Page 99] "one of the most widely shared sentiments of late-century writers" as "what motivational speakers today call 'retail therapy.' Olaudah Equiano and, to a lesser extent, Cugoano, following the early Quaker abolitionist Anthony Benezet, adopt this view. . . . In contemporary documents, consumption of English goods figures as a primary antidote to savagery and as the key to cultural assimilation with the British" (25).

8. The "climatological" explanation for race persisted far into the eighteenth century, according to Wheeler; however, philosophers like David Hume, Adam Ferguson, and others began to argue for "the influence of other external factors on those societies. In fact, mode of government or the extent to which a society was commercialized were increasingly offered as the most important factor shaping societal development" (20).

9. John Marrant, a free black man in whose narrative the trope is again revised, like Gronniosaw, rejects the religious orientation of his family. He leaves them, to wander in the South Carolina wilderness and preach among the Cherokee, abandoning his family after his conversion to Methodism, a change for which they "revile and ridicule" him (qtd in Weyler 47). See Karen Weyler's "Race, Redemption, and Captivity in the Narratives of Briton Hammon and John Marrant" in *Genius in Bondage: Literature of the Early Black Atlantic* (Eds. Vincent Carretta and Philip Gould. [Lexington: University Press of Kentucky, 2001] 39–53).

10. As Henry Louis Gates, Jr. observes, the 1770 edition of Gronniosaw's narrative claims that he "related" his tale "himself," while the 1774 edition claims to be "written by himself" (132–133). In the context of Gronniosaw's "intuition" about monotheism, it is at least reasonable to suspect that it may be a retroactive effect of the acquisition of literacy and Christian conversion. As Ong notes about the noetic changes instigated by literacy, "the mind does not enter into the alphabet or the printed book or the computer so much as the alphabet or print or the computer enters the mind, producing new states of awareness" (47).

11. See for example, Eric A. Havelock, *Preface to Plato* (Cambridge: Belknap P of Harvard University Press, 1963) and *The Muse Learns to Write: Reflections of Orality and Literacy from Antiquity to the Present* (New Haven: Yale University Press, 1986); Walter J. Ong, S.J. *The Presence of the Word* (New Haven: Yale University Press, 1967) and *Orality and Literacy: The Technologizing of the Word* (New York: Methuen, 1982); Jack Goody, *The Interface Between the Written and the Oral* (Cambridge: Cambridge University Press, 1987); Ivan Illich and Barry Sanders, *ABC: The Alphabetization of the Popular Mind* (San Francisco: North Point Press, 1988); and Albert Lord, *The Singer of Tales* (Cambridge: Harvard University Press, 1960).

12. For more on the specific connection between the cultural devaluation of women and the ascendancy of the alphabet, see Goux, 134–151. See also Leonard

Shlain's *The Alphabet Versus the Goddess: The Conflict Between Word and Image* (New York: Viking, 1998), 64–120.

13. Thus Equiano, as Gates has so thoroughly analyzed, is profoundly perceptive to represent his old self and new self in rhetorically different ways (153–157). See his discussion of Equiano's self-conscious use of "two distinct voices to distinguish . . . the simple wonder with which the young Equiano approached the New World of his captors and a more eloquently articulated voice that he employs to describe the author's narrative present" (153)

14. Sarah's compassionate musings do not exist in the 1973 edition of "Strong Horse Tea." That section of the story reads: "She was sipping something hot from a dish. When would this one know, she wondered, that she could only depend upon those who would come" (93). Also absent in the 1973 edition and present in the 1986 *Modern Stories of the South* are Sarah's earlier musings, while Rannie is conversing with the mailman, about the allure of an allegedly "superior" white culture:

> "White mailman, white doctor. White doctor, white mailman," she murmured from time to time, putting the poker down carefully and rubbing her shins.
>
> "You young ones will turn to them," she said," when it is *us* what got the power". (462)

15. To emphasize the point, Walker has Rannie echo Sarah's dictum, when she realizes that Sarah is the only help available: "How could she have thought anyone else could help her Snooks, she wondered brokenly, when you couldn't even depend on them to come!" (464)

16. In this context, Ong observes that "because writing carries within it always an element of death, the tragic literary work—or simply the serious written work in general, the work which deals with life and death honestly—often turns out to be in some way about itself. . . . That is to say, a work about death often modulates readily, if eerily, into a work about literature. For death inhabits texts" (238).

17. For an extensive examination of this correlation, see Goux, 9–63 and 213–244.

## WORKS CITED

Abram, David. *The Spell of the Sensuous: Perception and Language in a More-Than-Human World*. New York: Vintage Books, 1996.

Bennett, Michael. "Anti-Pastoralism, Frederick Douglass, and the Nature of Slavery." *Beyond Nature Writing: Expanding the Boundaries of Ecocriticism*. Ed. Karla Armbruster and Kathleen R. Wallace. Charlottesville: U of Virginia P, 2001. 195–210.

Cugoano, Ottobah. *Thoughts and Sentiments on the Evil of Slavery and Other Writings*. Ed. Vincent Carretta. New York: Penguin Books, 1990.

Davis, Charles T. and Henry Louis Gates, Jr., eds. *The Slave's Narrative*. Oxford: Oxford University Press, 1985.

Douglass, Frederick. *Narrative of the Life of Frederick Douglass, An American Slave Written by Himself*. Ed. Benjamin Quarles. Cambridge: Harvard University Press, 1960.

Equiano, Olaudah. *The Interesting Narrative of the Life of Olaudah Equiano, or Gustavus Vassa, the African. An authoritative text / written by himself*. 1794. Ed. Werner Sollors. New York: Norton, 2001.

Estes, David C. "Alice Walker's 'Strong Horse Tea': Folk Cures for the Dispossessed." *Southern Folklore* 50 (1993): 213–29.

Ewen, Stuart and Elizabeth Ewen. *Channels of Desire: Mass Images and the Shaping of American Consciousness*. 2nd ed. Minneapolis: U of Minnesota P, 1992.

Gates, Henry Louis, Jr. *The Signifying Monkey: A Theory of African-American Literary Criticism*. New York: Oxford University Press, 1988.

Goux, Jean-Joseph. *Symbolic Economies After Marx and Freud*. Trans. Jennifer Curtiss Gage. Ithaca: Cornell University Press, 1990.

Gronniosaw, James Albert Ukawsaw. *Narrative of the Most Remarkable Particulars in the Life of James Albert Ukawsaw Gronniosaw, An African Prince as Related by Himself*. Leeds: Davies and Booth, 1841. Microfilming Corp of America, 1980. Fiche# 13311.

Hyde, Lewis. *The Gift: Imagination and the Erotic Life of Property*. 3rd ed. New York: Vintage Books, 1983.

Ong, Walter J., S.J. *Interfaces of the Word: Studies in the Evolution of Consciousness and Culture*. Ithaca: Cornell University Press, 1977.

Walker, Alice. "Am I Blue." *Living by the Word: Selected Writings 1973–1987*. San Diego: Harcourt Brace Jovanovich, 1988. 3–8.

———. "The Black Writer and Southern Experience." *In Search of Our Mothers' Gardens: Womanist Prose*. San Diego: Harcourt Brace Jovanovich, 1983. 15–21.

———. "Everything is a Human Being." *Living by the Word: Selected Writings 1973–1987*. San Diego: Harcourt Brace Jovanovich, 1988. 139–152.

———. "Strong Horse Tea." *In Love and Trouble: Stories About Black Women*. San Diego: Harcourt Brace Jovanovich, 1973. 88–98.

———. "Strong Horse Tea." *Stories of the Modern South*. Expanded Edition. Eds. Ben Forkner and Patrick Samway, S.J. New York: Penguin Books, 1986. 459–466.

———. "The Universe Responds." *Living by the Word: Selected Writings 1973–1987*. San Diego: Harcourt Brace Jovanovich, 1988. 187–193.

Wheeler, Roxann. "Betrayed by Some of My Own Complexion: Cugoano, Abolition and the Contemporary Language of Racialism." *Genius in Bondage: Literature of the Early Black Atlantic*. Eds. Vincent Carretta and Philip Gould. Lexington: University Press of Kentucky, 2001. 17–38.

# Alice Walker Chronology

1944    Alice Walker is born on 9 February to Willie Lee and Minnie Tallulah Grant Walker, sharecroppers in Eatonton, Georgia.

1952    Walker loses the sight in one eye, the result of a bb-gun accident.

1965    Walker receives her B. A. at Sarah Lawrence College, one of six black students in her class.

1967    Walker marries Melvyn Leventhal, a civil-rights attorney, on 17 March. They have a daughter, Rebecca, two years later. They are divorced in 1976.

1968    Walker's first book, *Once: Poems* is published.

1968    Walker teaches black studies and literature at Jackson State College, Tugaloo College, Wellesley, and University of Massachusetts until 1973. She is active in the Civil Rights Movement and in the feminist movement.

1970    *The Third Life of Grange Copeland*, Walker's first novel, is published.

1976    Walker's second novel, *Meridian*, is published.

1979    Walker edits *I Love Myself When I Am Laughing: A Zora Neale Hurston Reader*, initiating a Hurston revival.

1982    Walker's third novel, *The Color Purple*, is published. It wins the Pulitzer Prize and the American Book Award.

1983   Walker's collection of feminist essays, *In Search of Our Mother's Gardens*, is published.

1984   With writer Robert Allen, Walker founds Wild Trees Press, which publishes books of "special insight," particular from a feminist perspective.

1985   Stephen Spielberg produces the movie adaptation of *The Color Purple*. It is nominated for Academy Awards in eleven categories, winning for best musical score.

1989   Walker's novel *The Temple of My Familiar* is on the New York Times Bestseller List for over four months.

1993   Walker co-produces *Warrior Marks*, a documentary movie about female circumcision.

2004   Walker publishes her ninth novel, *Now Is the Time to Open Your Heart*.

2005   A musical adaptation of *The Color Purple* opens on Broadway.

# *Contributors*

HAROLD BLOOM is Sterling Professor of the Humanities at Yale University. He is the author of 30 books, including *Shelley's Mythmaking* (1959), *The Visionary Company* (1961), *Blake's Apocalypse* (1963), *Yeats* (1970), *A Map of Misreading* (1975), *Kabbalah and Criticism* (1975), *Agon: Toward a Theory of Revisionism* (1982), *The American Religion* (1992), *The Western Canon* (1994), and *Omens of Millennium: The Gnosis of Angels, Dreams, and Resurrection* (1996). *The Anxiety of Influence* (1973) sets forth Professor Bloom's provocative theory of the literary relationships between the great writers and their predecessors. His most recent books include *Shakespeare: The Invention of the Human* (1998), a 1998 National Book Award finalist, *How to Read and Why* (2000), *Genius: A Mosaic of One Hundred Exemplary Creative Minds* (2002), *Hamlet: Poem Unlimited* (2003), *Where Shall Wisdom Be Found?* (2004), and *Jesus and Yahweh: The Names Divine* (2005). In 1999, Professor Bloom received the prestigious American Academy of Arts and Letters Gold Medal for Criticism. He has also received the International Prize of Catalonia, the Alfonso Reyes Prize of Mexico, and the Hans Christian Andersen Bicentennial Prize of Denmark.

LOUIS H. PRATT wrote *James Baldwin* (1978) and *Alice Malsenior Walker: An Annotated Bibliography, 1968–1986* (1988).

JOSEPH A. BROWN is director of Black American Studies at Southern Illinois University in Carbondale. He wrote *To Stand on the Rock: Meditations on Black Catholic Identity* (1998).

ALICE FARLEY, formerly Alice Hall Petry, teaches at Southern Illinois University, Edwardsville. She has written books on F. Scott Fitzgerald, Anne Tyler, and George Washington Cable.

LYNN PIFER is a professor of English at Mansfield University, Pennsylvania and the Director of Mansfield's Frederick Douglass Institute.

FELIPE SMITH is Assistant Professor of English at Tulane University, where he teaches African American and American literature. He wrote *American Body Politics: Race, Gender, and Black Literary Renaissance* (1998).

ROBERT JAMES BUTLER, Professor of English and director of College Honors at Canisius College, is the author of *Native Son: The Emergence of a New Black Hero* (1992).

GAIL KEATING is senior instructor in English at Pennsylvania State University, Worthington Scranton.

BONNIE BRAENDLIN is associate professor of English at Florida State University.

DEBORAH E. BARKER is Assistant Professor of English and Women's Studies at the University of Mississippi.

MARCIA NOE is a professor of English and Coordinator of Women's Studies at The University of Tennessee at Chatanooga. She wrote *Susan Glaspell: Voice from the Heartland* and is a senior editor of *The Dictionary of Midwestern Literature*.

MICHAEL JAYNES is a graduate student in English at The University of Tennessee at Chatanooga.

LAURIE MCMILLAN is assistant professor and writing coordinator at Marywood University.

DEBORAH ANNE HOOKER is assistant head of the English department at North Carolina State University.

# Bibliography

Banks, Emma Davis and Keith Byerman. *Alice Walker, An Annotated Bibliography 1968–1986*. New York: Garland Pub., 1989.

Barnett, Pamela E. "'Miscegenation,' Rape, and 'Race' in Alice Walker's Meridian." *Southern Quarterly: A Journal of the Arts in the South*, 39:3 (2001 Spring), pp. 65–81.

Bloom, Harold, ed. *Alice Walker's The Color Purple*. Philadelphia : Chelsea House, 2000.

———. *Alice Walker: Comprehensive Research and Study Guide*. Broomall, PA: Chelsea House, 2000.

Brooker, Will, and Deborah Jermyn, eds. *The Audience Studies Reader*. London, England: Routledge, 2003.

Butler-Evans, Elliott. *Race, Gender, and Desire: Narrative Strategies in the Fiction of Toni Cade Bambara, Toni Morrison, and Alice Walker*. Philadelphia : Temple University Press, 1989.

Cheung, King-Kok. "'Don't Tell': Imposed Silences in The Color Purple and The Woman Warrior," *PMLA*, 103 (March 1988): 162–174.

Christian, Barbara. "Novels for Everyday Use: The Novels of Alice Walker," in *Black Women Novelists: The Development of a Tradition, 1892–1976* (Westport, Conn.: Greenwood Press, 1980), pp. 180–238.

———. "Alice Walker: The Black Woman Artist as Wayward," in *Black Women Writers (1950–80): A Critical Evaluation*, edited by Mari Evans. Garden City, N.Y.: Anchor/Doubleday, 1984, pp. 457–477.

———. "The Contrary Women of Alice Walker: A Study of Female Protagonists in *In Love and Trouble*," in *Black Feminist Criticism: Perspectives on Black Women Writers*. New York: Pergamon Press, 1985, pp. 31–46.

211

Davis, Thadious M. "Alice Walker's Celebration of Self in Southern Generations," *Southern Quarterly*, 21 (Summer 1983): 38–53.

Erickson,Peter. "'Cast Out Alone/To Heal/And Recreate/Ourselves': Family-based Identity in the Work of Alice Walker," *College Language Association Journal*, 23 (Spring 1979): 71–94.

Fike, Matthew A. "Jean Toomer and Okot p'Bitek in Alice Walker's 'In Search of Our Mothers' Gardens,'" *MELUS*, 25:3–4 (2000 Fall–Winter), pp. 141–60.

Gaston,Karen C. "Women in the Lives of Grange Copeland," *College Language Association Journal*, 24 (March 1981): 276–286.

Gates Henry L. and K.A. Appiah, eds. *Alice Walker: Critical Perspectives Past and Present*. New York: Amistad, 1993.

Harris, Trudier. "From Victimization to Free Enterprise: Alice Walker's The Color Purple," *Studies in American Fiction*, 14 (Spring 1986): 1–17.

———. "On The Color Purple, Stereotypes, and Silence," *Black American Literature Forum*, 18 (Winter 1984): 155–161.

Howard, Lillie P. ed. *Alice Walker and Zora Neale Hurston: The Common Bond*. Westport, Conn.: Greenwood Press, 1993.

Kelly, Ernece B. "Paths to Liberation in Alice Walker's *The Color Purple* (1982)." Fisher, Jerilyn and Ellen S. Silber eds. *Women in Literature: Reading through the Lens of Gender*. Westport, CT: Greenwood, 2003, pp. 75–78.

Kim, Minjung. "The Subversiveness of the Letters from Africa: Alice Walker's *The Color Purple.*" *Feminist Studies in English Literature*, 8:2 (2001 Winter), pp. 105–129

McDowell, Deborah E. "The Self in Bloom: Alice Walker's *Meridian*," *College Language Association Journal*, 24 (March 1981): 262–275.

Noe, Marcia; Jaynes, Michael. "Teaching Alice Walker's 'Everyday Use': Employing Race, Class, and Gender, with an Annotated Bibliography." *Eureka Studies in Teaching Short Fiction*, 5:1 (2004 Fall).

Parker-Smith, Bettye J. "Alice Walker's Women: In Search of Some Peace of Mind," in *Black Women Writers (1950-80): A Critical Evaluation*, pp. 478–493.

Sol, Adam. "Questions of Mastery in Alice Walker's *The Temple of My Familiar.*" *Critique: Studies in Contemporary Fiction*, 43:4 (2002 Summer), pp. 393–404.

Stein, Karen F. "*Meridian*: Alice Walker's Critique of Revolution," *Black American Literature Forum*, 20 (Spring-Summer 1986): 129–141.

Wall, Wendy. "Lettered Bodies and Corporeal Texts in *The Color Purple*," *Studies in American Fiction*, 16 (Spring 1988): 83–97.

Watson, Reginald. "The Power of the 'Milk' and Motherhood: Images of Deconstruction in Toni Morrison's *Beloved* and Alice Walker's *The Third Life of Grange Copeland*." *CLA Journal*, 48:2 (2004 Dec).

Warhol, Robyn R. "How Narration Produces Gender: Femininity as Affect and Effect in Alice Walker's *The Color Purple.*" *Narrative*, 9:2 (2001 May), pp. 182–187

Washington, Mary Helen. "An Essay on Alice Walker," in *Sturdy Black Bridges: Visions of Black Women in Literature*, edited by Roseann P. Bell and others. Garden City, N.Y.: Anchor/Doubleday, 1979, pp. 133–149.

White, Evelyn C. *Alice Walker: A Life.* New York, NY: Norton, 2004.

Whitsitt, Sam. "In Spite of It All: A Reading of Alice Walker's 'Everyday Use'." *African American Review*, 34:3 (2000 Fall), pp. 443-59.

Winchell, Donna Haisty. *Alice Walker.* New York: Twayne, 1992.

# Acknowledgments

Pratt, Louis H., "Alice Walker's Men: Profiles in the Quest for Love and Personal Values," *Studies in Popular Culture*, 1989; 12 (1): 42–57. Reprinted by permission of the author's estate.

Brown, Joseph A., "'All Saints Should Walk Away': The Mystical Pilgrimage of *Meridian*," *Callaloo: A Journal of African American and African Arts and Letters*, 1989 Spring; 12 (2 (39)): 310–320. © Charles H. Rowell. Reprinted with permission of the Johns Hopkins University Press.

Petry, Alice Hall. "Alice Walker: The Achievement of the Short Fiction," *Modern Language Studies*, 1989 Winter; 19 (1): 12–27. Reprinted by permission of the publisher, *Modern Language Studies*.

Pifer, Lynn. "Coming to Voice in Alice Walker's *Meridian*: Speaking Out for the Revolution," *African American Review*, 1992 Spring; 26 (1): 77–88. Reprinted by permission of the author.

Smith, Felipe. "Alice's Walker's Redemptive Art," *African American Review*, 1992 Fall; 26 (3): 437–451. Reprinted by permission of the author.

Butler, Robert James. "Alice Walker's Vision of the South in *The Third Life of Grange Copeland*," *African American Review*, 1993 Summer; 27 (2): 195–204. Reprinted by permission of the author.

Keating, Gail. "Alice Walker: In Praise of Maternal Heritage," *Literary Griot: International Journal of Black Expressive Cultural Studies*, 1994 Spring; 6 (1): 26–37. Reprinted by permission of the author.

Braendlin, Bonnie. "Alice Walker's *The Temple of My Familiar* as a Pastiche," *American Literature: A Journal of Literary History, Criticism, and Bibliography*, 1996 Mar; 68 (1): 47–67. Reprinted by permission of the author.

Barker, Deborah E., "Visual Markers: Art and Mass Media in Alice Walker's *Meridian*," *African American Review*, 1997 Fall; 31 (3): 463–479. Reprinted by permission of the author.

Noe, Marcia. "Teaching Alice Walker's 'Everyday Use': Employing Race, Class, and Gender," with an Annotated Bibliography, *Eureka Studies in Teaching Short Fiction*, 2004 Fall; 5 (1): 123–136. Reprinted by permission of the author.

McMillan, Laurie. "Telling a Critical Story: Alice Walker's *In Search of Our Mothers' Gardens*," *Journal of Modern Literature*, 2004 Fall; 28 (1): 107–123. © 2004 Indiana University Press. Reprinted by permission of the publisher.

Hooker, Deborah Anne. "Reanimating the Trope of the Talking Book in Alice Walker's 'Strong Horse Tea,'" *Southern Literary Journal*, 2005 Spring; 37 (2): 81–102. © 2005 The Southern Literary Journal. Reprinted by permission of The Southern Literary Journal, University of North Carolina at Chapel Hill.

# Index